The Superiority of an Evangelical Model of Religious Liberty

The Superiority of an Evangelical Model of Religious Liberty

A Critique of Secular and Roman Catholic Conceptions

Daniel J. Trippie
Foreword by Daniel R. Heimbach

WIPF & STOCK · Eugene, Oregon

THE SUPERIORITY OF AN EVANGELICAL MODEL OF RELIGIOUS LIBERTY
A Critique of Secular and Roman Catholic Conceptions

Copyright © 2022 Daniel J. Trippie. All rights reserved. Except for brief quotations in critical publications or reviews, no part of this book may be reproduced in any manner without prior written permission from the publisher. Write: Permissions, Wipf and Stock Publishers, 199 W. 8th Ave., Suite 3, Eugene, OR 97401.

Wipf & Stock
An Imprint of Wipf and Stock Publishers
199 W. 8th Ave., Suite 3
Eugene, OR 97401

www.wipfandstock.com

PAPERBACK ISBN: 978-1-6667-4536-8
HARDCOVER ISBN: 978-1-6667-4537-5
EBOOK ISBN: 978-1-6667-4538-2

11/11/22

Scripture quotations marked (ESV) are taken from The ESV® Bible (The Holy Bible, English Standard Version®), copyright © 2001 by Crossway, a publishing ministry of Good News Publishers. Used by permission. All rights reserved.

for Dan Trippie Sr., I will see you in the morning.

Contents

Foreword by Daniel R. Heimbach | ix
Acknowledgments | xiii

1 Introduction | 1
    The Problem of Religious Liberty | 4
    Thesis | 7
    Philosophical Assumptions | 9
    Theological Method | 13
    Background | 18
    Components | 19

2 Utilitarianism: The Influence of John Stuart Mill on Modern Religious Liberty | 20
    John Stuart Mill (1806–1873) | 22
    Interpretations of *On Liberty* | 30
    Mill's Religious Liberty: Premise One | 33
    Mill's Religious Liberty: Premise Two | 43
    Mill's Religious Liberty: Premise Three | 49
    Mill's Religious Liberty: Premise Four | 53
    Summary | 54

3   Justice as Fairness: John Rawls's Contribution
    to Modern Religious Liberty | 56
        John Rawls (1921–2002) | 57
        Human Agency | 64
        The Priority of Right over the Good | 71
        Privatized Religion | 79
        Conclusion | 80

4   Natural Law Philosophy: John Courtney Murray's
    Contribution to Modern Religious Liberty | 81
        John Courtney Murray (1904–1967) | 82
        Natural Law Philosophy | 88
        Weakness in Relationship to the World | 93
        Weakness in Relationship to Time | 96
        Weakness in Relationship to Self | 99
        Conclusion | 105

5   The Evangelical Paradigm for Religious Liberty | 106
        Evangelicalism Rediscovered | 107
        Evangelical Structure for Religious Freedom | 110
        The Superiority of Evangelical Anthropology | 122
        The Superiority of Evangelical Cosmology | 132
        The Superiority of Evangelical Eschatology | 139
        Conclusion | 145

6   Summary Thoughts and Conclusion | 146
        Summary of Arguments | 152
        Further Research | 154
        Conclusion | 156

Bibliography | 159
Subject Index | 177
Scripture Index | 195

Foreword

Daniel R. Heimbach

Religious liberty has few friends in an age of perfectionism that tolerates no dissent. In the eighteenth and nineteenth centuries precursors of today's Evangelicals championed a vision of religious liberty that separated church and state without abdicating duty to influence governing for good. They meant neither to isolate themselves from public life nor to protect those inciting religiously-driven revolution. They rather challenged civil authorities to tolerate differences strengthening the common good while influencing and supporting good governing despite those differences.

But we now live in days when religious liberty no longer means what it did following the Protestant Reformation or when the American founders drafted the US Constitution. It then meant forgoing state-sponsored churches and allowing Christians to disagree without state interference. Today religious liberty is no longer defined in uniquely Christian terms. It now must include more than limiting the way government treats Christians and has to include treating all belief systems the same way. This comes with hazards because religious liberty must now be extended to faiths that reject extending it to others, and what needs guarding against no longer is Christians using civil power to suppress other Christians but secularists

Foreword

bent on marginalizing Christianity, religions bent on ruling the world, and ideologies bent on silencing all dissent.

As formerly conceived, religious liberty did not include protecting those denying it to others and did not mean privileging one faith over others. But treating all faiths the same these days risks protecting those denying others the same protection and risks nationalizing a single worldview or ethical framework at the expense of others. So, while religious liberty needs updating, it no longer is safe to assume it serves the common good or is blind to clashing ideological convictions. New conceptions occasioned by new circumstances need examining, not only to defend what was formerly achieved, but also to avoid dangers that did not exist before.

Trippie's *The Superiority of an Evangelical Model of Religious Liberty* addresses this need in a manner that is both thoroughly researched and readable. Recent writing on the subject is mostly shallow, emotional, and out of touch and Trippie corrects that deficiency. *The Superiority of an Evangelical Model of Religious Liberty* is so refreshingly original I think Trippie offers the greatest advance to understanding religious liberty since John Courtney Murray persuaded the Vatican to support religious freedom over state churches. For this see: *We Hold These Truths: Catholic Reflections on the American Proposition* (Sheed and Ward, 1960), and *Religious Liberty: Catholic Struggles with Pluralism* (Westminster/John Knox, 1993). Murray articulated religious liberty in a manner reconciling Catholicism with American democracy, and now Trippie reconciles religious liberty in today's world with how it was conceived by evangelical precursors drafting the US Constitution.

Religious liberty lies at the intersection of religion, civil law, and morality. It involves all three without reducing one to the other, and that makes it both strategic and complex. Religious liberty addresses whether those governing should leave religious life alone or try to control it because what people most value (worship) matters enormously to justice and social stability. In fact, the main reason religious liberty remains so challenging is it requires those in power to stay out of something that largely affects succeeding in what they do.

It is hard to advocate on behalf of something poorly understood, and religious liberty is more complex than most realize. It is experienced in personal and religious terms. But the principle is social and political, which means institutions—and government in particular—must recognize it in a civilly protected public manner. It concerns institutions (churches,

Foreword

synagogues, mosques) as well as individuals, has positive (freedom to evangelize) as well as negative (immunity from coercion) aspects, and applies as much to ideological systems (communism, progressive secularism, LGBTQ+ worldview ideology, antireligious atheism) as to ecclesial systems (Christianity, Judaism, Islam, Buddhism, Hinduism). It is important as well to understand that religious liberty is neither ideal nor eternal. It refers to things here and now that will not apply when Jesus returns and seeks civil immunity for things God punishes.

The ethics of religious liberty must therefore take a realist (not perfectionist) approach that separates political from religious power and distinguishes belief systems from civil governing (not just churches but organized ideologies as well). Nevertheless, this separation cannot be total and must always be qualified by how ethical perspectives all depend on belief systems that cannot be separated from politics without leaving it morally blind. The way governing power recognizes and supports religious liberty is balanced against the duty it has to protect peace and order. So, while recognizing and supporting religious liberty, good governing needs also to protect society from religiously-motivated actions (like human sacrifice and killing heretics) that threaten rather than serve the common good.

Idealists dislike religious liberty because it requires tolerating what they think wrong or hinders their goals. Perfectionists fear dissent, associate civil power with what they worship (most valued), and so confuse the role of government (defending justice and civil security) with the role of religion (solving spiritual problems). Religious liberty cannot survive without perpetual defending, and passing it on from one generation to the next is difficult and rare. Some countries follow how the US handles religious liberty. But most do not and support for religious liberty now is waning even in the US as trends in culture and politics lead more and more to consider it harmful and dangerous.

Cultivating and preserving religious liberty requires living with tension that cannot be resolved, and living with that tension is more challenging now than ever. On the one hand, religious liberty is a religious doctrine regarding the way people of faith relate to civil power. On the other hand, it is a civilly guaranteed right that stabilizes society better than other approaches. Thus it is religious (doctrinal) and political (practical) at the same time, and this tension makes it as challenging to gain support among unbending social warriors as among those wanting to impose all dimensions of God's kingdom rule immediately—especially when trying to coexist on equal terms with divergent ethical perspectives driven by incompatible belief systems.

As to this book I am not a neutral or independent observer. I mentored Trippie through doctoral studies and chaired his dissertation committee. Moreover, this book publishes Trippie's dissertation largely because I urged him to share it with a larger audience. But I recommend the book here for reasons beyond that personal connection. It is worth reading, first, because it takes on the sharpest thinking done on this important subject and does it extremely well. It is worth reading, second, because, while scholarly, the book never in the least compromises the faith. And, third, it is worth reading because religious liberty must be explained and defended in ways that account for political and cultural changes, and this is the only work I know that provides what is needed today.

May this book give you deeper understanding of what religious liberty truly involves, may it inspire in you greater appreciation for what makes religious liberty so important, may it encourage you to stand for religious liberty when opposition arises, and may it enable you to promote and defend religious liberty in today's world more effectively.

Acknowledgments

THE ENDEAVOR OF WRITING an academic book is a difficult task. One must exert tremendous amounts of mental and emotional energy. In addition to the mental vigor exercised, the scholar finds themselves isolated for hours on end. Thus, a book project such as this is an act of stamina and a test of intellect. Therefore, one who completes the task finds themselves grateful to all those who offered support.

First, I would like to thank my mentoring professor Daniel Heimbach. Dr. Heimbach has offered me constant encouragement and thoughtful critique. I am exceedingly grateful for Dr. Heimbach's kind spirit and guidance along my academic journey. Dr. Heimbach has been a genuine blessing in my life, and I am forever thankful.

Second, I would like to thank the elders of Restoration Church. Jim Murphy, Steve Snyder, and Peter Fredrick have offered continuous support and encouragement. In addition, the elders of Restoration Church provided time away from my pastoral responsibilities to research and write. This book is not possible without the support of these men.

Third, I owe Restoration Church a debt of gratitude for their support. The people of Restoration Church encouraged me even while I was frequently closed off in my study. Terri Saathoff spent countless hours reviewing, correcting, and editing many chapter drafts. I am indebted to Terri for her contribution. Restoration Church is an example of a congregation that loves a pastor well.

Acknowledgments

Fourth, I am grateful for my twin sons, Samuel and Dominick. Samuel and Dominick finished both of their undergraduate degrees while I was working on this project. Both my sons have been incredible study partners and tremendous encouragements. A father could not be prouder of his children.

Finally, words will not express my gratitude for my wife, Gina Trippie. Gina has walked faithfully with me since our days as high school sweethearts. Gina has sacrificed time, money, and many lonely nights as I worked on this project. Gina has endured much for the sake of the gospel; I am eternally indebted to my beloved wife.

Daniel J. Trippie Jr.
Buffalo, New York
April 2022

CHAPTER 1

Introduction

"IF THERE IS ANY fixed star in our constitutional constellation, it is that no official, high or petty, can prescribe what shall be orthodox in politics, nationalism, religion, or other matters of opinion or force citizens to confess by word or act their faith therein. If there are any circumstances which permit an exception, they do not occur to us."[1] With these words, Justice Robert H. Jackson in 1943 reinforced the long-standing tradition of religious liberty in American jurisprudence. The high court's ruling in *West Virginia State Board of Education v. Barnette* was one of many decisions that strengthened the vitality of religious liberty in the modern American age.

Religious freedom remains a great distinctive in American life.[2] In spite of accusations that religious freedom encourages bigotry, religious freedom, in principle, accommodates irreligion.[3] But religious liberty can often be an abstract concept.[4] And while religious liberty can often be an abstract concept, it is nonetheless a concrete constitutional principle and a social reality.[5] For the purpose of this book, religious liberty is defined as a principle whereby individuals and institutions are free in the eyes of human government to accept or reject religious doctrines based solely on

---

1. Board of Education v. Barnette, 319 U.S. 624 (1943).
2. Henry, *The Christian Mindset*, 11.
3. Henry, *The Christian Mindset*, 11.
4. Moore and Walker, *The Gospel and Religious Liberty*, 4.
5. Forte et al., *The Heritage Guide to the Constitution*, 399.

one's faculty of conscience; this freedom also includes the ability to exercise one's religious convictions and duties without fear of government or social coercion.[6] Religious liberty is the first principle that supports separation of church and state. But religious liberty and separation are different topics.[7] Religious freedom establishes the principles whereby respect of one's conscience is established. But church and state separation are the operative modes by which the state remains neutral toward religion.[8] Whereas religious freedom considers first principles, the conception of separation codifies the principles between institutional authorities. This book will primarily consider the theological, philosophical, and epistemological foundations that support religious liberty in general.

The ethical framework supporting religious liberty assumes three common axioms. First, religious freedom is necessary for pluralistic societies. Religious liberty affords governments the power to balance public order while providing diverse peoples the opportunity to exercise their religion in peaceful ways.[9] Second, religious freedom contributes to the overall common good of society. Religious freedom cultivates a society where ethical influence is gained through assent of the will—not coercion. Nations that recognize the religious rights of all its citizens are less violent than those who enforce religious conformity.[10] Third, religious freedom promotes an overall culture of equality.[11] This is not to say that religious liberty considers all truth claims as equally true. Religious freedom establishes principles that support an instrumental good that ensures all people the right to seek truth according to one's own conscience. A government that can impede

---

6. Another possible definition is found in Andrew Walker's dissertation: "Religious liberty is the principle that religious persons and institutions should have the ability to freely accept or reject religiously-inspired doctrines, and the corresponding freedom to exercise these religious convictions without fear of civil penalty or civil control" (Andrew Thomas Walker, "Religious Liberty in Contemporary Evangelical Social Ethics, 1n3).

7. The doctrine of separation is considered a matter of practical reason derived from the principle of religious liberty. Separation affirms the principles of free exercise by restricting state inference with particular doctrines and practices of free citizens and churches.

8. Maclure and Taylor, *Secularism and Freedom of Conscience*, 20.

9. Moore and Walker, *The Gospel and Religious Liberty*, 9.

10. US State Department Office of International Religious Freedom, "2019 Report on International Religious Freedom."

11. Equality ensures equal opportunity for all citizens. Equity is the progressive idea that all outcomes must be equal. The concept of equity cuts against religious freedom because it supposes that all truth claims must be equally regarded as true.

Introduction

someone else's religion is a government that can impede anyone's religion.[12] But governments that foster respect of conscience elevate the overall conditions of fairness across society. Consequently, religious liberty is assumed to promote overall human flourishing and social well-being.

Liberal political philosophers have a long history of championing religious liberty.[13] For the purpose of this book, I will use the terms "liberal" and "liberalism" in reference to classical liberalism before the mid-twentieth century. Classical liberalism argued for individual rights in religious, economic, and social spheres. It is a political framework that emerged as philosophers sought to acknowledge Christianity's cultural influence while applying Enlightenment rationalism. But after Roosevelt's New Deal, the term "liberalism" has been applied to the modern welfare state's progressive policies. This book will use the term "liberal" and "liberalism" in its former sense while understanding that the latter emerged from its deficiencies.

Moreover, I will use the term "secular" throughout this work with two considerations. First, political secularity relates to the removal of God from public spaces. Political secularity is the process by which the state remains independent from all religious influence.[14] Second, social secularity consists in the denial of public acts aimed toward the acknowledgment of God.[15] Social secularity seeks to erode the influence of religion in social practices and in the conduct of individual lives.[16] Secularism is an ideology that explains the universe in exclusively material terms. Thus, secularism denies all metaphysical realities. But this is not to suggest that secularism does not contain ultimate principles. In fact, it contains unspoken religious principles. Political philosopher Ronald Dworkin argues that secularism and theism both maintain a "deep, distinctive, and comprehensive worldview."[17] He contends that belief in a transcendent being is only one form of religious belief. Dworkin says, "Religion is whatever gives a person's universe purpose and order," so he calls himself a religious atheist.[18] Thus, secularism, properly

---

12. Moore and Walker, *The Gospel and Religious Liberty*, 18.

13. The term "liberal" in this book refers to classic liberalism. Classic liberalism stresses individual rights, limited government, and economic freedom. Classic liberalism is contrary to modern social liberalism which prioritizes progress social principles and a large government welfare state.

14. Maclure and Taylor, *Secularism and Freedom of Conscience*, 16.

15. Taylor, *A Secular Age*, 3–4.

16. Maclure and Taylor, *Secularism and Freedom of Conscience*, 16.

17. Dworkin, *Religion without God*, 1.

18. Dworkin, *Religion without God*, 1.

understood, is a religious system. Consequently, the idea of secularism relates to philosophies and ideologies that reject the existence of transcendent realities, divine special revelation, and metaphysics in general.

This book assumes that political secularity is fallacious. Political secularity believes that individuals can remain neutral regarding social ethics. But as Dworkin readily admits, secularity contains its own set of religious principles. St. Augustine rightly understood that there is no such thing as political neutrality. Augustine argued that two loves form the thoughts of humans: either the "earthly love of self, even to the contempt of God" or the "heavenly love of God, even to the contempt of self."[19] Therefore, the conception of political secularity is a misnomer.

The Problem of Religious Liberty

Political philosophers have long realized that religious freedom is essential for pluralistic societies. Ethicist John Rawls contends that religious toleration is necessary to establish a well-ordered society.[20] And political philosopher Martha Nussbaum argues that religious freedom is necessary to ensure fairness for minority groups.[21] Consequently, political philosophers and ethicists affirm the value of religious liberty. But the support of secular social ethics for religious freedom is entirely for its public utility. Classic liberals such as John Stuart Mill believed that free exchange of ideas helped increase society's intellectual temperature. Mill argued that the free exchange of ideas moved society toward greater freedom.[22] And the American Civil Liberties Union contends that religious liberty is essential for protecting against theocratic statism.[23]

Nevertheless, secular frameworks for religious freedom contain pathologies that metastasize because they are founded exclusively on an autonomous human reason that rejects theological surety. C. F. Henry noted that secularism's ideological displacement of supernatural theism unwittingly invited the emergence of profane religions like Nazism and communism.[24] Henry properly realized that secular thought imposes its

19. Augustine, *The City of God*, 283.
20. Rawls, *A Theory of Justice*, 192.
21. Nussbaum, *Liberty of Conscience*, 4.
22. Mill, *On Liberty*, 17.
23. American Civil Liberties Union, "Religious Liberty."
24. Henry, *God, Revelation, and Authority*, 6:8.

Introduction

own preferred values and readily sacrifices the lives and freedoms of innumerable millions of humans. He contended that secular ideology rejects every alternative to totalitarian control because it redefines the meanings of progress, truth, and right.[25] Consequently, secular social ethics cannot establish absolute universal moral principles, and this eventually results in social instability and a reduction of freedom.

Roman Catholic social ethics contain absolute universal moral principles derived from nature. Catholic natural law posits that nature is sufficient for regulating social relationships. It is founded on two self-evident principles: the maxim "*Suum cuique*," and the broader principle "Justice is to be done and injustice avoided."[26] Catholic moral philosopher John Courtney Murray appealed to natural law as the foundation for his religious liberty model.[27] But Catholic natural law is too optimistic about humanity's ability to perceive specific transcendent principles. Natural law without divine revelation is incomplete because it can only study visible forces while it speculates about values.[28] Therefore, Roman Catholic natural law succumbs to similar problems found in secularism; natural law is insufficient because it lacks a revelatory bridge to the secular world.[29]

Evangelical scholars Carl F. H. Henry, Os Guinness, Daniel Heimbach, and Albert Molher all champion the value of religious liberty. These scholars argue that ethics are grounded in divine revelation; thus, evangelical ethics can establish absolute universal moral principles, which allow for enduring freedom for all peoples. While Scripture does not explicitly command religious freedom, the principles of religious freedom are evident. Roger Williams, founder of the Baptist Church in North America, contended that Matt 13:30–38 established religious liberty for all people.[30] Baptist pastor Isaac Backus also drew directly from Scripture in his 1773 work titled *An Appeal to the Public for Religious Liberty*. More recently, evangelical scholar Barrett Duke posits that Scripture's major doctrines demonstrate that God grants all humankind freedom of choice.[31] Because evangelical social ethics are grounded in a transcendent authority attested to in Scripture, evangelical

---

25. Henry, *God, Revelation and Authority*, 6:8.
26. Murray, *We Hold These Truths*, 297.
27. Murray and Hooper, *Religious Liberty*, 175.
28. Del Noce, *The Crisis of Modernity*, 175.
29. Murray and Hooper, *Religious Liberty*, 175.
30. Backus, *Appeal to the Public*, 86.
31. Duesing et al., *First Freedom*, 14.

The Superiority of an Evangelical Model of Religious Liberty

ethics can provide universal moral principles. Consequently, the principles found in Scripture provide a necessary foundation that offers religious liberty for all peoples.

Evangelical social ethics maintain that religious liberty is fundamentally part of Christian anthropology, cosmology, and teleology. But until recently, no systematic evangelical framework for religious freedom existed. The absence of a cohesive framework has hampered evangelical scholarship in two ways: first, evangelical scholars have failed to provide a comprehensive critique of secular and Roman Catholic frameworks for religious freedom. A literature review reveals that evangelical scholars often cite problems in alternative frameworks, but they fail to present how an evangelical paradigm is superior. Second, the lack of a comprehensive framework has hindered Evangelicals in the public square. Kenneth Kantzer argues that the weakness of evangelical influence is not due to cultural changes, but rather to too few evangelical intellectuals in the public square.[32] Attorney Luke Goodrich also suggests that the lack of evangelical scholarship regarding religious freedom has cost Evangelicals credibility in the public square.[33] In his book *Free to Believe*, Goodrich claims that non-believers often see religious liberty as a thin disguise to maintain Christian dominance cloaked in the language of rights. Non-believers often argue that evangelical support for religious liberty means "religious rights for me and not for thee."[34] Subsequently, the lack of a systematic framework for religious freedom has weakened the perception of Evangelicals in the public square.

Recently, however, Andrew Walker has provided a systematic framework for Evangelicals. In his 2018 dissertation, Walker formed a cohesive paradigm for religious liberty founded in the evangelical categories of anthropology, Christology, and eschatology. Walker's work creates a consistent and comprehensive model that allows for a fuller critique of secular and Roman Catholic paradigms. And his model provides warrants for why the evangelical concept of religious liberty is superior. This book will expand on Walker's work by comparing and contrasting an evangelical paradigm for religious liberty against secular and Roman Catholic concepts.

---

32. Henry, *The Christian Mindset*, 24.
33. Goodrich, *Free to Believe*, 17.
34. Franke, "Religious Freedom for Me, but not for Thee."

Introduction

Thesis

This book critiques the frameworks of religious freedom put forth by John Stewart Mill, John Rawls, and John Courtney Murray. It will examine the philosophical and theological assumptions of each and their contributions to religious freedom. It will offer both positive and negative responses to each theory. The argument is that secular and natural law philosophies offer many helpful principles to shape religious freedom, but they are inferior to the principles found in the evangelical perspective of religious freedom. The thesis of this book is that the evangelical paradigm on religious liberty is superior to frameworks provided by John Stuart Mill, John Rawls, and John Courtney Murray because it recognizes a personal transcendent being in a way that provides a balance between individual and collective freedoms.

This book argues that secular frameworks of religious liberty collapse on two points. First, the utilitarian theory of John Stuart Mill is unstable and breaks in two directions: radical libertarianism or paternal collectivism. Utilitarian conceptions of religious freedom eventually reduce to religious toleration. Religious toleration is distinctly different from genuine religious freedom. Religious tolerance cannot provide the full expression of one's religious beliefs because it assumes minority beliefs are inherently harmful. Religious freedom advocate David French notes that "tolerance" implies that something is necessarily wrong and must be tolerated.[35] Religious tolerance assumes that majority beliefs are inherently right, and minority beliefs are potentially harmful to the common good. Consequently, religious toleration ultimately restricts the full expression of minority beliefs, values, and practices.

Moreover, utilitarian philosophy centers authority in the autonomous individual, which creates social tension. Daniel Heimbach recognizes the internal conflict that exists when individual autonomy and communal authority clash.[36] In his article titled "Religious Liberty and Religious Autonomy," Heimbach says, "Consequently, this view poses a dilemma—law must either deny autonomous liberty in order to maintain social order or allow autonomous liberty to increasingly undermine the rule of law leading eventually to complete social chaos."[37] In order to avoid anarchy, utili-

---

35. French, *Divided We Fall*, 186.
36. Heimbach, "Understanding the Difference Between Religious Liberty and Religious Autonomy," 131.
37. Heimbach, "Understanding the Difference Between Religious Liberty and Religious Autonomy," 134.

tarianism favors a majority religion or ideology, which undermines true religious freedom. Utilitarian political philosophy apart from divine special revelation moves toward paternalism at best and tyranny at worst. While utilitarian philosophies may protect the existence of minority religions, it cannot foster genuine religious freedom.

Second, John Rawls's theory offers a procedural framework for religious freedom. But his theory ultimately privatizes religion, and privatized religion diminishes individual and corporate freedoms because it restricts religious practice from public spaces.[38] Religious liberty is an ordered liberty constrained by shared moral obligations.[39] Rawls rightly recognizes religious liberty as such.[40] But because he forbids the public acknowledgment of divine authority, he undercuts the necessary elements needed for ordered liberty. Rawls rightly acknowledges the concept of ordered authority,[41] but he mistakenly places the locus of authority in society and not in God. For Rawls, community consensus serves as the highest order of authority; therefore, all freedom is derived from society. Rawls's theory ultimately deifies the collective. This is not to say that individuals and institutions are not free to exercise their religion. But the location of religious exercise is determined by community authority. Rawls's ideal theory recognizes the value of religion for the individual, but it does not permit religious ideas in the public sphere. Rawls contends that individual religious ideas will disrupt social consensus; therefore, they must not enter the public domain.

Nevertheless, because it is virtually impossible for one to shed one's religious beliefs, Rawls's theory creates a religious idealism in secular form. The evangelical perspective argues that ordered liberty starts with God; therefore, institutional and individual moral obligations are governed by a transcendent moral authority. Evangelicals contend that both civil and ecclesiological authority is delegated from God. Consequently, Rawls's collectivist vision of religious freedom can only allow for privatized religion because anything else would disrupt community consensus.

Roman Catholic natural law puts forth a compelling framework for religious freedom.[42] The Roman Catholic doctrine of natural law supports religious liberty within the particular structures of Catholic political

38. Rawls, *A Theory of Justice*, 7.
39. Duesing, *First Freedom*, 13.
40. Rawls, *A Theory of Justice*, 178.
41. Rawls, *A Theory of Justice*, 178.
42. Murray and Hooper, *Religious Liberty*, 21.

Introduction

theology. But natural law divorced from divine revelation is insufficient in the public square because it presumes upon humanity's ability to perceive specific transcendent principles. Natural law assumes upon divine special revelation but remains silent in the public square; therefore, natural law theory yields its power. Consequently, Catholic natural law is inferior because it remains silent regarding its scriptural assumptions, and it lacks a revelatory bridge to the secular world.

Philosophical Assumptions

This book presumes politics and culture are not hermetically sealed categories. Protestantism often defines culture as humanity's normative activity resulting from one's status as an image-bearer.[43] Humans engaging in family life, art, and education are considered part of culture; thus, culture is a pre-fall condition. Martin Luther contended that God instituted temporal authorities to restrain evil following humanity's fall.[44] Because police, criminal courts, and penal systems are a matter of politics, politics are often considered a post-fall condition. For this reason, some Protestants regard politics as a post-fall condition. Therefore, if humans had not sinned, there would be no need for politics.

However, politics viewed as post-fall misses the underlying meaning of political life.[45] Politics are concerned with governance, and governance is an essential aspect of God's command to subdue the earth. While Luther properly recognized that coercion was a post-fall necessity, one cannot assume that politics on the whole were not part of the pre-fall order. Protestantism does not consider politics and culture separately. Instead, rightly understood, Protestantism recognizes politics as the activity of governance, and this is included in the cultural mandate of Gen 1:28. Therefore, this book assumes that humanity's call to subdue the earth included the activity of governance.

Roman Catholic theologian Joseph Ratzinger also recognizes the unity between politics and culture. He contends that biblical revelation provided proper insight for governance.[46] Ratzinger notes that Western political culture was historically supported on two legs: the Jerusalem

---

43. Skillen, *The Good of Politics*, xix.
44. Luther, *Luther's Works*, 45:xiii.
45. Skillen, *The Good of Politics*, xix.
46. Ratzinger, *Western Culture Today and Tomorrow*, 9.

The Superiority of an Evangelical Model of Religious Liberty

leg—that of Biblical revelation—and the Athenian leg—that of reason.[47] But Enlightenment philosophy kicked out the Jerusalem leg and thus left the Athenian leg wobbly.[48] Liberal frameworks of social ethics are now founded upon the assumptions of reason divorced from the powers of divine special revelation, and this has created two problems.[49] First, liberal social ethics misunderstands freedom. Second, liberal social ethics lacks absolute universal moral values. Consequently, the liberal social ethics are left with a crisis of equilibrium—namely how to balance individual rights while maintaining social cohesion.

The crisis of equilibrium becomes most volatile when individual religious convictions collide with collective interests. Christian theology and Greek philosophy traditionally understood freedom in terms of personal restraint. Political theorist Patrick Deneen says,

> Liberty is a word of ancient lineage, yet liberalism has a more recent pedigree, being arguably only a few hundred years old. It arises from a redefinition of the nature of liberty to mean almost the opposite of its original meaning. By ancient Christian understanding, liberty was the condition of self-governance, whether achieved by the individual or a political community. Because self-rule was achieved only with difficulty—requiring an extensive habitation in virtue, particularly self-command and self-discipline over base but insistent appetites—the achievement of liberty required constraints upon individual choice.[50]

But modern liberalism conceives of liberty in the opposite form; modern liberalism conceives of liberty as a revolt against immaterial and material constraints. Modern liberalism primarily seeks to revolt against the immaterial restraint of God's authority, and this logically leads to liberalism's desire to cast off the material restraints found in nature. Thus, Italian social philosopher Augusto Del Noce argues that it was liberalism's redefinition

---

47. Ratzinger, *Western Culture Today and Tomorrow*, 9.

48. Ratzinger, *Western Culture Today and Tomorrow*, 10.

49. The term "modern" will refer to the philosophical assumptions that emerged with the European Enlightenment. Today's "post-modern" era may be defined as "late modernity" because it expands upon the modern assumptions; therefore, "post-modernity" is merely the natural progression of rationalism divorced from divine revelation. This work will use the term "modern" to address issues relating to reason untethered from the belief in a personal transcendent being.

50. Deneen, *Why Liberalism Failed*, xiii.

Introduction

of freedom that helped ignite the sexual revolution.[51] Del Noce believes that the quest for ever-expanding libertine freedom culminates in the casting off of all sexual restraint. He believes that sexual freedom was nothing more than a vain attempt of humanity to overthrow the constraints of the human body.[52] Modern liberalism's redefinition of freedom has weakened public understanding of the church and its role in society. Del Noce says, "The church is tolerated only to the extent that she does not take any stance on the moral exultations . . . she must be a spectator, without even being granted the right to criticize a new sexual morality."[53] The clash between libertine freedom and religious rights was most notable in the oral arguments in *Obergefell v. Hodges*. In this case, the solicitor general Donald Verrilli acknowledged that same-sex marriage would be an "issue" for the religious freedom of institutions.[54]

Additionally, liberalism's redefinition of freedom also undermines absolute universal morality. Enlightenment thought moved from the biblical concept of God in a twofold direction: First, God, the creator who had continually upheld and sustained the world, had become the one who simply started the universe. Second, the concept of special revelation had been abandoned.[55] Joseph Ratzinger argues that Protestant Christianity at first had no trouble allowing room for the liberal idea of autonomous reason.[56] Protestant social ethics was supported, for a time, by a broad Christian consensus. But as the pathology of libertine freedom metastasized, Protestant social ethics collapsed under the weight of relativism. Therefore, individuals left to pursue their own moral truths cannot answer questions regarding universal goodness.

Nevertheless, Ratzinger is only partially correct. He rightly understands that the power of Protestant social ethic was able to support libertine freedom for a while. Indeed, the Protestant principle of work, rightly understood, created a powerful social ethos that fostered individual freedom while it promoted self-restraint. And he properly recognizes the pathology in libertine conceptions of freedom. But Ratzinger is wrong to insinuate that Protestantism fostered the conditions for libertine freedom. Ratzinger

---

51. Del Noce, *The Crisis of Modernity*, 133.
52. Del Noce, *The Crisis of Modernity*, 159.
53. Del Noce, *The Crisis of Modernity*, 163.
54. Anderson, *Truth Overruled*, 3.
55. Ratzinger, *Western Culture Today and Tomorrow*, 53.
56. Ratzinger, *Western Culture Today and Tomorrow*, 30.

The Superiority of an Evangelical Model of Religious Liberty

is wrong because he fails to distinguish the difference between classic Protestantism and liberal Protestantism.

Liberal Protestantism throughout the nineteenth century rejected the authority of Scripture, resulting in the ascent of relativism. Carl F. H. Henry noted that liberal Protestantism collapsed under the weight of relativism because it rejected the core principles of Protestant theology itself—*Sola Scriptura*.[57] Consequently, Ratzinger's suggestion that classic Protestantism gave way to relativism is a misrepresentation of Protestant principles.

Moreover, social scientist Christian Smith posits that secular ethics founded on autonomous reason may provide a "modest good," but they cannot establish an absolute universal moral good.[58] Because modern liberalism is detached from divine special revelation, it cannot maintain absolute values. Smith contends that secular ethics cannot explain why a person would seek freedom for another person if they are unknown or live at a distance.[59] He says, "Naturalism may well justify many important substantive moral responsibilities but not, as far as I can see, a commitment to honor universal benevolence and human rights."[60] Because liberal social ethics are not grounded in special divine revelation or metaphysics, they have no universal measurement for determining the value of goodness. Thus, one can now understand how Vladimir Lenin was able to claim, "Morality is whatever serves the success of the proletarian revolution."[61] Therefore, liberalism's ambition for ever-expanding freedom is hollowed out by its inability to establish universal moral values.

Furthermore, ethics are lived in a physical world. But as liberalism denied special revelation and the metaphysical world, it enslaved itself to empiricism. Secular ethics are bound to material calculations as the only source of moral authority; therefore, good and evil are dependent on a calculus of consequences. A society that cuts itself off from transcendent realities will eventually have nothing left but the positivistic criterion of the majority principle, leading to the decadence of law governed by statistics alone.[62] Consequently, liberal social ethics take on a distinctly utilitarian hue.

---

57. Henry, *Christian Personal Ethics*, 529.
58. Smith, *Atheist Overreach*, 24.
59. Smith, *Atheist Overreach*, 32.
60. Smith, *Atheist Overreach*, 9.
61. Lenin, *Collected Works of Vladimir Lenin*, 283.
62. Ratzinger, *Western Culture Today and Tomorrow*, 122.

Introduction

Finally, secular liberalism ultimately requires expansive state control. As individual freedoms increase and universal values decrease, large state structures are required to preserve social order. Because secular philosophies do not draw upon first principles of divine revelation or metaphysics, secular ethics must rely on state power to regulate individual and institutional moral choices. Patrick Deneen argues this point in his book, *Why Liberalism Failed*. Deneen says,

> Statism enables individuals, individualism demands statism. For all the claims about the electoral transformations—for "Hope and Change"—and "Making America Great Again"—two facts are naggingly apparent: modern liberalism proceeds by making us both more individualistic and more statist. This is not because one party advances individualism without cutting back on statism while the other does the opposite; rather both move simultaneously in tune with our deepest philosophic premise.[63]

Secular liberalism's philosophical premise is constructed on the idea of expanding freedom untethered from God. But when societies are confronted with the frailty of autonomous reason, they easily fall victim to dictatorships.[64] Therefore, secular liberal social ethics collapses when they are confronted with the frailty of human reason.

Nevertheless, this book does not suggest that classic liberalism is necessarily wrong. Classical liberalism offers the best opportunities for individuals and communities to flourish. But this book assumes that classic liberalism can only flourish when the moral conscience is shaped by Scripture.[65] Therefore, this book contends that Evangelicalism contributes to overall human flourishing through its prophetic witness.

Theological Method

The following book argues for the superiority of an evangelical vision of religious freedom. I will argue that the evangelical paradigm is cognitively defensible regardless of whether it is accepted or rejected by non-believers. This work makes a distinction between evangelical ethics and other forms of Christian ethics. First, evangelical ethics believe that Scripture is the

---

63. Deneen, *Why Liberalism Failed*, 17.
64. Ratzinger, *Western Culture Today and Tomorrow*, 35.
65. Ratzinger, *Western Culture Today and Tomorrow*, 35.

The Superiority of an Evangelical Model of Religious Liberty

ultimate authority for divine revelation. Evangelicalism recognizes the power of general revelation according to Rom 1:18–32. But evangelical theology does not believe that general revelation alone is sufficient for salvation. General revelation is adequate to render humankind guilty before God. But general revelation alone is inadequate for specific moral guidance. General revelation cannot provide details concerning holiness, worship, or nuanced moral living in a pluralistic society. Evangelical ethics believe that submission to God's authority is an act of worship; therefore, evangelical ethics are founded in the special revelation given through Scripture.

Moreover, Evangelicals believe that Scripture is taken on its own terms. Scripture speaks for itself.[66] In contrast, biblical ethics uses the Bible as a part of its ethical structure. But they give other elements equal authority. Biblical ethicists often mix Scripture with philosophy, and this undermines the potency of God's revelation.[67] Therefore, evangelical ethics are more stable because it submits to Scripture as its final authority.

Second, evangelical ethicists believe that God's self-revelation comes fully in Jesus Christ. The Baptist Faith and Message 2000 asserts, "All Scripture is a testimony to Christ, who is Himself the focus of divine revelation."[68] Evangelical ethicists believe that all Scripture attests to Christ, which is distinctly different from neo-Orthodoxy or liberal Protestantism that reject propositional statements about Christ.[69] Consequently, evangelism is fixed in the reality that God has revealed himself through Jesus Christ, the divine *Logos*.

Evangelicalism's strength and weakness is that it allows for intramural disagreements.[70] Evangelicalism's diversity serves to advance its potency. Carl F. H. Henry argued that the evangelical mind, enlightened by Scripture, can employ the canons of reason to interpret reality in amazingly diverse ways and expound competing views with compelling force.[71] But Evangelicalism's diversity often lacks consensus. Because Scripture does not specifically mention religious liberty per se, Evangelicals have been slow to

---

66. Henry, *God, Revelation, and Authority*, 6:13.

67. For example, biblical ethicists such as J. Philip Wogaman, Harry Hueber, Stanley Hauerwas, and John Howard Yoder use the Bible as part of their ethical frameworks. But Scripture is either equal or subservient to other authorities.

68. Baptist Faith and Message 2000, "Article I: The Scriptures."

69. Henry, *God, Revelation, and Authority*, 6:439.

70. Calvinism and Arminianism, dispensationalism and covenant theology are examples of intramural disagreements.

71. Henry, *God, Revelation, and Authority*, 6:90–91.

Introduction

develop a comprehensive and unifying framework for religious freedom. This absence has been a stunning oversight because evangelical social ethics must assume religious freedom if it is to advocate in the public square.[72] Andrew Walker argues, "The ability, for example, to advocate for the unborn—whether praying in front of an abortion clinic or casting one's vote in a referendum on the issue—assumes some framework that makes such activity possible."[73] Consequently, Walker unifies the three themes common among Evangelicals to create a comprehensive evangelical framework for religious liberty. Walker forms a framework around the motifs of the kingdom of God, the image of God, and the mission of God.

The method used in this book will build upon the evangelical framework established by Andrew Walker. Walker formed a Christological schematic utilizing three elements of consensus within evangelical theology: first, the kingdom of God serves as an orienting doctrine.[74] Second, the image of God serves a practical guide.[75] Third, the mission of God serves as a cultural apologetic.[76] I will work within the boundaries put forth in Walker's paradigm. But because this book is a critique, it must intersect with classic liberal and Roman Catholic thought. Therefore, I will focus my attention on what Walker calls a "cultural apologetic" using the tools of ethicist Oliver O'Donovan. O'Donovan notes,

> Ethics is necessarily an architectural enterprise, bringing trains of thought together which differ with inner logics, the practitioner must be able to function polymorphously, now telling a narrative, now mounting an argument that proceeds to valid inference, now depicting reality adequately from many sides.[77]

Because liberal thought denies divine revelation, I will use categories of thought that are familiar for non-believers. Therefore, while I will focus my analysis under the cultural apologetic element of Walker, I will also nuance my argument using the categories of self, world, and time.

Oliver O'Donovan's categories of self, world, and time serve as a helpful conduit to critique liberal, Roman Catholic, and evangelical thought. The categories of self, world, and time provide evangelical answers to

72. Walker, "Religious Liberty in Contemporary Evangelical Social Ethics," 4.
73. Walker, "Religious Liberty in Contemporary Evangelical Social Ethics," 4.
74. Walker, "Religious Liberty in Contemporary Evangelical Social Ethics," 25.
75. Walker, "Religious Liberty in Contemporary Evangelical Social Ethics," 28.
76. Walker, "Religious Liberty in Contemporary Evangelical Social Ethics," 28.
77. O'Donovan, *Self, World, and Time*, x.

The Superiority of an Evangelical Model of Religious Liberty

questions regarding anthropology, cosmology, and teleology. O'Donovan's anthropology, cosmology, and teleology overlap within the evangelical pattern put forth by Andrew Walker. O'Donovan's categories of self, world, and time emerge from his seminal work *Resurrection and the Moral Order*.[78] And his classifications intersect with liberal and Roman Catholic thought in several key ways. First, O'Donovan's theory of self contends that the resurrection of Christ awakens individuals to a renewed agency.[79] Evangelicals and Roman Catholics agree that image bearing above all includes the ability to make real choices. Regardless of theological nuances, both Evangelicals and Roman Catholics believe that God acts to energize the human will. Classic liberalism rejects God's activity regarding human will. But classic liberalism agrees that humans are capable of free-will decision making. In effect, liberal theory is based on the philosophy of voluntarism. Liberalism defines freedom as unfettered and autonomous free choice.[80] Liberalism often claims neutrality about the choices people make because it is a defender of the individual's "right to choose" over and above any particular concept of the "good."[81] Classic liberalism is established on the belief that expanding choices leads to increasing freedom.[82] Classic liberalism believes that the role of government is to expand libertine freedom by protecting individual choice. Therefore, the category of human agency, regardless of one's belief concerning Jesus Christ, serves as a point of contact.

Second, O'Donovan's category of world posits that the resurrection of Christ provides a foundation for objective truth.[83] O'Donovan argues that humans exist in an ordered world, and this ordering provides objective truth.[84] The cosmology of the world makes sense in light of the resurrection of Christ. O'Donovan's natural law theology is different from natural law philosophy found within Roman Catholicism because he explicitly draws attention to the resurrection of Christ. O'Donovan argues that the resurrection of Christ properly orders the universe, and this truth exists regardless of one's assent or rejection. Both Evangelicals and Roman Catholics can agree that a natural objective order exists. Yet some strains of classic

78. O'Donovan, *Self, World, and Time*, xii.
79. O'Donovan, *Self, World, and Time*, 7.
80. Deneen, *Why Liberalism Failed*, 31.
81. Deneen, *Why Liberalism Failed*, 34.
82. Deneen, *Why Liberalism Failed*, 31.
83. O'Donovan, *Self, World, and Time*, 10.
84. O'Donovan, *Self, World, and Time*, 10.

Introduction

liberalism reject natural law and natural rights theory.[85] For example, Jeremy Bentham and John Stuart Mill loathed natural law theology and natural right philosophy.[86] They rejected the idea that an ordered universe tells one anything about morality. But even classic liberalism founded in utilitarian social ethics recognizes the existence of objective reality. Utilitarian social ethics are founded on the principle that actions can be measured based upon objective results. Therefore, the category of world provides a point of contact regardless of one's beliefs about Christ.

Third, O'Donovan's method reorients time based on the resurrection of Christ.[87] O'Donovan's method recognizes that individual agency and the objective world are co-present in moments of time, and this opens individuals for action.[88] Evangelicals and Roman Catholics both agree that time has a beginning and end point. Evangelicals and Catholics also agree that Christ's incarnation joins past, present, and future time. Yet classic liberalism rejects the incarnation. Classic liberalism denies metaphysical realities; therefore, the incarnation is reduced to Christian mythology. But modern liberal philosophy is a project that is dependent upon time. Patrick Deneen posits that liberalism is about redefining the human perception of time. It is an effort to transform the experience of time, and in particular the relationship of past, present, and future.[89] Augusto Del Noce argues that Marxism's revolutionary spirit is a quest to overthrow the past and advance toward a utopian future.[90] Del Noce says,

> The question whether objective truth can be attributed to human thinking is not a question of theory but is a practical question. In practice men must prove the truth, i.e., the reality and the power, the "this sightedness" of his thinking. The dispute over the reality or the non-reality of his thinking which is isolated from practice is a purely scholastic question. In other words, the truth of philosophy is verified by the historical reality it is able to produce.[91]

---

85. Within classic liberalism several political philosophies exist. Libertarian political philosophies may be constructed on the concept of natural rights, while utilitarian and Kantian political philosophies deny natural law and natural rights.

86. Jeremy Bentham, "Anarchical Fallacies," 896.

87. O'Donovan, *Self, World, and Time*, 15.

88. O'Donovan, *Self, World, and Time*, 15.

89. Deneen, *Why Liberalism Failed*, 72.

90. Del Noce, *The Crisis of Modernity*, 63.

91. Del Noce, *The Crisis of Modernity*, 106.

The Superiority of an Evangelical Model of Religious Liberty

Because secular philosophies reject divine revelation and metaphysics, they are dependent upon history to establish reality. Therefore, regardless of classic liberalism's beliefs about the resurrection of Christ, classic liberalism must acknowledge the historical Jesus marked a new ethical reality in time.

Moreover, all ethics are lived out in moments of real time. O'Donovan posits that making a moral choice includes deliberating about future consequences.[92] But the act of deliberating assumes one reflects upon past choice and consequences, and this is something that classic liberals can also affirm. Therefore, O'Donovan's triadic structure of self, world, and time provides a distinctly evangelical method for evaluating secular theory and natural law philosophy, and it allows for points of contact with non-believers.

Background

This book comes at a time when many are calling for Christians to exit the public square. Following Rod Dreher's 2015 book titled *The Benedict Option: A Strategy for Christians in a Post-Christian Nation*, some Evangelicals have argued that it is time to withdraw from public engagement. But disengagement undermines Evangelicalism itself. The word "evangelical" comes from the mandate to "bring good news." Evangelical disengagement would be catastrophic on two points. First, disengagement would reduce evangelism to merely personal evangelism. Carl F. H. Henry argued that the church's mission must not be limited to a preoccupation with personal evangelism at the expense of public concerns.[93] Evangelical congregations lose opportunity and credibility for personal evangelism when they ignore the problems of our communities. Because Evangelicals recognize Scriptural authority, Evangelicals can speak to cultural issues as a prophetic witness. Evangelicals have a responsibility to proclaim the words of truth regardless of the outcome. Evangelicals stand today as Moses, Daniel, and Paul speaking truth to power. Second, disengagement would weaken overall missionary activity. In 2014, the International Mission Board released its strategy for tent-making missionaries.[94] At the heart of this strategy was the concept of fully mobilizing all of God's people. Today, thousands of Evangelicals are tent-makers in the institution of government. A call to disengage would not only secede public policy to unregenerate minds, but

---

92. O'Donovan, *Self, World, and Time*, 15.
93. Henry, *The Christian Mindset*, 39.
94. International Mission Board, "Engineering: A Guide for IMB Students."

Introduction

it also undermines one's individual missionary calling. Therefore, this book emerges as a work of mission.

Components

This book will prove that the evangelical perspective of religious freedom is superior to the approaches found in secular and Roman Catholic paradigms. Chapter 1 serves as an introduction to the definition of terms and provides the thesis of this book. Also, chapter 1 introduces philosophical and epistemological problems found within secular social ethics. Chapter 1 also presents a method of analysis developed by Oliver O'Donovan. Chapter 2 will offer a brief biography of John Stuart Mill and then explain key aspects of his philosophy. After this, chapter 2 will critique Mill's consequentialist philosophy. This is followed by the negative conclusion that utilitarianism only provides religious toleration. In chapter three, the book considers the political philosophical method of John Rawls as set forth in *A Theory of Justice*. Additionally, chapter 3 will provide a biographical sketch of Rawls's major works and his contribution to American social ethics. After this, it will critique Rawlsian theory and present a negative response. Chapter 3 will demonstrate that Rawls's ideal theory privatizes religion; therefore, it removes the benefit of religion from the public square. Chapter 4 will consider the value of John Courtney Murray's natural law philosophy. It will summarize the Roman Catholic Church's problem with religious freedom throughout church history. Then it will offer a biography of John Courtney Murray SJ, and it will consider his influence on Vatican II. After this, the book will critique Murray's use of natural law philosophy and offer both positive and negative responses. Chapter 4 will present a conclusion that natural law philosophy is incomplete. Chapter 5 will present an evangelical perspective of religious freedom. It will prove that Evangelicalism offers a comprehensive theory of religious freedom. Chapter 5 will use the structure put forth in Andrew Walker's "Religious Liberty in Contemporary Evangelical Social Ethics: An Assessment and Framework" and explain why it is superior to secular and natural law perspectives. Chapter 6 will offer a summary and a final analysis. Finally, the chapter will argue for the need of an evangelical perspective in the public square.

CHAPTER 2

Utilitarianism

The Influence of John Stuart Mill on Modern Religious Liberty

LIBERALISM HAS HISTORICALLY SUPPORTED religious liberty. John Locke is considered the father of liberalism, and scholars such as Jim Powell argue that Locke significantly influenced Thomas Jefferson, Thomas Paine, George Mason, James Madison, and Benjamin Franklin.[1] As a Christian, Locke believed that religious liberty was the chief mark of the true church.[2] But as a philosopher, Locke sought a liberal justification for religious freedom. Locke's notion of liberty reflects his commitment to theology and philosophy.[3] But Locke's use of philosophy was submitted under divine revelation.[4] Locke used Scripture to form his argument for religious liberty.

Jeremy Bentham was not Christian, nor was he sympathetic to biblical revelation.[5] Bentham loathed the doctrine of divine revelation and the idea of natural rights. He believed that natural rights philosophy incited the revolutions in America and France. Bentham feared revolution would come to England; therefore, he sought to undermine natural rights philosophy,

---

1. Powell, "John Locke," line 1–4.
2. Ahdar and Leigh, *Religious Freedom in the Liberal State*, 15.
3. Gewirth, *Political Philosophy*, 18.
4. Locke sought to use reason as he contended for religious liberty. But Locke's use of reason was submitted to the Scripture; therefore, he was Augustinian in the sense that he "believed to understand."
5. Bentham, "Anarchical Fallacies," 896.

calling it "rhetorical nonsense" and "nonsense on stilts."[6] But Bentham supported religious liberty even though he opposed Christianity. Jeremy Bentham defended the rights of all people, regardless of religious expression, because he believed religious freedom was good for the collective.[7]

Immanuel Kant contended for religious liberty based on his categorical imperative.[8] In a notable but not well-known book on religious belief, Kant argued with Prussian authorities about the right to religious opinion for all people.[9] For Kant, religious liberty was a matter of human freewill exercised through the faculty of reason. Kant believed that humans were rational and self-determining; therefore, humans are subjected to their own laws, and they make their own moral choices.[10] Kant grounded his argument for religious freedom exclusively in intellectual power and not biblical revelation or natural law.

Liberal paradigms of religious freedom based exclusively on human reason are unstable. Liberal philosophy, untethered from Scripture, struggles to maintain the fragile balance between individual autonomy and corporate concern. Oliver O'Donovan notes the insufficiency of philosophy for social ethics, stating,

> Philosophy is not as such text-based, though it may read philosophical texts and learn from them; its task is to render an account of reality, and in doing so, it will take its concepts where it finds them. Theology, avoiding philosophy's hazardous smash-and-grab tactics, insists on having primary concepts issued and duly signed for out of the scriptural inventory.[11]

O'Donovan argues that philosophy, cut off from divine revelation, maintains internal inconsistencies and fragmentizes ethics, leaving the ethicist with only a loose form of utilitarianism.[12] John Stuart Mill recognized the irregularities in the utilitarian philosophy handed down to him. Mill sought to strengthen utilitarian philosophy by solving the problem of autonomous rights and social cohesion.[13] But because Mill's philosophy was

---

6. Bentham, "Anarchical Fallacies," 914.
7. Bentham, "Anarchical Fallacies," 927.
8. Kant, *Complete Works of Immanuel Kant*, 402.
9. Houlgate, *Understanding Immanuel Kant*, 11.
10. Houlgate, *Understanding Immanuel Kant*, 73.
11. O'Donovan, *Self, World, and Time*, 6.
12. O'Donovan, *Self, World, and Time*, x.
13. Houlgate, *Understanding John Stuart Mill*, 21.

entirely secular, his work remained fragile and inconsistent. John Stuart Mill's utilitarian model of religious liberty splits along two poles. Libertarians often appeal to Mill to support a form of radical individualism, and progressives use Mill to encourage egalitarianism.

The purpose of this chapter is to critique the principles that ground John Stuart Mill's utilitarianism and prove his model inferior to those emerging from divine revelation. This chapter will argue that utilitarianism fails to provide a full-orbed understanding of one's relationship to self, one's knowledge of the surrounding world, and one's understanding of time. Therefore, utilitarianism cannot sufficiently provide a sustainable vision of religious liberty. And utilitarianism is not inclusive enough to answer the challenges presented by increasing pluralism and technological advances. The chapter will offer a brief biographical sketch of John Stuart Mill considering his secular motivations for religious liberty. After this, the chapter will explore the contours of religious liberty put forward in Mill's *On Liberty*. Additionally, the problem of authority, the harm principle, and prejudice are analyzed and contrasted against evangelical foundations. Finally, chapter 2 will conclude with a focus on the deficiencies and dangers of the utilitarian model for religious liberty.

John Stuart Mill (1806–73)

"Each is the proper guardian of his own health, whether bodily or mental and spiritual. Mankind are greater gainers by suffering each other to live as seems good to themselves, than by compelling each to live as seems good to the rest."[14] With these words, John Stuart Mill declared his philosophy for religious liberty. John Stuart Mill was a British utilitarian philosopher, political activist, and member of the English Parliament who lived during a time of significant cultural and political change.[15] Mill came of age in a nation recovering from the wars with Napoleonic France. He lived in a transitionary period when the populace was growing fearful of the exclusive and elitist political system of nineteenth-century Europe. Additionally, the emerging industrial system created uncertainties for the lives of common men and women.[16] John Stuart Mill sought to protect the rights of individuals from two forms of tyranny. First, Mill wanted to protect society

---

14. Mill, *On Liberty*, 15.
15. Patrick, *An Analysis of John Stuart Mill's Utilitarianism*, 9.
16. Mill, *On Liberty*, ix.

Utilitarianism

from the power that a ruler could exercise over a community.[17] Second, Mill wanted to protect individuals from the power of democratic tyranny.[18] Mill argued that democracies necessarily assume a majority rule, and this rule tends toward oppressing people in the minority. John Stuart Mill did not advocate for religious freedom because he necessarily valued religion per se—Mill was a devoted atheist—but Mill contended for faith because he believed freedom of thought was essential for human progress. Consequently, Mill defined freedom as "doing what one desires."[19]

Mill was a committed Humean philosopher,[20] which meant he believed human reason was subservient to human passions. Mill also rejected metaphysics; therefore, he denied theoretical reason.[21] He also contended that practical reason required empirical evidence, and this belief ultimately caused him to reduce human reason to mere instrumentality. John Stuart Mill was a product of nineteenth-century rationalist philosophy, and in this regard his political persuasion was thoroughly perfectionist.[22]

John Stuart Mill was a child prodigy raised under the tutelage of his father, James Mill.[23] Mill's education and upbringing lacked several vital components. First, Mill's childhood was absent of religion. Mill's father regarded it as his duty to keep his son from Christianity. In his autobiography, John Stuart Mill describes himself as "one who has not thrown off religious belief, but I never had it."[24] James Mill believed that it was a logical fallacy to think that an all-powerful, all-wise, and all-good being could exist and, at the same time, allow evil. Thus, John Stuart Mill lacked exposure to genuine Christian faith. But this does not mean that Mill lacked a religion in practice. Mill wrote in his autobiography that when one discovered the principle of utility, it was a religious experience. Mill states,

> The "principle of utility," understood as Bentham understood it, and applied in the manner in which he applied it through these

---

17. Mill, *On Liberty*, 6.
18. Mill, *On Liberty*, 9.
19. Gregg, *On Ordered Liberty*, 5.
20. Gregg, *On Ordered Liberty*, 5.
21. The term "metaphysics" will be used throughout this chapter to refer to non-material realities, including human conscience and emotions. The term "theoretical reason" will be used in reference to thinking about truth claims.
22. Mill, *John Stuart Mill Autobiography*, 180–81.
23. Patrick, *An Analysis of John Stuart Mill's Utilitarianism*, 6.
24. Mill, *John Stuart Mill Autobiography*, 49.

> three volumes, fell exactly into its place as the keystone which held together the detached and fragmented component parts of my knowledge and beliefs. It gave unity to my conception of things. I now had opinions; a creed, a doctrine, a philosophy; in one among the best senses of the word, a religion: inculcation and diffusion of which could be made the principal outward purpose of life.[25]

Utilitarianism became John Stuart Mill's functional religion.

Second, John Stuart Mill's education lacked emotional awareness. Mill's father rejected theism and replaced it with Greek philosophy.[26] James Mill adopted the principles of the Stoics, Cynics, and the Epicureans. Consequently, the elder Mill taught his son to ignore emotions. But as creatures created in the image of God, humans are endowed with an inner spirit that cannot be ignored. Theologian Anthony Hoekema notes that the human mind includes all aspects of the inner person, including conscience, will, and emotion.[27] Moral reasoning cannot be cut off from emotions because the inner person responds emotionally to morality. Virtues such as justice, courage, prudence, and temperance correlate with emotions. For instance, injustice often produces anger. The virtues of courage and temperance often provoke fear; prudence can often produce feelings of loneliness. Emotions often motivate moral actions; therefore, emotions and motives cannot be uncoupled from ethics. O'Donovan notes that humans are awakened to their responsibility as a moral agent through the emotional pangs of conscience.[28] Therefore, any framework of morality that seeks to deaden the inner person will be severely impaired, and this proved true in the life of the young philosopher. John Stuart Mill's lack of emotional awareness left him unequipped to deal with non-rational personal motivation.[29] At the age of twenty, John Stuart Mill descended into a severe depression and mental crisis. Mill's own words ironically echo those of Qohelet when he states,

> Suppose that all your objects in life were realized; that all the changes in institutions and opinions which you are looking forward to could be completely affected at this very instant; would this be a great joy and happiness to you? And an irrepressible self-consciousness distinctly answered, "No!" At this, my heart

---

25. Mill, *John Stuart Mill Autobiography*, 68.
26. Mill, *John Stuart Mill Autobiography*, 54.
27. Hoekema, *Created in God's Image*, 206–7.
28. O'Donovan, *Self, World, and Time*, 36.
29. Mill, *John Stuart Mill Autobiography*, 8.

Utilitarianism

sank within me: the whole foundation on which my life was constructed fell down. All my happiness was to have been found in the continual pursuit of this end. The end had ceased to charm, and how could there ever again be any interest in the means? I seemed to have nothing left to live for.[30]

The utilitarianism handed down to John Stuart Mill could not bridge the gap between a generalized social happiness and individual happiness.[31] John Stewart Mill's moral philosophy left him disoriented and depressed.

Mill's Utilitarian Project

Mill never wavered in the conviction that happiness was the test by which morality was judged.[32] Mill made it his goal to perfect the inconsistencies within the utilitarianism of Bentham and the elder Mill. He turned to the Romantics and English poets to educate himself about human emotion. It was through romanticism that Mill developed a scale to judge pleasure, pain, and ultimate happiness.[33]

Nevertheless, while John Stuart Mill learned the importance of emotions, he did not believe feelings were sufficient to establish the first principles of morality.[34] Mill rejected any moral theory that derived first principles from *a priori* knowledge.[35] Mill strongly opposed Kant's categorical imperative and Locke's natural right theory because they failed to provide sufficient empirical evidence for determining the rightness or wrongness of an act.[36] Commenting on Kant's logic, Mill states,

> So act, that the rule on which thou actest would admit of being adopted as a law by all rational beings. But when he begins to deduce from this precept any of the actual duties of morality, he fails, almost grotesquely, to show that there would be any contradiction, any logic (not to say physical) impossibility, in adoption by all rational beings of the most outrageously immoral rules of conduct.

---

30. Mill, *John Stuart Mill Autobiography*, 8.
31. Mill, *John Stuart Mill Autobiography*, 8.
32. Mill, *John Stuart Mill Autobiography*, xiv.
33. Mill, *John Stuart Mill Autobiography*, xiv.
34. Houlgate, *Understanding John Stuart Mill*, 19.
35. Mill, *On Liberty*, 118.
36. Houlgate, *Understanding John Stuart Mill*, 23.

> All he shows is that the consequence of their universal adoption would be such as none would choose to incur.[37]

Mill reasoned that Kantian philosophy lacked direct proof because *a priori* knowledge does not contain empirical properties. Therefore, Mill set out to strengthen historic utilitarianism by developing an experiential framework to judge the morality of an act.[38] Mill maintained that actions are morally right if they promote a general overarching happiness and morally wrong if they encourage the reverse.[39]

But Mill's theory contains significant fallacies. First, Mill reasoned that what is true for the whole is true for the part. He claimed that the general happiness of society leads to greater individual happiness. But because he ordered reason as submissive to passion, rights are the invention of collective passions. As an example, if the general population determined that starving brown-haired people would lead to overall happiness, then the happiness of the majority would supersede the rights of all brown-haired people. Mill failed to explain how general happiness can exist when some individuals are deprived of happiness.

Because Mill rejected biblical theology and metaphysics, he failed to grasp the complex nature of the human relationship within an ordered ecosystem. In *Resurrection and the Moral Order*, Oliver O'Donovan affirms that in the natural order of creation creatures are interdependent so that the ordering-to of any particular being is a function of its ordering-alongside a member of a kind.[40] An evangelical framework of ethics balances the tension between part and world by placing humanity within the network of creation. The creation narrative answers the problem of correlation between part and whole. The opening chapters of Genesis reveal humanity's interconnectedness with the world, the animal kingdom, the human world, and the supernatural sphere. The Christian doctrine of the fall posits that individual moral actions connect to other spheres of reality. Evangelical ethics are superior to Mill's ethics because they answer the relational and ordering questions left silent in Mill's secular paradigm. Mill cannot address the problem of individuals cut off from general happiness; neither does he discuss how these individuals may affect the general happiness of the whole.

37. Mill, *On Liberty*, 118.
38. Patrick, *An Analysis of John Stuart Mill's Utilitarianism*, 31.
39. Patrick, *An Analysis of John Stuart Mill's Utilitarianism*, 30.
40. O'Donovan, *Resurrection and Moral Order*, 38.

Second, Mill's utilitarian consequentialism is teleologically flawed. Mill does not answer how one would or could know which actions would bring about future happiness. Finite humans cannot determine with certainty how one moment in time will influence the next. Humans may deliberate on how an action might result in future happiness, but these deliberations do not determine outcomes. Solomon recognized this when he wrote, "The heart of man plans his ways, but the Lord establishes his steps" (Prov 16:9). Solomon did not explain the nuances of God's sovereignty and human agency—the ancient mind was superior in its ability to appreciate paradox.[41] But Solomon did recognize that divine power governs human agency. However, Mill's theory denies the influence of any transcendent being, and this denial results in a false assumption that humankind can predict future happiness with certainty. Utilitarian ethics ascribes divine omniscience to finite human creatures, which leads to a false sense of human deification.

Mill's theory about future happiness was ironic. The irony emerges when one considers Mill's fervent rejection of Kantian and Lockean ethics. Mill rejected Kant's and Locke's frameworks because he believed they lacked empirical evidence.[42] He contended that *a priori* knowledge is insufficient for moral reasoning. But Mill's consequentialism also assumes knowledge before empirical evidence. Mill's utilitarianism requires that an act take place before one can determine the value of the experience; therefore, his consequentialism lacks the same proof he demanded from others. Mill recognized the inconsistency, so he redefined the word "proof." Mill admitted that "questions of ultimate ends are not amenable to direct proof."[43] So he claimed that when something is deemed as good, it is because it is a means to something else that is good, or it is good in itself.[44] Mill argued that "considerations may be presented capable of determining the intellect either to give or withhold assent to the doctrine: and this is equivalent to proof."[45] For Mill, the concept of proof is a matter of means, not ultimate ends. Political philosopher Alan Gewirth notes that utilitarian reason is calculative of means and ends, and utilitarianism has no inherent moral significance except insofar as the calculations of self-interest may

---

41. Lennox, *Proverbs*, 162.
42. Houlgate, *Understanding John Stuart Mill*, 25.
43. Mill, *On Liberty*, 118.
44. Houlgate, *Understanding John Stuart Mill*, 26.
45. Mill, *Considerations on Representative Government*, 118.

coincide with what is for the public interest.[46] Mill's theory results in an ethic of "the end justifies the means." Consequently, John Stuart Mill's utilitarian ethic falls short and commits a teleological fallacy because he has no way to prove happiness before an action.

Third, Mill's utilitarian ethic reduces freedom to materialistic freedom. Mill located the origins of liberty within human appetites.[47] In Mill's writing about freedom, he said, "Liberty consists in doing what one desires."[48] And he said, "In part, which merely concerns himself, his independence is, of right, absolute. Over himself, over his own body and mind, the individual is sovereign."[49] In one regard, Millian theory attempts to elevate the status of human reason and individual autonomy. But because he denied divine revelation, he could not balance the dualistic nature of human experience. For Mill, happiness was thought to be the promotion of pleasure and the absence of pain. His definition assumes that pleasure is freedom from physical pain. But this definition is reductionist because it does not leave open the possibility for dueling experience. For instance, a cancer patient may suffer extreme pain and, at the same time, experience profound happiness. The dual experience of suffering and joy prompted James to say, "Count it all joy, my brothers, when you meet trials of various kinds" (Jas 1:3). Consequently, utilitarian theory fails to recognize the fullness of humanity as embodied spirits.

Additionally, Mill's definition of happiness assumes that pleasure is the end for which all people strive—pleasure is humanity's ultimate end. Mill's claim that humanity seeks happiness is not distinct from the claims of others made throughout church history. But Christian theologians recognize that happiness is the result of a proper relationship with God and others; Christian theology locates the source of happiness in the person of God. John Piper notes that God is the object of happiness, and all those who have a right relationship with God find happiness communicated through experiencing his love.[50] But Mill's secular philosophy entirely rejects the idea of a transcendent being and metaphysics; therefore, Mill's utilitarianism makes happiness a self-validating experience based only on natural pleasures. As a result, Mill's utilitarian concept of happiness is logically

46. Gewirth, *Political Philosophy*, 16.
47. Mill, Considerations on Representative Government, 118.
48. Mill, *Considerations on Representative Government*, 118.
49. Mill, *On Liberty*, 9.
50. Piper and Edwards, *God's Passion for His Glory*, 3.

Utilitarianism

independent, which causes a split in two directions.[51] Utilitarianism collapses into egoism, in which individuals become self-determining agents of happiness. Or utilitarianism expands along on a corporatist axis in which the collective determines general happiness for society. This split was apparent in the nineteenth and twentieth centuries when many interpreters hailed Mill as a libertarian and others considered him a collectivist.

Because utilitarianism is self-determining, it ultimately deifies either the individual or the collective. Mill's definition of happiness seeks to contort the created order toward one's hedonistic desires, and this is why Mill's contemporaries often called his paradigm a "swine" ethic.[52] Consequently, Mill's classification of happiness is self-referential and ultimately reduces happiness to individual experience.

John Stuart Mill's philosophy contains many inconsistencies and fallacies. But his utilitarian philosophy has become tremendously influential in Western political philosophy.[53] Robert P. George notes that by the mid-1960s, "the spirit of Mill's philosophy had perhaps acquired the status of orthodoxy among academic elites."[54] Political philosopher Samuel Gregg says, "Much of the modern case for freedom is encumbered by a continuing reliance, implicit or otherwise, upon the utilitarian premises and methodology."[55] Mill's views on liberty, happiness, and political order significantly shaped the thought of Western democracies.

But while some may celebrate Mill as the secular saint of religious liberty, Maurice Cowling contends that Millian philosophy ultimately results in intolerance toward Christianity.[56] Maurice Cowling argues that Mill's paradigm for religious liberty results in "moral totalitarianism" because its goal is to establish reason as a new modern religion.[57] Cowling recognized that Mill's secular model for religious liberty is a competing secular religion in which the power of unregenerate human reason becomes the highest form of worship. Consequently, Mill's framework for religious liberty established a temporary conduit for freedom of thought. But because his theory

---

51. Gewirth, *Political Philosophy*, 8.
52. Mill, *On Liberty*, 121.
53. Patrick, *An Analysis of John Stuart Mill's Utilitarianism*, 9.
54. George, *Making Men Moral*, 75.
55. Gregg, *On Ordered Liberty*, 6.
56. Cowling, *Mill and Liberalism*, xiii.
57. Cowling, *Mill and Liberalism*, xlviii.

denies a transcendent divine being, it eventually falls under the weight of human depravity.

Interpretations of *On Liberty*

The principles found in *On Liberty* are clear, but Mill's motivation is not as obvious. Mill unequivocally stated his goal was to delineate the nature and limits of the power that can legitimately be exercised by society over the individual.[58] Mill advocated for the rights of the individual against society during an era when people were rapidly coming to believe that the individual had no absolute rights against society.[59] Mill saw that the French Revolution was not just an assertion of human liberty but was also the unfortunate consequence of the natural right theory.[60] He believed the French monarchy and aristocracy deserved what they got in revolution, but he did not admire the destruction that went with it.[61] In the French Revolution, Mill saw that social order must be protected from the tyranny of opinion as well as tyranny from the magistrate.[62] Mill's goal in the essay *On Liberty* was to define and set boundaries for the relationship between individual freedom and society.

Controversies surround John Stuart Mill's *On Liberty*. Henry Sidgwick notes that Mill's utilitarian ethic is dominated by the problem of "dualism of practical reason."[63] Sidgwick realizes that Mill's ethic does not provide a substantive reason for pursuing general happiness over and above individual happiness. Hence, Sidgwick recognizes two forms of hedonism that emerge from Mill: egoism and universal intemperance.[64] The problem of practical dualism in Mill allows some commentators to interpret *On Liberty* individualistically and others universally. Scholars such as Daniel Jacobson understand Mill as a libertarian.[65] Jacobson argues that Mill's motivation was to preserve "self-regarding acts."[66] "Self-regarding

---

58. Mill, *The Complete Works of John Stuart Mill*, 9.
59. Mill, *The Complete Works of John Stuart Mill*, 7.
60. Cowling, *Mill and Liberalism*, 6.
61. Cowling, *Mill and Liberalism*, 6.
62. Mill, *The Complete Works of John Stuart Mill*, 10.
63. Sidgwick and Singer, *Essays on Ethics and Method*, xxii.
64. Kilner, *Why People Matter*, 18.
65. Jacobson, "Mill on Liberty, Speech, and the Free Society," 275.
66. Jacobson, "Mill on Liberty, Speech, and the Free Society," 280.

acts" are actions that primarily deal with one's personal happiness over and above social concerns. Jacobson believes Mill's primary intent was to preserve individual autonomy from state and cultural power. He contends that it is wrong to interpret Mill through the consequentialism of his later disciples.[67] David Boaz understands Mill on a libertarian spectrum. He argues that *On Liberty* was motivated by Mill's belief in individual "alternative lifestyles."[68] Boaz says, "Mill's *On Liberty* argued that the full flourishing of the individual requires not only freedom but 'a manifoldness of situations,' by which he meant that people should have available to them a wide variety of circumstances and living arrangements."[69] But libertarian interpretations of Mill seem to consider only a portion of his work. When one studies the full catalog of Mill's work, one notices his progressive ambitions.

Mill certainly believed in the perfectibility of society.[70] And he realized that progress toward perfection does not happen spontaneously. Mill said,

> But as soon as mankind has attained the capacity of being guided to their own improvement by conviction or persuasion (a period long since reached in all nations with whom we need here concern ourselves), compulsion, either in the direct form or in that of pains and penalties for non-compliance, is no longer admissible as a means to their own good, and justifiable only for the security of others.[71]

Mill argued that despotism was not only legitimate but needed until humanity advanced to a higher state of being. For this reason, scholars such as David Owen Brink and Maurice Cowling note that Mill's motives were progressive and open to forms of paternalism.

Maurice Cowling contends that three events set the foundation for Mill's thinking. First, the breakdown of a universal church meant no superstructure existed to provide social unity.[72] Second, the rise of democracy meant that rulers were beholden to the people, and this meant rulers now had a duty to the social interest of the people. Mill saw that democracy easily can become a tyranny of the majority.[73] Third, the rise of the entre-

---

67. Jacobson, "Utilitarianism without Consequentialism," 167.
68. Boaz, *Libertarianism*, 48.
69. Boaz, *Libertarianism*, 48.
70. Mill, *On Liberty*, 14.
71. Mill, *On Liberty, Utilitarianism and Other Essays*, 14.
72. Cowling, *Mill and Liberalism*, 8.
73. Cowling, *Mill and Liberalism*, 9.

preneur resulting from the Industrial Revolution meant individuals may become consumed with the struggle for wealth.[74] Mill believed the Industrial Revolution coarsened society and, if left unchecked, would eventually lead to a cultural breakdown. Mill's motives for liberty seem to be driven by a fear that the Industrial Revolution would hinder social progress and restrict intellectual advancement. Subsequently, Cowling believes Mill wanted to create a "civil religion" to advance human reason and build social cohesion. Because Mill rejected Christianity, Cowling argues that Mill needed a unifying ideology that would appeal to all; therefore, Mill sought to establish a religion founded on human reason. Cowlings says,

> The situation Mill feels called on to deal with—the historic mission it is his business to fulfill—is to provide a body of commanding doctrine which, by stimulating the higher intelligence of all citizens, will produce, as a consequence, not individualistic anarchy, but that sense of active participation which well-regulated societies alone are capable of providing.[75]

Cowling's interpretation is compelling and consistent with Mill's autobiographical work. In his autobiography, Mill expressed a deep affection for the philosophy of Auguste Comte.[76] Comte believed that human knowledge passed through three phases of development—theological, metaphysical, and positive. Mill looked forward to a future stage when "unanimity of sentiment, firmly grounded in reason and true exigencies of life, that they shall not, like all former and present creeds, religious, ethical, and political, require to be periodically thrown off and replaced by others."[77] Cowling's interpretation of *On Liberty* considers the underlying progressive motive throughout the work of Mill.

David Owen Brink also recognizes Mill's progressive first principles.[78] He notes that Mill was a philosopher steeped in nineteenth-century radicalism and progressive thought; therefore, any interpreter of *On Liberty* must also consider his utopian ambitions.[79] Brink makes a compelling argument that libertarians misunderstand Mill because they interpret his thoughts in *On Liberty* through a lens of psychological egoism and hedonism. But to

74. Cowling, *Mill and Liberalism*, 9.
75. Cowling, *Mill and Liberalism*, 12.
76. Mill, *John Stuart Mill Autobiography*, 132.
77. Mill, *John Stuart Mill Autobiography*, 133.
78. Brink, *Mill's Progressive Principles*, xi.
79. Brink, *Mill's Progressive Principles*, ix.

do so is to misunderstand the first principles in Mill's classic essay *Utilitarianism*.[80] Brink persuasively illustrates that Mill's commitment to collective utility underlines every aspect of his political philosophy.

But Mill was not as libertarian as some would like to suggest. Mill was willing to restrict individual freedom if liberty became an obstacle to social good.[81] He insisted on justifying restrictions to personal freedom according to the "greatest happiness of the greatest number" principle.[82] Consequently, Mill's vision for autonomous liberty was submissive to a commitment to the happiness of the collective.

John Stuart Mill's philosophy is unstable; it contains overlapping principles of individualism and collectivism, which allows both libertarians and progressives to claim his doctrine. But the polarity of interpretations serves as more evidence that Mill's theory is unsound. Because Mill's philosophy denies divine revelation, his work is often inconsistent, and thus future interpreters relativize his arguments. Libertarians can interpret him to support radical individualism, and progressives can appeal to him for a socialist vision. Therefore, Mill's failure to articulate a substantive foundation left him open to "cherry-picking" by many future commentators.

Mill's Religious Liberty: Premise One

Traditional utilitarian theory argues that human reason is the foundation of liberty. John Stuart Mill understood reason as the unifying principle that joins all humanity. He posited that freedom of thought and freedom of expression contributed to "the mental well-being of humankind."[83] Mill argued that freedom of opinion contributed to social progress because the process of debate raised the general intellect of society.[84] Four premises construct the framework for Mill's religious liberty. First, Mill argued that a silenced opinion might be true. Mill wrote,

> The opinion which it is attempted to suppress by authority may possibly be true. Those who desire to suppress it, of course deny its truth; but they are not infallible. They have no authority to decide the question for all mankind, and exclude every other person from

80. Brink, *Mill's Progressive Principles*, 28.
81. Mill, *On Liberty*, 94.
82. Gregg, *On Ordered Liberty*, 6.
83. Houlgate, *Understanding John Stuart Mill*, 126.
84. Mill, *On Liberty*, 22.

> the means of judging. To refuse a hearing to an opinion, because they are sure that it is false, is to assume that their certainty is the same thing as absolute certainty. All silencing of a discussion is an assumption of infallibility.[85]

At first, one is tempted to argue that Mill commits the fallacy of self-refutation. His claim against absolute certainty appears as a claim of absolute certainty, but this is not the case. Mill's argument was one of epistemology, not ontology. Mill's first premise rightly recognizes the limitations of human reason. In Rom 1:12, the apostle Paul notes three different ways the human mind is fallible: the mind became vain in its reasoning, the heart was turned toward foolishness, and the soul was darkened.[86] Mill would not have affirmed the theological category of sin. Nonetheless, through common grace, he correctly recognized the noetic effects of sin.

Mill's premise is ultimately reductionist because he simply assumed the non-existence of an omniscient being. He rejected the possibility that a divine person could exist who possessed absolute certainty, and he rejected the possibility that a being with absolute certainty is capable of communicating absolute knowledge to his creatures. Not only did Mill reject divine transcendence, and he also dismissed metaphysics. Therefore, he placed epistemological knowledge in the realm of the unknowable. For Mill, the means to epistemological knowledge came through experience.

Moreover, Mill's first premise is anthropologically reductionistic. Ironically, John Stuart Mill desired to champion human reason, but by rejecting divine revelation and metaphysics, he did the opposite. The apostle Paul affirmed that humans are creatures with the capacity for moral reasoning. Romans 2:15 notes that "the work of the law is written on the heart," and the "conscience also bears witness." Paul's premise contains insights about the inner life of humans: first, creatures made in the image of God are endowed with specific knowledge mediated by their creator. Paul acknowledges that certain first principles are written on the heart. Second, creatures made in the image of God have the capacity for practical reason. Humans intuitively know some actions are morally repugnant, and others are proximally good. Thomas Aquinas noted that through conscience, humans could discern some forms of morality. Aquinas believed the conscience was a power fixed within human reason. He categorized the mental powers of moral reason

---

85. Mill, *On Liberty, Utilitarianism and Other Essays*, 19.
86. Schreiner, *Romans*, 87.

as *synderesis* and *conscience*.⁸⁷ He thought the conscience provided both "intuitive reason" and "practical wisdom."⁸⁸ While evangelical scholars debate the exact categories of human reason and the effect of sin on moral reasoning, the Christian tradition holds a more robust view of human reason than the secular philosophy of Mill. Historically, Christian scholarship has recognized that the regenerated mind can know both theoretical reason and practical reason.

Mill weakened the concept of human reason by rejecting all forms of divine revelation and intuitive knowledge. He rejected the belief that humans are born with a moral conscience. Mill argued that the conscience was created through interacting with people in the community. He did not believe the conscience was something innate in the person. For Mill, conscience was formed person to person, not person to God.⁸⁹ Therefore, conscience is subject to social pressure and social change. Instead, Mill argued that conscience evolved as humans create, interpret, and internalize laws.⁹⁰ For Mill, right and wrong, as well as truth and falsehood, become matters of experience.⁹¹ Mill reduced human reason to mere instrumental reason. Instrumental reason is only concerned with outcomes, and this focus on outcomes ultimately diminishes human value because it does not consider the inner person. Consequently, because Mill rejected biblical anthropology, he held a diminished view of human reason.

Problem of Authority

Mill's utilitarianism holds perfectionist assumptions. His philosophy fixes its perfectionist hopes in the dialectic between oneself and the surrounding world. But Mill's instrumental reason undercuts his project in two ways. First, Mill's theory displaces authority. In his initial premise, Mill argued that no one could claim absolute certainty because no one is infallible. Mill was correct to assert human fallibility; fallibility is common to all humanity. But if all humans are fallible, as Mill rightly concedes, then where does one find the locus of authority? Mill sought to answer this question, stating,

---

87. Aquinas, *Summa Theologica*, 1314.

88. Aristotle called intuitive reason the ability to discern, and practical reason deliberates on morals.

89. Brink, *Mill's Progressive Principles*, 54.

90. Mill, *On Liberty, Utilitarianism and Other Essays*, 116.

91. Houlgate, *Understanding John Stuart Mill*, 23.

> The human mind, the source of everything respectable in man is either as an intellectual or as a moral being, namely, that his errors are corrigible. He is capable of rectifying his mistakes by discussion and experience. Not by experience alone. There must be discussion to show how experience is to be interpreted.[92]

Mill placed the locus of authority in the process of rational discussion and experience.[93] But how does a dialectic between fallible people contribute to the advancement of knowledge? Imperfect people discussing ideas and experiences have no way to move beyond themselves; therefore, his argument commits a circular fallacy and fails in his ambition to advance society.

Mill was right to believe that communication plays a part in establishing authority structures. King Solomon's counsel in Prov 19:20 encourages the wise to seek advice and instruction from others. One who seeks advice ascribes authority to the person or the group of inquiry.[94] Oliver O'Donovan also notes, "Authority is an event in which reality is communicated to practical reason by social communication."[95] Therefore, Mill was not entirely wrong when he sought to establish authority for ideas through a communicative process.

But Mill's rejection of divine authority left him open to a naturalistic fallacy. Individuals discussing ideas and experiences tell one nothing of the *oughtness* of an act. Moral authority becomes unstable and subjective when it is cut off from fixed and objective foundations. Mill's instrumental reason can only describe morality. And because Mill rejected theoretical reason and metaphysics, these descriptions have no tie to foundational truth. Consequently, Mill's theory can only provide opinions about morality, and this limitation severely undercuts liberty because there is nothing concrete to which we can appeal to defend liberty.

To this point, Samuel Gregg notes, "The Nazis cannot be held accountable for their choices because they acted according to their preferences, they showed real commitment to their opinions; and who in any case is to judge that what they did was wrong?"[96] Evangelical ethics posits that authority is derived from God's communication to humans, and this establishes an objective foundation to measure one's ideas and experiences.

---

92. Mill, *On Liberty, Utilitarianism and Other Essays*, 22.
93. Mill, *On Liberty, Utilitarianism and Other Essays*, 22.
94. O'Donovan, *Self, World, and Time*, 53.
95. O'Donovan, *Self, World, and Time*, 53.
96. Gregg, *On Ordered Liberty*, 31.

Mill's theory cannot build such a foundation; therefore, Mill's theory provides no substance to measure justice.

Additionally, Mill's theory falsely attempts to make the quality of an experience universal. Ethicist John Frame, commenting on John Stuart Mill's theory, notes, "No method could qualify these pleasures so as to permit calculation. We can measure a feeling of cold or hot, by windchill calculations and such, but even that will vary from individual to individual."[97] Because Mill denied the certainty of truth claims, his theory has no universal framework for cross-cultural engagement. Nations that enter economic treaties must share some certain knowledge if they are to cooperate. Subsequently, one sees again that Mill conflated the distinction between part and whole, and this weakens his argument for liberty.

Like other nineteenth-century skeptics, Mill sought to unify society through skepticism. The skeptic believes that if knowledge were deemed "uncertain," then no one religion, opinion, or class of people would rise to dominance. Mill's first premise was to protect society from the tyranny of a majority. However, without a commitment to certain knowledge, genuine free choice is an impossibility.[98] Skepticism ultimately reduces human choices to mere animalistic instincts, which diminishes one's genuine freedom. Skepticism becomes deterministic because it enslaves humans to passions and appetites; one can only do what his or her impulses dictate. Consequently, like other secular philosophies, Mill's theory promises to enhance human reason and protect from tyranny, but it betrays that promise.

Second, Mill's qualifications for authority undercut his project. Mill's doctrine often sounds individualistic, but ultimately, he created a paternalistic structure. Mill located moral authority in a particular class of people.[99] Those who had the opportunity to experience higher qualities of pleasure were deemed worthy of judging the quality of experience. Mill said, "The test of quality, and the rule for measuring it against quantity, being the preference felt by those who, in their opportunities of experience, to which must be added their habits of self-consciousness and self-observation, are best furnished with the means of comparison."[100] For Mill, these "higher pleasures" were pleasures associated with intellect and reason. Only those who had experienced both lower and higher forms of pleasure were capable

---

97. Frame, *The Doctrine of the Christian Life*, 98.
98. Gregg, *On Ordered Liberty*, xii.
99. Mill, *On Liberty, Utilitarianism and Other Essays*, 126.
100. Mill, *On Liberty, Utilitarianism and Other Essays*, 126.

of judging the quality of each.[101] Mill believed that mental cultivation led to greater happiness. He defended his theory for liberty on the assumption that liberty would ultimately promote the "higher" pleasures of human reason. Therefore, he created a hierarchy in which the intellectual minority determined the type, the quantity, and the quality of pleasure that was good for the majority.

Mill desired to preserve autonomy, but his theory contains paternalistic elements that restrict liberty. Mill scholar and political philosopher David Owen Brink insists that Mill's philosophy was egalitarian because it emphasized that everyone's happiness matters equally.[102] Brink contends that Mill's skepticism preserves plurality because no one group could claim ultimate truth. But Brink later concedes that Mill's ethical theory measures the moral quality of an act by its consequence; therefore, there is no reason to believe that respecting individual liberties is always optimal.[103] Brink acknowledges that Mill's calculation of pleasure requires qualified judges to authorize the quality of each pleasure. Therefore, moral judges may restrict liberty if they deem that one's pleasure obstructs social advancement.

Moreover, Mill's concept of liberty does not ensure enduring liberty. Maurice Cowling notes in his critique of Millian liberty, "The demand for liberty is not the assertion of a fundamentally binding end, but the designation of a means to the end—the end of allowing men to approach as close as possible to the highest of all pleasures which comes from mental cultivation of the closest approximation possible to knowledge of what is true."[104] Cowling notices that Mill's philosophy does not produce binding liberty; liberty is only a means toward mental cultivation as one pursues the truth. But because utility was the central principle that guided Mill, Mill allowed restrictions on liberty if liberty was thought to hinder social progress. For Mill, freedom was derived from specific properties located in human personhood; liberty was an instrument to bring about certain ends. Subsequently, Mill's paradigm of liberty required authoritative judges to approve what discussions, truth claims, and religious practices enhance mental cultivation, and this makes liberty subservient to positive law.

Mill's high esteem for the faculty of reason informed his beliefs about individual liberty. He believed reason was the power that united humanity.

---

101. Patrick, *An Analysis of John Stuart Mill's Utilitarianism*, 33.
102. Brink, *Mill's Progressive Principles*, 10.
103. Brink, *Mill's Progressive Principles*, 218.
104. Cowling, *Mill and Liberalism*, 42.

Utilitarianism

But J. P. Day recognizes inconsistencies in Mill's logic.[105] Day notes how Mill's theory for liberty contains two principles. First, individual liberty ought to be protected. Mill believed that thoughts and words were inseparably linked through the power of reason; therefore, to restrict one's speech was equivalent to restricting one's thought.[106] Second, the general happiness of society must be safeguarded. Mill reasoned that words contain the power to incite action.[107] He reasoned that speech must have limits because he saw a link not only between thoughts and words but between words and actions. Mill said, "No one pretends that actions should be as free as opinions. On the contrary, even opinions lose their immunity when the circumstances in which they are expressed are such as to constitute their expression a positive instigation to some mischievous act."[108] Mill reasoned that the relationship between speech and physical actions was contingent, whereas he believed the link between thought and word was inseparable. Therefore, Mill believed that if an idea was potentially harmful to the social order, then it was permissible to suppress speech. But at the same time, he argued that the suppression of potentially dangerous speech did not necessarily destroy one's thought. Mill's distinction between words and actions allowed him to advocate for the tolerance of any opinion as long as it was not spoken openly.

Mill's skepticism left him no objective standard to discern what words may harm society. He argued, once again, that circumstances must determine what speech is permissible. For example, Mill claimed that it was not tolerable for an angry mob to say that corn dealers starve the poor while standing in front of the corn dealer's house.[109] Mill argued that limiting free expression, when it is a "nuisance to other people," does not harm one's ability to maintain individual opinions.[110] Oliver Wendell Holmes would later use Mill's theory to support his ruling in *Schenck v. The United States*.[111] Holmes ruled that the circumstances of war allow for restrictions to free

---

105. Day, "More about Mill on Free Expression," 189.
106. Mill, *On Liberty, Utilitarianism and Other Essays*, 55.
107. Day, "More about Mill on Free Expression," 190.
108. Mill, *On Liberty, Utilitarianism and Other Essays*, 55.
109. Mill, *On Liberty, Utilitarianism and Other Essays*, 55.
110. Mill, *On Liberty, Utilitarianism and Other Essays*, 57.
111. Schenck v. United States, Baer v. United States, 249 U.S. 47; 39 S. Ct. 247 (1919).

expression.[112] Mill's rejection of absolute knowledge meant that arbitrary conditions determine the measure of one's individual liberty.

Therefore, Mill's logic seems flawed. Mill was correct to acknowledge the link between thoughts, speech, and actions. But because he rejected divine revelation and metaphysics, he was limited in how he conceived of the relationship. Mill only thought in terms of material science; therefore, the link connecting thoughts, speech, and acts was a conjoining of physical and mental energy. Mental energy animates both speech acts and physical acts. One may argue that some physical acts are reflexive, yet they still exert mental energy. And one might say that speech acts often happen without careful reason, but mental energy still animates the process of speaking. It is clear that mental energy runs through all three exercises—thinking, speaking, and acting. But Mill saw that the link between speech and a physical act as a contingent link, whereas the relationship between thought and speech was inseparable. If physical and mental energy are exerted in all three exercises, how can it be said that the link between thought and word is inseparable while the link between word and action is contingent? Mill's original claim for liberty of speech was based on the connection between thought and word. But if mental energy animates all three exercises, would it not form a consistent link across all activities? If intellectual reason joins thoughts, words, and acts, then would not a barrier to one affect the quality of them all? It is difficult to see how Mill could argue that thought and speech are inseparably linked and therefore free, and at the same time argue that words that are potentially harmful acts are less free. Mill's concept of inseparability was flawed because he never explained why the link between speech and physical acts is contingent. One might assume he thought physical acts are matters of free choice, but his skepticism logically undercut free choice. And, as argued earlier, skepticism is by nature deterministic. Mill did not have categories to understand the dualistic nature of humans as body and spirit; therefore, he had no way to explain the self-limiting nature of moral agents.

Evangelical anthropology provides a grander vision of liberty. Genesis 1 reveals a trinitarian structure that displays the inseparable link of ideas, words, and actions. The creation narrative reveals the interconnectedness of God's thoughts, words, and actions. Augustine noted that each member of Trinity was on display in God's act of creation.[113] God the Father is the

---

112. The decision of *Schenck v. The United States* was later overturned.
113. Augustine, *The City of God*, 233.

energy of thought, Christ is the energy of speech, and the Holy Spirit is the energy that formed matter. Within the Holy Trinity exists an inseparable link that joins thoughts, words, and actions. But this inseparable link is one of relationship.

Moreover, God created humans in his own image; therefore, this trinitarian structure animates the mind of humans. Dorothy Sayers notes that the inseparable nature of the Trinity is present within all human reason. She contends that the energy of memory, the energy of understanding, and the energy in the will are derived from trinitarian unity.[114] Sayers notes that image bearing includes formulating ideas and articulating words, thus making new forms of creation. Therefore, a primary function of image bearing is to express the inseparable link between thoughts, words, and actions.

Mill was correct to notice an inseparable link within human reason. But because he denied divine revelation, metaphysics, and certain knowledge, he did not have a device to regulate harmful expressions. Evangelical anthropology proves superior because its authority is rooted in a living being who communicates to regenerated minds. God's Spirit communicates to individual believers; therefore, harmful speech is regulated by an external living being. Through the Holy Spirit, the word of God pierces the conscience and infuses it with the ideas of God. For this reason, regenerated believers are made aware of corrupt communication and are empowered by the Spirit to restrain themselves. Millian theory has no internal motivation for self-restraint; therefore, it must rely on arbitrary external restraints. Consequently, at best, Mill's thought can prove tolerance of ideas but not genuine free expression.

Religious Tolerance vs. Religious Expression

Toleration and free expression are not the same. Jay Newman notes, "Toleration is a half-hearted attitude towards something that is not liked, loved, respected, or approved of."[115] Moreover, toleration necessarily assumes that one party is right, and the other party is wrong; therefore, the correct party grants privilege to the erring party. In Millian theory, human rights originate in the government for social utility. And because John Stuart Mill fixed authority in a small class of social judges, his theory must institute a system in which a few governing judges determine the good for the

---

114. Sayers, *The Mind of a Maker*, 42.
115. Newman, *Foundations of Religious Tolerance*, 4.

majority. Minority opinions are tolerated only so far as they are not disruptive to the general happiness of the majority.

Toleration inevitably weakens a pluralistic society. The ideology of the majority often accommodates the lowest common denominator of ethical principles, which lowers general morality.[116] Additionally, Mill's misplacement of authority meant that an arbitrary group determines what privileges are afforded to minority groups. Ultimately, Mill's framework is paternalistic, undermining individual dignity. Moreover, while religious toleration may permit minority opinions, these opinions must be privatized to ensure the majority remains undisrupted. Consequently, Mill's rejection of divine revelation created structures that only allow for an inferior form of religious toleration, not genuine religious freedom.

Genuine free expression appreciates the complexity of humans. Humans are embodied spirits, and as image-bearers, this means they are self-aware. Humans can perceive themselves and think beyond themselves. And because humans are made from dust, they are finite beings. John Kilner notes that the ability for self-perception means that humans have a degree of self-transcendence.[117] Those with physical disabilities can transcend physical limitations as they imagine themselves apart from their bodies. Humans are not merely objects; humans can think beyond their physical boundaries. And because humans are made from matter, they are limited by history and space. They do not live in a mental state only, but they extend our agency as they engage with a physical world. Kilner notes, "When we think of a human being, we have to think of one who is neither purely a self-transcending spirit nor simply a finite body—but somehow the union of both."[118] Therefore, free expression serves to balance the finite against the infinite.

Religious freedom recognizes that worship is an activity that connects one with his or her creator, themselves, and the surrounding world. Worship engages the link between thoughts and words, and it combines one's physical body to actions in the material world. Moreover, worship is not exclusively an individual act. Worship is not merely thoughts and words; worship engages the body as well. Free religious expression recognizes that one's acts also connect them to space and history. Whereas religious toleration privatizes thoughts and opinions, religious expression allows humans

---

116. Newman, *Foundations of Religious Tolerance*, 14.
117. Kilner, *Why People Matter*, 21.
118. Kilner, *Why People Matter*, 22.

to extend thoughts and opinions into the physical world. As one worships with body and spirit, one fulfills his or her purpose of image bearing. Worship becomes a conduit between God and humanity, and humanity and the world. Religious expression fully allows humans to imagine God through thoughts and words. But also, through creative acts, people fulfill their purpose as makers in the world. Consequently, Mill's rejection of certain truth undermines human reason, misplaces authority, and ultimately affords only an implicit form of religious tolerance.

Mill's Religious Liberty: Premise Two

Mill's second premise for liberty builds upon his first. He contended that all opinions help to establish the truth; therefore, if a silenced opinion is false, "it may contain a portion of the truth."[119] Mill wrote,

> We have hitherto considered only two possibilities: that the received opinion may be false, and some other opinion, consequently, true; or that, the received opinion being true, a conflict with the opposite error is essential to a clear apprehension and deep feeling of its truth. But there is a commoner case than either of these; when the conflicting doctrines, instead of being one true and the others false, share the same truth between them; and nonconforming opinion is needed to supply the remainder of the truth, of which the received doctrine embodies only a part. Popular opinions, on subjects not palpable to sense are often true, but seldom or never the whole truth.[120]

Mill believed that a clash of diverse ideas was essential for the establishment of truth. Because Mill did not accept the certainty of epistemological knowledge, he assumed that truth was always incomplete and continuously moving from error to correction. He contended that personal opinions always add something to the truth, even if those opinions prove to be wrong.[121] For Mill, the truth was a subset of human progress; therefore, moral reality is never fixed. Consequently, Millian theory conceives of truth as a social construct, and this makes truth fundamentally unstable.

Mill was correct to recognize the expansive nature of truth. The biblical narrative moves along a horizon of progressive revelation. In the New

---

119. Houlgate, *Understanding John Stuart Mill*, 126.
120. Mill, *On Liberty, Utilitarianism and Other Essays*, 45.
121. Mill, *On Liberty, Utilitarianism and Other Essays*, 46.

Testament, Heb 1:1–2 reveals the progressive nature of truth culminating in Christ. Second Peter 3:18 commands that one is to "grow in the grace and the knowledge of our Lord and Savior Jesus Christ." Scripture supports the infinite nature of truth. Therefore, Mill properly perceived the unfolding aspect of truth.

Nevertheless, because Mill rejected divine revelation, he failed to distinguish the difference between adding to truth and dividing of truth. Because the truth is fixed in the person of Jesus, truth is a matter of division. Paul notes in 2 Tim 2:15 that followers of Jesus are charged to "rightly handle the word of the truth." Paul used the word ὀρθοτομέω, implying that the word of truth is something to be cut open and plumbed.[122] Biblical revelation fixes truth in the divine nature of Jesus; therefore, truth is a set reality that infinitely unfolds as one grows in a relationship with Christ. Subsequently, evangelical ethics understands truth as a communication from a divine source to infinite humanity—humans are recipients of truth, not creators of it.

Moreover, because utilitarian ethics rejects divine revelation and natural law, it has no way to balance values. Those with a libertarian guise value individual liberty over egalitarian visions. And those inclined toward progressivism elevate equality to the highest value. Mill's vision of liberty breaks toward the latter. Subsequently, his framework for liberty assumes all opinions equally construct truth.[123]

Moreover, Mill reasoned that minority opinions should be favored because they are the ones most often suppressed.[124] Mill claimed that suppressed opinions harm the mental good of individuals and the collective because an element of truth is neglected. For this reason, he contended that all opinions deserve a free voice. This is not to say that Mill accepted an absolute right to individual free expression. As stated earlier, Mill believed there are no indefeasible moral rights.[125] He allowed for the interference of individual liberty based on a speculative calculation of harm. According to Mill, all opinions that do not cause harm to others ought to be given free expression. His focus on harm created a universal principle that judged moral actions and governed free expression. Consequently, his second principle for liberty was balanced by his concept of harm and its effect on the greater society.

---

122. Bauer and Danker, *A Greek-English Lexicon of the New Testament*, 722.
123. Mill, *On Liberty, Utilitarianism and Other Essays*, 46.
124. Mill, *On Liberty, Utilitarianism and Other Essays*, 47.
125. Day, "Mill on the Moral Right to Free Expression of Thought," 41.

Utilitarianism

Harm Principle

John Stuart Mill never named his universal principle, but later commentators would unanimously call it the harm principle or, more accurately, the harm-to-others principle.[126] Mill's harm principle is essential for modern social ethics because it has become a significant standard for rights in liberal jurisprudence.[127] In short, the harm principle argues that individuals are at liberty to do what they want as long as they do not harm other individuals or society in general.[128]

But John Stuart Mill recognized that one's responsibility not to harm others might come into conflict with social interests. When this conflict happens, then the greatest balance of pleasure over pain should determine the proper course of action. Moreover, when more significant social concerns are not in view, individuals are left to decide questions of liberty based on the calculation of increasing pleasure and reducing pain. Laurence Houlgate notes, "There is not only a rule or obligation not to harm another in their life, but also a rule or obligation not to harm another in their liberty."[129] The harm principle assumes that the pain of those who are harmed is balanced by the pain suffered by those who desire to harm. Mill calculated that the right action will always favor the one who is harmed over the one who desires to harm; therefore, one is not justified to take a life, unless it is for self-defense.[130] Consequently, utilitarian philosophers appeal to the harm principle as the scale to balance individual liberty and societal action.

The harm principle appears to provide a practical standard for regulating individual liberty. Legal philosopher Joel Feinberg argues that there is no more effective principle for reducing harm to different persons (other than the actor) and preserving the greater values of others than the harm principle.[131] But when one examines Mill's definition of harm, one realizes that his principle lacks stability. Mill divides harm into two categories: physical harm and interference harm.[132] Interference harm is the pain

---

126. Houlgate, *Understanding John Stuart Mill*, 106.

127. Plessis, "The Legitimacy of Using the Harm Principle in Cases of Religious Freedom within Education," 349.

128. Plessis, "The Legitimacy of Using the Harm Principle in Cases of Religious Freedom within Education," 349.

129. Houlgate, *Understanding John Stuart Mill*, 111.

130. Houlgate, *Understanding John Stuart Mill*, 112.

131. Feinberg, *Offense to Others*, xii.

132. Mill, *On Liberty, Utilitarianism and Other Essays*, 121.

caused when one is obstructed in his or her pursuit of pleasure. But Mill's category of interference is vague and opens the door for subjective claims of harm. David Brink notes that Mill intended a broad definition of harm.[133] Brink contends that harm includes anything that "sets one back" in his or her important interest.[134] Therefore, harm may consist of psychological harm and emotional harm resulting from a personal offense.

Georgia Plessis also recognizes that the harm principle seeks to leave open an array of possible harms, including emotional pain.[135] It would be unfair to accuse Mill of including minor offense in his definition of harm. Mill seemed to reject the regulation of minor offenses.[136] But his vagueness easily allowed for the conflation of harm and offense in the work of other utilitarians. Feinberg contends that the link between offense and harm is close; therefore, the establishment of an offense principle is instrumental in the effort to reduce harm.[137] Consequently, offensive may also be numbered among Mill's category of harms.

Raphael Cohen-Almagor, in his book *Speech, Media, and Ethics: The Limits of Free Expression*, appeals to the harm principle as a foundation for limits on free expression. Cohen-Almagor says, "There are certain utterances which do not induce anyone to take a harmful action but which should still be excluded from the protections of free speech because of their imminent offensive effects on those who are exposed to them"[138] Cohen-Almagor reasons that there are grounds for abridging free expression not only when one's speech may provoke physical harm, but also when it is designed to inflict psychological offense.[139] Cohen-Almagor contends that physical harm and psychological harm are equally damaging; therefore, the harm principle must regulate language that may potentially harm one's emotional state.

Additionally, Robert Mark Simpson argues that certain types of speech create identity-based social hierarchies, and these structures may

---

133. Brink, *Mill's Progressive Principles*, 173.

134. Brink, *Mill's Progressive Principles*, 189.

135. Plessis, "The Legitimacy of Using the Harm Principle in Cases of Religious Freedom within Education," 336.

136. Brink, *Mill's Progressive Principles*, 175.

137. Feinberg, *Offense to Others*, 1.

138. Cohen-Almagor, *Speech, Media and Ethics*, 7.

139. Cohen-Almagor, *Speech, Media and Ethics*, 6.

Utilitarianism

result in oppression and racism.[140] In societies where egalitarian equality is the highest value, any notion of inequality is thought to be the utmost of harms. For instance, in the United Kingdom, Canada, France, and Australia, speech that is deemed abusive, threatening, insulting, or that is targeted at someone based on race, religion, or sexual orientation is restricted by hate speech laws. Hate speech is thought not only to cause emotional and psychological trauma, but also it is believed to create systems of hierarchical oppression.[141] Therefore, liberal democracies that rely on the harm principle must maintain tight controls on the types of speech allowed in the public sphere, presenting challenges for religious freedom.

Free speech is essential for religious liberty because it ensures that all views are given full voice. Freedom of speech honors human dignity because it allows both the speaker and listener to exercise human agency. But because the harm principle must balance competing claims of harm, conscientious judges are left to determine which words and values are permissible, undermining human choice. Offensive speech must be struck from public debate if it has the potential to harm unsuspecting listeners, therefore robbing listeners of the opportunity to determine the legitimacy of claims. Ironically, Mill's second principle of liberty lauds competing ideas. But because utilitarianism has no foundation for an epistemic reason, it has no consistent scale to weigh competing harms in public debate. Subsequently, without an objective standard, there is no means to measure one person's offense over another.

Moreover, in societies where egalitarian equality is the highest value, all truth claims must be treated equally. This is not to say that all claims are measured evenly in content. Reasonable people can undoubtedly judge what is nonsensical. But competing claims must be treated equally regarding demonstration. Societies that value egalitarian equality necessarily must allow all ideas equal voice. But the harm principle cannot provide this kind of freedom. The harm principle does not allow a person to act in a manner that may harm or offend another.

Moreover, the harm principle has no means to determine why one person's psychological harm outweighs another; therefore, it cannot provide robust free expression. For instance, if A's religion requires proselytizing, it would be psychological harm to A to restrict proselytizing. But evangelism necessarily assumes that A possesses truth that B does not; therefore, B

---

140. Simpson, *Harm and Responsibility in Hate Speech*, 3.
141. Simpson, *Harm and Responsibility in Hate Speech*, 13.

will encounter psychological harm when A corrects B of their error. Moreover, B may incur emotional or psychological harm (or at least offense) if A presents the need for personal repentance. Repentance necessarily infers that one changes his or her life plans, and this would undoubtedly involve a "setback" to one's important interest. Therefore, the harm principle may restrict evangelism if A's claim to truth offends B's life choices, and thus limits freedom of speech.

Free speech is essential for religious liberty. Free speech safeguards religious liberty because it protects not only religious language but also public expression. But the harm principle moralizes harm, which ultimately elevates harm above free speech and free expression. Consequently, utilitarian social ethics governed by the harm principle can only provide a narrow form of religious freedom.

Evangelical Balance

The evangelical paradigm of truth is rooted in foundational certainties. The apostle Paul explains in Rom 1:18–23 that humans possess an awareness of their place in the world. This argument presupposes two realities. First, truth is not ordered under harm; harm is the result of suppressing the truth. Paul argues that as one reflects upon the created world, they will collide with objective truth. The collision that takes place as one reflects and deliberates serves to illustrate that objective truth exists independently from opinion. The very process of human reflection presupposes an objective physical and metaphysical reality exists.[142] To this point, Francis Schaeffer noted that truth is not found in synthesis but antithesis.[143] Schaeffer understood that some things are true, and their opposite is untrue. Mill's second premise of liberty recognizes that the collision of diverse opinions is necessary for the discovery of truth.[144] But Mill never explained how a false opinion maintains a "portion of the truth" and how a "collision" of alternative opinions releases that portion.[145] The evangelical understanding of truth recognizes truth and lies cannot be synthesized. And the evangelical paradigm acknowledges that truth is a fixed reality; therefore, harm may be judged universally and objectively.

142. O'Donovan, *Common Objects of Love*, 13.
143. Schaeffer, *How Should We Then Live?*, 163.
144. Mill, *On Liberty, Utilitarianism and Other Essays*, 52.
145. Houlgate, *Understanding John Stuart Mill*, 129.

Second, Heb 11:3 affirms that humans encounter fixed realities as they reflect on the created world. Human consciousness allows one to grasp the whole shape of things.[146] This ability infers that creatures fixed in the material world do not add to the truth—they are made aware of it. Oliver O'Donovan recognizes that as one reflects on his or her place in the created world, one does not add moral truth to moral truth; one can only repent of false perceptions of the moral order and turn to a truer one.[147] This is not to say that humans can gain salvific knowledge of Christ, nor can they independently bridge the gap between nature and morality. But this is to say that the search for truth constantly confronts humans with their proper position in the universe. And as one faces his or her place in creation, one is compelled to seek ultimate concerns. The evangelical understanding of truth is fixed, and so all humans may fulfill their purpose as truth-seekers—not truth-creators. Religious expression is essential to human dignity because it enables individuals to test their beliefs against the fixed realities of truth. Therefore, evangelical paradigms of truth allow for more widespread expressions, whereas utilitarian frameworks are limited.

Mill's Religious Liberty: Premise Three

Mill's third premise for liberty is founded on the idea of prejudice. Mill argued that claims to exclusive truth necessarily produce partiality, and this results in the impulse of dominance.[148] He wrote, "Even if the received opinion be not only true, but the whole truth; unless it is suffered to be, and actually is, vigorously and earnestly contested, it will, by most of those who receive it, be held in the manner of a prejudice, with little comprehension or feeling of its rational grounds."[149] Mill assumed that exclusive truth claims result in two forms of prejudice. First, exclusive truth leads to intense partisanship, and intense partisanship ultimately creates an unequal distribution of power. Moreover, those who claim to hold exclusive truth eventually end up enforcing their beliefs on the minority class. Mill reasoned that "exclusive pretensions" are absolutizing and thereby require enforcement.[150] Additionally, he contended that the implementation of exclusive religious

---

146. O'Donovan, *Resurrection and Moral Order*, 91.
147. O'Donovan, *Resurrection and Moral Order*, 92.
148. Mill, *On Liberty, Utilitarianism and Other Essays*, 51.
149. Mill, *On Liberty, Utilitarianism and Other Essays*, 52.
150. Mill, *On Liberty, Utilitarianism and Other Essays*, 51.

The Superiority of an Evangelical Model of Religious Liberty

claims produces a servile nature in the populace. Mill argued that the Christian command to obey all authority inherently restricted social progress. He claimed that Christianity necessarily "inculcated" submission to authority even when the authority commanded what religion forbids.[151] He reasoned that the exclusive claims of Christianity necessitate absolute enforcement. This absolute enforcement results in demanding passive acceptance rather than providing the necessary challenges that advance social progress.

Second, Mill believed prejudice of opinion weakened the opinion of those who held it. Mill contended that any opinion held without deep comprehension lacked conviction, weakening the belief itself. According to Mill, one's lack of conviction will result in enforcement through dominance instead of a peaceful debate of ideas.[152] Consequently, Mill saw that exclusive religious claims produced a prejudice that harmed both opponents and adherents.

Mill's antidote for exclusive religious claims was syncretism. He believed that free expression of religious ideas served to merge beliefs, which would chasten the prejudicial spirit of absolutism. Mill argued that Christian ethics emerged from the moral gaps in the pagan and Old Testament worlds.[153] According to Mill, Jesus added moral truth to the preexisting truth of his day; therefore, the ethics of Jesus were progressive additions and not absolute foundations. According to Mill, the church forsook the practice of its founder when it claimed exclusive truth.[154] He argued that the church's exclusive prejudice cut ethics off from moral progress. And Mill contended that the only solution for ensuring progress was to "infuse" Christianity with secular ideas.[155] He believed syncretizing secular beliefs with Christian values would neuter the church's exclusive pretensions and at the same time allow ethics to progress. Consequently, Mill's third argument for religious freedom was rooted in a desire to undermine absolutism.

However, Mill's view of Christianity was wrong. His belief that Christianity "inculcated" absolute submission was misleading. First, biblical anthropology contends that creatures made in the image of God can make free choices. Anthony Hoekema notes, "The understanding that human beings have this capacity for choice, and that they retain this capacity even

---

151. Mill, *On Liberty, Utilitarianism and Other Essays*, 51.
152. Mill, *On Liberty, Utilitarianism and Other Essays*, 51.
153. Mill, *On Liberty, Utilitarianism and Other Essays*, 48.
154. Mill, *On Liberty, Utilitarianism and Other Essays*, 50.
155. Mill, *On Liberty, Utilitarianism and Other Essays*, 50.

after the Fall, is, therefore, an essential emphasis in the Christian doctrine of man."[156] Whereas the Bible does command absolute submission to God, that submission is always one of impassioned voluntary choice.[157] Psalm 51:16–17 affirms that submission not a passive experience; rather, submission is the overflow of a fervent heart. From Eden to the New Jerusalem, Scripture compels individuals to "choose whom they will serve" (Josh 24:14–15). Mill's claim of "inculcated submission" reveals his ignorance of the Christian faith. Second, where Scripture does command submission to earthly authority, that submission is never absolute. Indeed, the apostle Paul did command Christians to be subject to the governing authority (Rom 13:1), but this submission was fenced by Peter's declaration in Acts 5:29, "We must obey God rather than men." Martin Luther noted the distinction between compliance and absolute submission in his letter to the City of Stettin Wittenberg on January 11, 1523, in which he said the following,

> In Romans 13:1 Paul says: "Let every person be subjected to the governing authority," and, "Pay taxes to whom taxes are due and revenue to whom revenue is due." St. Peter teaches in the same way. No one is exempt from this commandment, be he priest or layman, unless he wishes not to be a Christian. The canons may argue that the emperor and the secular authorities have given their agreement and consent in this matter. It is obvious, however, that the emperor cannot give away that which does not belong to him.[158]

The Christian command to submission is always one that is ordered under a hierarchy of values. Additionally, Christian history is filled with martyrs, and martyrdom can hardly be categorized as passivity. Consequently, Mill's claim that exclusive pretensions result in impassioned dominance and excessive passivity was not based on genuine Christianity.

Prejudice

Mill's third premise for religious liberty arose from his fears of religious prejudice. He believed that prejudice ultimately leads to the oppression of minorities. There can be no doubt that the presence of sin has led to religious persecution throughout history. As Roger Williams noted, "The

---

156. Hoekema, *Created in God's Image*, 229.

157. Note the author's use of the term "voluntary choice" within the tradition of Particular Baptist theology.

158. Luther, *Luther's Works*, 45:27.

blood of so many hundred thousand souls of Protestants and Papists, spilled in the wars of present and former ages for their respective conscience, is not required nor accepted by Jesus Christ, the Prince of Peace."[159] But prejudice does not necessarily mean that one's biases will result in oppression or evil acts. Humans are created as moral agents, and all practical reasoning includes some form of bias. No person makes decisions from an unadulterated libertine free will. Every choice reflects a preference over its alternative. Therefore, one may say that every choice includes some degree of prejudice. But the evangelical doctrine of regeneration recognizes that the Christian mind has the power to distinguish destructive prejudice from righteous prejudice. The Christian mind is influenced by the word of God, one's relationship to his or her neighbor, and God's goal for redemptive history. The triadic structure of one's relationship with God, the world, and time forms an objective standard for weighing prejudice. John Stuart Mill's definition of prejudice assumes the acceptance of opinion without proper justification. But this definition is reductionistic because it does not recognize that all moral reasoning contains some degree of bias.

Synchronization

Moreover, because Mill believed that epistemological truth was mutable, he assumed that syncretizing opinions ultimately leads to the purest form of truth. But Mill committed the fallacy of middle ground, which assumes that the middle point between two extremes is always the purest form of truth. While middle positions are often helpful for resolving policy disputes, one can hardly employ a middle ground position when dealing with ultimate questions. Because Mill denied divine revelation, natural law, and metaphysics, synchronization was a simple solution. But synchronization assumes that all religious beliefs are essentially the same, and this is simply not the case. Synchronization essentially changes the character of both substances. The Roman Catholic Church's experiment with Christianity and Santeria in Latin America reveals the fallacy of synchronization. Therefore, Mill's third premise for religious liberty ultimately undermines the uniqueness of religion, thereby fundamentally altering its fundamental nature. His third premise cannot ultimately lead to genuine religious liberty.

---

159. Davis, *On Religious Liberty*, 86.

Utilitarianism

Mill's Religious Liberty: Premise Four

John Stuart Mill's fourth premise is an extension of the third.[160] Mill argued that coerced opinions lose conviction, thus weakening the doctrine itself.[161] He contended that dogma would become a mere formal profession, thereby rendering it inefficacious for good and preventing any growth from real and heartfelt conviction from reason or personal experience.[162] Mill's premise was rhetorically brilliant. As a devoted atheist living in Christian England, Mill found himself in the minority position.

Mill's opponents were able to accept his premise because it preserved their doctrinal purity. Additionally, Mill observed that when one toiled to develop a doctrine, one was more fervent to spread that doctrine.[163] He noticed that general opinions lack vitality because they do not produce controversy. According to Mill, controversy leads to progress. But if a doctrine becomes a general opinion, then it ceases to spread further and gradually dies away. He argued that mental vitality produces a conviction, and conviction resulted in an impulse to win converts. Mill skillfully appealed to the evangelizing spirit of his Christian opponents to win approval. Consequently, Mill's fourth premise for religious liberty appealed to established evangelical beliefs of the day.

Ironically, John Stuart Mill's fourth premise echoes that of Puritan theologian Roger Williams. One can find no specific evidence stating that Mill relied upon Williams. But Williams's theological contributions concerning the human conscience greatly influenced seventeenth-century political thought in England. Roger Williams's 1645 treatise *Christenings Make Not Christians* and his 1652 treatise *The Bloody Tenet of Persecution for Cause of Conscience* contributed significantly to American and European concepts of religious freedom.[164] Therefore, it seems highly likely that John Stuart Mill was exposed to at least the general thoughts of Williams.

Roger Williams recognized that coerced doctrine loses the power of conviction. In the *Bloody Tenet of Persecution*, Williams argued that the Council of Trent enforced the reading of selected prayers.[165] Roman

---

160. Houlgate, *Understanding John Stuart Mill*, 127.
161. Mill, *On Liberty, Utilitarianism and Other Essays*, 52.
162. Mill, *On Liberty, Utilitarianism and Other Essays*, 52.
163. Mill, *On Liberty, Utilitarianism and Other Essays*, 39.
164. Williams, *On Religious Liberty*, 21.
165. Williams, *On Religious Liberty*, 97.

The Superiority of an Evangelical Model of Religious Liberty

Catholic leaders believed forced readings would neutralize the spread of Protestantism in Roman Catholic lands and inevitably result in devout Catholics. But Williams recognized that the practice did neither. Moreover, the practice of forced prayer stripped the prayer of its meaning.[166] According to Williams, forced prayer diminished one's fellowship with God.

Additionally, Williams argued a similar point in *Christenings Make Not Christians*. Here Williams argues for the respect of conscience about the Native Americans. In this treatise, Williams contends that most of Christendom—Protestant and Catholic—exhibits no more faithfulness to the true message of Christ than the Native Americans, and thus most people under Christendom remain every bit as "heathen" as the natives themselves.[167] Williams recognized that a coerced doctrine does nothing but give the appearance of faith, which eventually diminishes the vitality of the doctrine itself. Therefore, Williams seemed to have come to the same conclusion as Mill nearly two hundred years earlier.

Nearly two centuries separated Roger Williams and John Stuart Mill. But the potency of Williams's ideas influenced the milieu that surrounded religious freedom in the seventeenth and eighteenth centuries. Whether or not Mill was influenced by Williams is a matter left to other researchers. But both Williams and Mill certainly recognized that coerced faith cuts one off from one's conscience, ultimately harming the individual and the doctrine itself. Therefore, Mill's fourth premise for religious liberty is not dissimilar from the evangelical arguments that previously circulated.

Summary

John Stuart Mill sought to defend religious freedom on reason alone. And while Mill's utilitarian ethic did provide for religious toleration, it ultimately proves unstable. Because Mill denied divine revelation, he had no objective foundations. Also, Mill's rejection of natural law further relativized his framework, therefore leaving his theory vulnerable to paternalism. While Mill is to be applauded for seeking to balance individual right and social concern, his ethical model remains inferior to those found in Roman Catholic natural law and evangelical foundationalism. Subsequently, John Stuart Mill's utilitarian model of religious freedom cuts one off from the robust operation of conscience. Also, Mill's theory over-realizes the

---

166. Williams, *On Religious Liberty*, 97.
167. Williams, *On Religious Liberty*, 157.

potentiality of humans in civil relationships. Finally, the progressive nature of Mill's theory wrongly assumes that time ultimately leads to truth.

CHAPTER 3

Justice as Fairness

John Rawls's Contribution to Modern Religious Liberty

It is generally agreed that John Rawls was one of the most important political philosophers of the last one hundred years.[1] His seminal work, *A Theory of Justice*, has sold over 400,000 copies and has been translated into twenty-eight languages.[2] John Rawls supervised more than thirty doctoral dissertations and influenced prominent scholars such as Thomas Nagel, David Lyons, and Martha Nussbaum. And his *A Theory of Justice* (hereafter *TJ*) has resulted in an estimated five thousand additional secondary works.[3] In 1999, President Bill Clinton awarded Rawls the National Humanities Medal. And Rawlsian principles were instrumental in laws such as Patient Protection and the Affordable Care Act (Obamacare). His definition of equality significantly shaped the Supreme Court's ruling on same-sex marriage.[4] And John Rawls's framework for social ethics influences many of today's conceptions of religious liberty. This chapter begins with a brief biographical sketch of John Rawls. I will highlight the key events and influences that shaped his thought. I will take up his purpose for writing *TJ*. I then present critical elements to his theory of justice focusing on the original position, two principles, and overlapping consensus. I next critique his

1. Graham, *Rawls*, vi.
2. Pogge, *John Rawls*, 3.
3. Graham, *Rawls*, 1.
4. Foss, "John Rawls," 1.

concept of human agency, the priority of right over the good, and the privatization of religious beliefs. Finally, I will offer a summary that explains the insufficiency of his paradigm for lasting religious freedom.

John Rawls (1921–2002)

John Rawls was the second of five sons born to William and Anna Rawls.[5] Rawls's father was a distinguished attorney, and his mother a charter member of the League of Women Voters and an advocate for women's rights.[6] Rawls's parents helped shape his concern for social ethics. But how John Rawls understood fairness was significantly affected by the death of his two brothers. Bobby Rawls and Tommy Rawls both died within twenty-four months due to a disease contracted from John.[7] At an early age, John Rawls was confronted with the unfairness of life.

Moreover, John Rawls grew up in the former slaveholding state of Maryland.[8] Although Maryland was not part of the Deep South, the heritage of his home state left him unsettled.[9] Paul Graham says, "For John Rawls, the slavery of the South and the failure after the Civil War to grant effective rights to black Americans became the paradigm of injustice."[10] Rawls believed that his educational opportunities and life prospects were superior to that of impoverished blacks in Maryland. In his biography, John Rawls said that these childhood experiences made a lasting impression on him and awakened his senses to injustice.[11]

Rawls proceeded to Princeton University in 1939, where he studied philosophy. Here he was exposed to the utilitarian philosophies of John Stuart Mill, Henry Sidgwick, and Walter T. Stace. But Rawls was most significantly influenced by Kant's *Groundwork of the Metaphysics of Morals*.[12]

During his time at Princeton, Rawls became deeply religious, and he even considered becoming an Episcopal priest.[13] But World War II signifi-

---

5. Pogge, *John Rawls*, 4.
6. Pogge, *John Rawls*, 5.
7. Pogge, *John Rawls*, 5.
8. Graham, *Rawls*, 2.
9. Graham, *Rawls*, 3.
10. Graham, *Rawls*, 3.
11. Pogge, *John Rawls*, 7.
12. Pogge, *John Rawls*, 10.
13. Rawls, *John Rawls*, 1.

cantly altered Rawls's religious beliefs.[14] Rawls was sent to the Pacific theater after enlisting in the US Army. Here Rawls was exposed to the aftermath of Hiroshima; he experienced first-hand accounts of Allied forces liberating concentration camps, and he witnessed the deaths of fellow servicemembers.[15] In a recorded interview with Thomas Pogge, Rawls retold the event that finally caused him to abandon orthodox Christianity. Rawls recounted a sermon given by a Lutheran pastor immediately following combat operations. Rawls said,

> The pastor, during his service, gave a brief sermon in which he said that God aimed our bullets at the Japanese while God protected us from theirs. I don't know why this made me so angry, but it certainly did. I upbraided the pastor (who was a First Lieutenant) for saying what I assumed he knew perfectly well—Lutheran that he was—were simply falsehoods about divine providence. What reason could he possibly have had but his trying to comfort the troops? Christian doctrine ought not to be used for that, though I knew perfectly well it was . . . To interpret history as expressing God's will, God's will must accord with the most basic ideas of justice as we know them. For what else can the most basic justice be? Thus, I soon came to reject the idea of a supremacy of the divine will as also hideous and evil.[16]

Like many other twentieth-century moral theologians and philosophers, Rawls changed his system of beliefs due to the war.[17] Consequently, Rawls abandoned the Christian faith after the war but continued to pursue a graduate degree in moral philosophy.

The Purpose of Rawls's Work

American society contains competing notions of the good life, and Rawls believed this resulted in different definitions of justice. America's diversity also leads to conflict. Rawls sought to create a theory of justice where everyone could agree without giving up personal convictions about the good

---

14. Rawls, *John Rawls*, 1.
15. Rawls, *John Rawls*, 262.
16. Rawls, *John Rawls*, 262–63.
17. Reinhold Niebuhr, Karl Barth, and Dietrich Bonhoeffer are a few significant theologians who were influenced by horrors of WWII.

life.[18] Moral philosophy in the twentieth century reflected two trends: utilitarianism or intuitionism. But Rawls did not believe these moral philosophies provided a standard of justice that could balance competing concepts of good. He believed utilitarianism and intuitionism ultimately privileged one concept of good over another. First, he thought that classic utilitarianism failed to recognize the distinctions that exist between persons.[19] Rawls argued that utilitarianism was unable to respect that each individual life has unique value. The majority cannot sacrifice a person's life because of the interests of others.[20] Also, he argued that classic utilitarianism contained perfectionist principles because it made happiness its ultimate end.[21]

Moreover, Rawls rejected teleologic moral philosophy because he believed it was perfectionist.[22] Teleological philosophy understands the "good" as the "realization of human excellence" in various cultural forms. Rawls contended that teleologic moral philosophy's perfectionist principles were unrealistic and ultimately led to an unfair distribution of social goods.[23] Ironically, Rawls scorned perfectionist principles, but his justice as fairness theory contained perfectionist principles. Thomas Pogge notes that Rawls's *TJ* models a "realistic utopia."[24] Pogge argues that *TJ* provides an inspiration that can banish the dangers of resignation and cynicism, and *TJ* enhances the value of our lives even today.[25] Consequently, Rawls's work contains the inconsistencies he sought to correct.

Second, Rawls rejected intuitionism. He contended that intuitionism created a plurality of first principles, which leads to conflict in particular cases.[26] He thought that intuitionism could not provide universal primary rules for structuring institutions. Rawls said, "Intuition includes no explicit method and no priority rules for weighting principles against one another: we are simply to strike a balance by intuition, by what seems to us most nearly right."[27] Finally, Rawls also rejected virtue ethics and divine

18. Foss, "John Rawls," 1.
19. Rawls, *A Theory of Justice*, 163.
20. Lovett, *Rawls' A Theory of Justice*, 118.
21. Rawls, *A Theory of Justice*, 286.
22. Graham, *Rawls*, 49.
23. Rawls, *A Theory of Justice*, 287.
24. Pogge, *John Rawls*, 27.
25. Pogge, *John Rawls*, 27.
26. Rawls, *A Theory of Justice*, 30.
27. Rawls, *A Theory of Justice*, 30.

command theory because he believed these also contained perfectionist principles, and in a pluralistic society citizens have competing visions of good. He thought that social ethics founded on natural rights or divine commands overrode the welfare of some; therefore, divine commands or natural rights are inherently unfair. Rawls focused his postgraduate work on creating a theory that would replace metaphysical and utilitarian moral theory. He endeavored to blend the principles of deontology with principles of naturalistic teleology. Consequently, he sought to establish a society with a strong commitment to the duty of fairness without sacrificing the diverse choices of its citizens.[28]

Rawls concentrated his work on two questions: First, how is it possible for a culture to be just? Second, how can human life be treated as worthwhile?[29] Rawls argued that the answer to these two questions determined the fair distribution of goods in society. For Rawls, basic goods are not merely material resources, such as income, but also freedom, political power, and self-expression.[30] Therefore, he contended that the fair distribution of goods required a particular basic structure.

Rawls's *TJ* falls within the political structure of social contract theory. But he believed the traditional social contract theories of Locke, Rousseau, and Kant contained fundamental flaws.[31] In *TJ*'s preface, Rawls argued that he wanted to take traditional social contract theories to "a higher order of abstraction."[32] Rawls believed traditional social contract theories contained three problems.[33] First, traditional social contract theory was based on an imaginary point in history called "the state of nature." But because the state of nature is imaginary, Rawls believed that it did not help determine the fair distribution of goods.[34] Second, social contract theories are inherently selfish. Rawls argued that any society that views itself in terms of "self-interest" and "mutual egoism" is headed for certain destruction.[35] But Rawls did

---

28. Rawls attempted to syncretize deontology and naturalistic teleology without an appeal to divine revelation. Ethics fixed in divine revelation can unify principles of deontology and teleology as witnessed in John Frame's *Doctrine of the Christian Life*.

29. Pogge, *John Rawls*, 4.

30. Graham, *Rawls*, vi.

31. Rawls, *A Theory of Justice*, 10.

32. Foss, "John Rawls," 5.

33. Rawls, *A Theory of Justice*, 11.

34. Rawls rejected biblical revelation for establishing political principles; therefore, any discussion of prelapsarian or postlapsarian conditions were irrelevant.

35. Rawls, *John Rawls*, 189.

Justice as Fairness

not ultimately reject contractarianism. He argued for balance in the social contract whereby the public's sense of justice ensured cooperation.[36] Third, social contract theories rest on an original contract between a ruler and subjects.[37] The original compact required a coronation oath where rulers agree to rule justly, and people pledge obedience to their commands.[38] But Rawls argued that people do not often choose their government. Citizens are generally born into a society without much choice. And because citizens never have an opportunity to accept or reject the terms of a social contract, how can it create genuinely free and equal citizens?[39] Rawls believed that the flaws in traditional social contract theory caused it to collapse into modern utilitarianism. Subsequently, Rawls sought to replace the "state of nature" concept with something he considered more stable.

Rawls believed that society is a system of cooperation.[40] Cooperation assumes that all members of society work for one another's mutual benefit; therefore, those in the upper class serve the best interest of the lower and vice versa. A society structured on cooperation requires basic structures to ensure justice, fair distribution, and orderly collaboration. For Rawls, basic social structures include political constitutions, principled economic institutions, and social arrangements. He argued, "The basic structure of society, or more exactly the way in which the major social institutions distribute fundamental rights and duties, determines the division of advantages for social cooperation."[41] Simply stated, the basic social structure of a society establishes and maintains social cooperation. And because basic structures govern social cohesion, all systems must be founded upon universally agreed-upon principles. Rawls contended that citizens could only cooperate when they universally agree on the founding principles that support their social structures. But because traditional social contract theory does not afford citizens the right to choose these principles continually, it cannot provide the basic principles of cooperation needed for social stability. Subsequently, Rawls replaced the concept of social contract with a theory he called the "original position."[42]

36. Rawls, *A Theory of Justice*, 5.
37. Lovett, *Rawls' A Theory of Justice*, 8.
38. Lovett, *Rawls' A Theory of Justice*, 8.
39. Rawls, *A Theory of Justice*, 19.
40. Lovett, *Rawls' A Theory of Justice*, 24.
41. Rawls, *A Theory of Justice*, 6.
42. Lovett, *Rawls' A Theory of Justice*, 9.

The Superiority of an Evangelical Model of Religious Liberty

Original Position

Rawls argued that just principles are those which would be chosen in a situation in which agents are free and equal.[43] Rawls called this situation the "original position." The original position is purely a hypothetical situation where rational agents select the basic principles of social cooperation. But because rational agents will likely disagree on basic principles, the validity principles are derived from the chosen procedure. Rawls argued that a veil of ignorance establishes the proper setting to select principles of justice.[44] The essential feature of the original position is that no one knows his or her place in society. Agents behind a veil of ignorance do not know their natural assets, abilities, intelligence, strength, social standing, race, or religion. Therefore, because all agents are similarly situated, no one can design principles to favor a particular condition. Rawls believed this procedure resulted in a fairest agreement for all people.

Agents in the original position are free to choose any principle. But these principles must achieve consensus before they can be assumed. Rawls argued that rational agents would agree on two fundamental basic principles. First, each person is to have an equal right to the most extensive scheme of equal basic liberties compatible with a similar scheme of liberties for others.[45] In short, each person must have equal access to a basic set of primary goods. Rawls defined primary good as follows: (1) political liberty (the right to vote and hold public office) and freedom of speech and assembly; (2) liberty of conscience and freedom of thought; (3) freedom of person, which includes freedom from psychological oppression and physical harm; (4) the right to hold private property; and (5) freedom from arbitrary arrest and seizure. The second principle states, "Social and economic inequalities are to be arranged so that they are both (a) reasonably expected to be to everyone's advantage, and (b) attached to positions and offices open to all."[46] Simply stated, all inequalities must work to skew to the advantage of the least unfortunate of society. Rawls recognized that material inequalities would inevitably happen in a liberal democracy, but where inequality exists, it must be arranged to benefit everyone. Rawls's first principles of justice reflect Kant's categorical imperative; therefore, his theory blended

---

43. Graham, *Rawls*, 29.
44. Rawls, *A Theory of Justice*, 11.
45. Rawls, *A Theory of Justice*, 53.
46. Rawls, *A Theory of Justice*, 53.

deontology and contractarian ethics. And his second principle was a form of reversed utilitarianism (the greatest good is calculated in benefits to the disadvantaged few). Here, one notices his synchronization with naturalistic teleological principles.

Anthropological Assumptions

When one considers Rawls's social ethic, two anthropological assumptions are evident. First, Rawls assumed humankind's most significant problem is community-corrupting egoism. In his 1942 senior thesis, he defined sin as "the corruption and destruction of community . . . and it is not caused by any factor which is not communal in essence."[47] Rawls denied the Augustinian concept of sin; therefore, he reduced sin to acts of selfishness that destroy the community.[48] Rawls argued that closed groups in a society are the apex of community killing sin. He said,

> Closed groups are now tearing that civilization to pieces. The development has seen several stages: (a) the religious closed groups, as exemplified by the Roman Catholic Church who called everyone outside the pale heretics; (b) the cultural closed groups such as the Italian humanists already mentioned; or the phenomenon of 18th-century cultural distinctions; (c) In Marxism the determinant falls to the economic level, and a person's group is determined by his economic status; and (d) finally, the determinant is biological. In Nazism, we find that what condemns us or exalts us is the sort of blood we have in our veins.[49]

Rawls contended that closed groups are a source of corrupting pride. And this belief informed how he conceived of religious toleration. Rawls officially renounced his Christianity in 1945; therefore, one does not find Rawls making explicit theological claims in his *TJ*. Neither does one find Rawls using the language of sin, per se. But one can recognize how his early theological studies influenced his later work. Throughout Rawls's career, he continued to believe that religious principles are valid for political

---

47. Rawls, *John Rawls*, 189.

48. Augustine's concept of sin was more broad. Augustine recognized that sin permeates desires as well as actions; therefore, motives are included in traditional Augustinian ethics.

49. Rawls, *John Rawls*, 197.

philosophy when they align with common reason. Therefore, one can recognize how his concept of sin influenced his social ethics.[50]

Second, Rawls attempted to answer questions of redeemability by focusing his work in the political realm. Pogge says, "Rawls' life work was focused on the question of whether, and to what extent, human life is redeemable—whether it is possible for human beings, individually and collectively, to live so that their lives are worth living."[51] Rawls rejected Christianity years earlier. But he remained troubled with the problem of evil in the human character.[52] In Pogge's final analysis he notes, "By modeling a realistic utopia as a final moral goal for our collective life, political philosophy can provide an inspiration that can banish the dangers of resignation and cynicism and can enhance the value of our lives even today."[53] Rawls envisioned a world where social structures could save collective life by eliminating closed groups. Thus, religious freedom was not about individuals discovering transcendent truths. Religious freedom was a means of ending social inequalities. Therefore, Rawls's theory of justice recognizes the problem of human egoism, but it expects political structures to provide salvation. Ultimately, Rawls was a utopian thinker who believed the purpose of government is to rectify every injustice.

Human Agency

Religious freedom established on concrete principles is most stable. Natural law theory provides sufficient principles. But Scripture offers the most concrete principles. Yet, John Rawls rejected the principles of natural law and divine revelation; therefore, he fixed religious freedom in the arbitrary

---

50. In Rawls's "My Religion" (published posthumously) he argued that the concept of "God's will" was barbaric because it conceived of God as a wrathful and punishing being; therefore, he rejected the God of orthodox Christianity. But Rawls rejected outright atheism as well. He argued that if one completely denies God's existence, then one must also deny principles of justice. Rawls adopted a view called *nonvoluntarist theism*. In this view, moral and political values are consistent with God's reason. Rawls contended that God's reason and human reason are consistent; therefore, believers and unbelievers can agree on basic principles of justice. Rawls's *nonvoluntarist theism* closely resembled eighteenth-century deism.

51. Pogge, *John Rawls*, 26.

52. Pogge, *John Rawls*, 26.

53. Pogge, *John Rawls*, 27.

Justice as Fairness

principles of reason. Subsequently, Rawlsian principles of religious liberty come exclusively from his original position theory.

In the original position, moral agents are cut off from cultural, historical, and religious influences; agents are disconnected from their own identity.[54] Individuals behind the veil of ignorance are limited only to the power of reason. In Rawlsian thought, the definition of good is rationality.[55] Rawls said, "A person's good is determined by what is for him the most rational plan of life given reasonably favorable circumstances."[56] Therefore, behind the veil of ignorance, only two powers of reason exist, and these two powers set the terms for society by establishing primary goods.

The first power of reason is empathy. Rawls argued that rational agents want primary goods first and foremost for themselves.[57] Therefore, a reasonable person desires religious freedom in the original position because behind the veil of ignorance one would not be aware if they are religious. One recognizes religious freedom as a social good because one would desire it for themselves. Rawls assumed that self-motivation is the source of empathy.

The second power of reason is self-authentication. Rawls argued that individuals could judge for themselves the validity of truth claims.[58] Individuals have the capacity to determine for themselves what is good; therefore, individuals have the power to define separate categories of good. Individuals define good based upon their subjective preference because Rawls detached good from nature and divine revelation. His theory of the good is general enough that any pleasure freely chosen neatly fits into a good category as long as it does not violate principles of justice. Rawls believed that every person maintains these two internal powers of reason. Therefore, one's sense of empathy and ability to decide good establish the "fair terms" for structuring social cooperation.[59]

Additionally, these two internal powers of reason allow an agent to consider themselves and others. Rawls's method presupposes a distinction

---

54. While it is impossible to be disconnected from identity, Rawls imagines a hypothetical situation where individuals do not draw upon their self-knowledge in regard to class, experience, religion, etc.
55. Rawls, *A Theory of Justice*, 347.
56. Rawls, *A Theory of Justice*, 347.
57. Graham, *Rawls*, 36.
58. Rawls, *Political Liberalism*, 32.
59. Rawls, *Political Liberalism*, 19.

between the rational and the reasonable.[60] Rawls said, "The rational is a distinct idea from the reasonable and applies to a single unified agent, either individual or corporate person."[61] Rationality harnesses the power of judgment and deliberation so that one can seek their own ends and interests.[62] Therefore, pure rationality is when an individual assesses a particular good and the political system that supports that good from their own standpoint.

However, reasonability requires viewing a good from each person's standpoint who will be affected by it. One has to put themselves in the shoes of another person and ask oneself, "If I were that person, would I agree that this particular system protects their concept of good?"[63] Hence, among a plethora of perceived goods, one is not asked to judge the actual virtue of another's vision of good; one is only to consider, "Is that concept of good reasonable from their position?" Regarding social ethics, only arguments about reasonability are permissible—not arguments about values. Jerome Foss says, "Rawls wants to limit debate to terms that all 'reasonable' people can accept. To be considered reasonable, one must agree not to root one's arguments for law in any philosophical or religious view that is not commonly shared by everyone."[64] Therefore, community consensus determines social ethics in Rawlsian theory.

Furthermore, Rawls's categories of rationality and reasonability set the terms for public engagement. Rawls argued that reasonability is the power that allows rational agents to enter the public world of others; therefore, it is a public power.[65] But rationality is the capacity to deliberate and form one's vision of good, which is a personal power. Therefore, in the Rawlsian method, religious freedom is a primary good because (a) individuals can privately reason that they would want this freedom outside of the original position; and (b) it is reasonable to believe that if one desires religious freedom, then others do as well. Hence, the Rawlsian argument for religious freedom is based exclusively on the power of human reason.

---

60. Graham, *Rawls*, 23.
61. Rawls, *Political Liberalism*, 50.
62. Rawls, *Political Liberalism*, 50.
63. Graham, *Rawls*, 23.
64. Foss, "The Hidden Influence of John Rawls on the American Mind," 5.
65. Rawls, *Political Liberalism*, 53.

Justice as Fairness

Problem One: Agency and Time

Rawls's original position theory suffers from two anthropological problems. The first deals with the connection between time and ethical reasoning. The second concerns itself with the relationship between human will and reason. Consequently, Rawls's desire to elevate social cooperation undermined critical elements of human agency.

First, Rawlsian thought does not fully respect the connection between time and moral reasoning. Humans are creatures that make ethical decisions in real time. Moral agents make decisions by deliberating on potential future consequences, and this includes engaging with previous experience. Oliver O'Donovan describes the intersection of human agency and time as follows: "Time lies before him (the moral agent) as his way through the world lies before him; time and the world are co-involved, so that as he approaches the one, he approaches the other. Time lies behind him too . . . time before him is not determined, as time behind him is determined."[66] O'Donovan recognizes that moral reasoning includes both deliberation and reflection, and both actions traverse time. One's past experience shapes how one perceives future consequences. Reflection is the activity of contemplating past experience, and these experiences include individual and communal matters. Michael E. Bratman argues that adult human agents persist over time.[67] One's practical thinking concerns itself with and plays a central role in the organization and coordination of their activities over time.[68] Bratman's claim is a statement more clearly by the writer of Ecclesiastes. Ecclesiastes 3:11 argues that moral agents reflect and deliberate as they consider the universe because eternity is written on their hearts. Qohelet revealed that deliberation and reflection are inseparably linked actions. Therefore, one cannot deliberate on the future without reflecting upon the past.

But Rawls's original position cuts moral agents off from the activity of reflection in the original position. And this hinders the agent's ability to deliberate. Rawls's theory restricts the process of reflection, leaving agents with no means to imagine the future. Again, Bratman rightly recognizes that deliberation is not truly deliberation if it does not engage actively in the process of reflection. Bratman says, "An agent moved by desires of which he

---

66. O'Donovan, *Self, World, and Time*, 15.
67. Bratman, "Two Problems about Human Agency," 320.
68. Bratman, "Two Problems about Human Agency," 320.

is unaware, or on which he is incapable of reflecting, or from whose role in action he is, as we sometimes say, estranged, seems himself less the source of the activity than a locus of forces."[69] Therefore, one who is cut off from serious reflection cannot fully engage in deliberation.

Additionally, one cannot be held fully accountable for actions if one does not have access to the full process of reflection and deliberation. Moral agents can predict, to a certain degree, the consequences of a particular act when one reflects on similar events in the past. Humans are not merely motivated to act in various ways; they can also step back and critically reflect on that motivation.[70] For instance, one knows that specific moral actions will produce pangs of guilt because one has experienced the sensation of guilt in the past. The human conscience continually processes previous actions and weighs them against future consequences. Thus, it seems that an order of critical reflection is central to an agent's deliberation process. But Rawls takes this away from agents in the original position; one is left only with blind guesses as they consider future consequences. Therefore, individuals would not be wrong to plead ignorance when their actions led to harm. How can one be genuinely responsible if they are not fully informed of potential consequences? Subsequently, Rawls's original position undermines individual accountability, rendering individuals accountable for only procedural correctness rather than moral goodness.

Moreover, the process of deliberation also includes motivations. Bratman argues that the initial act of deliberation occurs because an agent desires a particular end.[71] Human agents are typically motivated by desires because they see these desires as associated with justifying reasons.[72] But Rawls's original position naively argues that human agents can put off desire and become purely disinterested so that fairness can be achieved.[73] Here Rawls encounters logical problems. For instance, in the original position, how can one know that fairness is a good to be desired? And how can individuals "turn off" desire and at the same time want fairness? Rawls is not logically coherent on this point. Frank Lovett points out, "Rawls does not draw a sensible line between information excluded by the veil of

---

69. Bratman, "Two Problems about Human Agency," 313.
70. Bratman, "Two Problems about Human Agency," 316.
71. Bratman, "Two Problems about Human Agency," 311.
72. Bratman, "Two Problems about Human Agency," 312.
73. Rawls, *A Theory of Justice*, 12.

ignorance in the original position, and information not excluded."[74] Rawls tried to get around this problem by claiming that a "thin good" is permissible initially in the original position.[75] He said, "The theory of the good used in arguing for the principles of justice is restricted to the bare essentials."[76] Even so, because Rawls denied divine revelation and natural law, he gave no substantive justification for why fairness is desirable above any other virtues. An evangelical ethic can argue that Christ's law of love compels fairness. But a Rawlsian ethic, fixed only in the arbitrary nature of reason, cannot answer why fairness is more desirable than power or domination. Yet, for Rawls's theory to work, he must start with fairness as the foundation for deliberation. Consequently, because Rawls separated the process of deliberation and reflection and detached desire and ends, his theory offers a reduced concept of human agency.

Problem Two: Volition and Cognition

Second, Rawls's theory also contains a relational problem relating to the ordering of will and cognition. In the original position, Rawls assumes that volition takes precedence over rationality. Rawls says, "The self is prior to ends which are affirmed by it."[77] For Rawls, fairness must be the fundamental primary good because fairness protects an individual's right to choose their own ends.[78] And this means, in Rawlsian thought, that humans are not created for an ultimate end, such as glorifying God or happiness. For Rawls, ends are the result of one's volition. Michael Sandel's influential critique of *TJ* notes that Rawls's theory fixes one's identity in the choices one makes.[79] Sandel astutely recognizes that in Rawls's paradigm of human agency, one's life plan is not an *interest in the self*, but they are *interests of a self*.[80] His human agency theory depicts humans as agents of

---

74. Lovett, *Rawls' A Theory of Justice*, 99.
75. Rawls, *Political Liberalism*, 178.
76. Rawls, *A Theory of Justice*, 348.
77. Rawls, *A Theory of Justice*, 560.
78. Rawls allows the principle of fairness to enter the original position calling it a "thin good." Michael Sandel notes that Rawls's thin theory of the good is distinguished from the full theory of the good in that the thin theory can provide no basis for judging or choosing between various particular values or ends.
79. Sandel, *Liberalism and the Limits of Justice*, 55.
80. Sandel, *Liberalism and the Limits of Justice*, 54.

choice separated from one's ends, attributes, talents, values, character, and commitments. And this is separate from all the particular or individual qualities that one may possess.[81] Matthew Arbo notes that three factors give shape to Rawls's concept of human agency.[82] First, human agents have a conception of the good. Second, human agents have a free voice to live out one's claim of the good. Third, human agents are free to take responsibility for their own ends.[83] Subsequently, Rawls reduces the human person to a series of abstract choices.

Moreover, if the self is separate and prior to one's ends, morality is volitional rather than cognitive.[84] Simply stated, one not only chooses what is moral and immoral; one also chooses one's identity. Rawlsian thought assumes that human identity is created through individual choices rather than discovered through religion or family. Rawls's claim that "self is prior to ends" necessarily ascribes a transcendent quality to fairness. If one creates one's identity through free choices leading to personal ends, then restricting one's choices would be the utmost of sins. In Rawls's theory, a subtle stigma is attached to anyone perceived to be against fairness. Therefore, Rawls's belief that human agents create their identity through volition ultimately deifies the idea of fairness, because human agents are considered creators of self.

Furthermore, Rawls's concept of human agency leads to social splintering. Humans naturally identify with groups that hold similar preferences. Humans will naturally gravitate toward people and groups centered on common beliefs, traditions, and origins.[85] And when one's identity is a matter of volition, one tends to form strong social bonds around those who make similar life choices. Jerome Foss argues that when one chooses one's identity, it results in tribalization and social splintering.[86] Foss says, "Rawls's theory ignores the problems of societal splintering while justifying and thereby encouraging the growth of identity politics in America. The original position in particular envisions citizens and representatives who act primarily on the basis of group identity."[87] Consequently, Rawls's con-

---

81. Baker, "Sandel on Rawls," 898.
82. Arbo et al., "Much More Than Fairness" 51.
83. Arbo et al., "Much More Than Fairness," 51.
84. Arbo et al., "Much More Than Fairness," 52.
85. Foss, "The Hidden Influence of John Rawls on the American Mind," 6.
86. Foss, "The Hidden Influence of John Rawls on the American Mind," 6.
87. Foss, "The Hidden Influence of John Rawls on the American Mind," 6.

cept that "self is prior to the ends" ultimately undermines social cohesion and fosters destructive identity politics.

Nevertheless, a biblical view of human agency stands in dramatic contrast to Rawls in three ways. First, identity is given and not chosen. Genesis 1:26–28 reveals that God made humans in his image. Among the many things that God's image may signify and imply, one of them is that people are delegated a role (function) in the world where he places them.[88] As God's representative agents, humans are bestowed with attributes, talents, values, and character, and these are essential aspects of one's identity. Second, one's self is not disconnected from one's ends. As image-bearers, human beings have been designed by God to have a destiny of conforming to the beauty and the wisdom of Christ, who *is* the image of God (Col 1:15).[89] Third, identity is discovered using the faculty of cognition illuminated by the Holy Spirit. To this point, John Calvin said,

> It is evident that man never attains to a true self-knowledge until he has previously contemplated the face of God, and come down after such contemplation to look into himself. For (such is our innate pride) we always seem to ourselves just, and upright, and wise, and holy, until we are convinced, by clear evidence, of our injustice, vileness, folly, and impurity.[90]

A biblical view of human agency posits that identity is discovered through an illuminated cognitive process rather than volitional acts. Therefore, a biblical understanding of human agency is more stable because it brings the human self into internal unity—identity, cognition, and volition are all joined to achieve one's designed end.

The Priority of Right over the Good

Religious freedom is a good before it is a right. Religious freedom is a good before it is a right because it respects God's active and continuous engagement with his world. God's dynamic engagement with creation gives an order to all aspects of creation and exists prior to political structures. Therefore, religious freedom is an essential good before it is a right.

---

88. Walton, *The Lost World of Genesis One*, 67.
89. Kilner, *Why People Matter*, 81.
90. Calvin, *Institutes of the Christian Religion*, 48.

The Superiority of an Evangelical Model of Religious Liberty

The ordering of good before the right is essential in the formation of law. The role of law is the protection of the good. Robert George argues,

> I wish to suggest that the good is prior to right, and indeed, to rights. To be sure, human rights, including the right to religious liberty, are among the moral principles that demand respect from all of us, including governments and international institutions (which are morally bound not only to respect human rights but also to protect them). To respect people, to respect their dignity, is to, among other things, honor their rights, including the right to religious freedom. Like all moral principles, however, human rights (including the right to religious liberty) are shaped, and given content, by the human goods they protect.[91]

But Rawlsian ethics argue in the opposite direction. Rawls argued that right is prior to the good.[92] Rawls defined "right" as "a set of principles in the general form that are universally applied, and can be publicly recognized as a final court of appeal for ordering conflicting claims of persons."[93] Rawlsian ethics contend that right comes before the good because good is a matter of individual choice. In Rawls's framework, the right to choose one's definition of good takes priority over the good itself. Subsequently, Rawls's framework posits that the purpose of law is to create good.

John Rawls wanted to ensure that social structures do not originate from any particular "comprehensive doctrine" (worldview) such as natural law or religious doctrine.[94] He believed that it is unfair to create social structures from a specific vision of the good in a world of competing goods. Rawls posited that if a single comprehensive doctrine is allowed to shape political structures, it will necessarily increase social tension.[95] Social tension occurs because citizens with opposing views may find themselves disadvantaged. And disadvantaged citizens will see their self-worth diminished. In the original position, self-worth is considered a primary good.[96] Therefore, any political structure that reduces one's sense of self-worth is contrary to good.

---

91. George and Glendon, *Conscience and Its Enemies*, 122.
92. Rawls, *A Theory of Justice*, 347.
93. Rawls, *A Theory of Justice*, 117.
94. Rawls, *Political Liberalism*, xix.
95. Rawls, *Political Liberalism*, xvii.
96. Nozick, *Anarchy, State, and Utopia*, 241.

Rawls sought to shield political structures from comprehensive doctrine by appealing to the value of fairness.[97] He argued that fairness is the one value whereby all rational people intuitively recognize their obligation.[98] Therefore, Rawls established a framework that prioritized the right (duty to fairness) over the good (individual conceptions of good) because he assumed this ordering established the best principles for social cooperation.

Nevertheless, Rawls's ordering of right over the good has problems. First, right over the good absolutizes the value of fairness. Michael Sandel notes that Rawls's framework over-realizes the importance of fairness.[99] Sandel says,

> Justice (fairness) is not merely one important value among others, to be weighed and considered as the occasion requires, but rather the means by which values are weighed and assessed. It is in this sense the "value of values," so to speak . . . justice is the standard by which conflicting values are reconciled and competing conceptions of the good accommodated if not always resolved.[100]

The Rawlsian model of syncretizing principles of deontology, and a naturalistic teleology is unstable. His theory collapses into a purely deontological model whereby fairness becomes the ultimate value. Consequently, Rawls's priority of right over the good imputes a totalizing quality to the value of fairness.

Second, the priority of right over the good restricts religious beliefs from affecting public policy, which creates biases against people of faith. In Rawlsian thought, one's religious beliefs are products of one's arbitrary choice, and that is what makes them good. But because religious beliefs fall into a category of good, they must consent to the primacy of right (fairness). For instance, in *US v. Windsor*, the Supreme Court argued that only "animus" could explain opposition to homosexual marriage.[101] The influence of Rawlsian thought barred religious beliefs from influencing the court even while a majority of Americans at the time favored traditional marriage based on their religious beliefs. Paul Graham argues that where

---

97. Rawls, *A Theory of Justice*, 96.
98. Rawls, *A Theory of Justice*, 96.
99. Baker, "Sandel on Rawls," 15.
100. Sandel, *Liberalism and the Limits of Justice*, 16.
101. Parks et al., "Can Human Beings Have Intrinsic Dignity or Equality without God?," 78.

right is prior to the good, the state must enforce neutrality.[102] He says, "In a society where fairness has primacy, the state is legitimate insofar as its laws and policies are couched in terms that are neutral between those conflicting conceptions of the good, rather than justified by appeals to any particular conception of the good."[103] Therefore, a purely secular state becomes the ultimate arbitrator in matters of fairness, and all religious claims must yield in terms of public policy.

Overlapping Consensus

Religious people will not easily lay aside their deeply held moral convictions. Rawls recognized that ordering right over good created problems for a pluralistic society. He received scholarly criticism from both secular and religious critics. Therefore, in Rawls's later work, *Political Liberalism*, he introduced the concept of overlapping consensus in hopes of winning over critics.

The idea of overlapping consensus argues that political concepts may contain principles derived from one's concept of good, so long as those ideas are considered reasonable. Rawls relied on his distinction between reason and reasonability to establish his claim. He contended that if one's concept of the good is considered "reasonable from his or her point of view" and consistent with the values that all reasonable people can affirm, then one is free to appeal to one's conception of the good.[104] For example, while it might be irrational to set out to become rich by going to seminary school, it might not be irrational to set out to become a good Christian by going to seminary school: the latter plan is logically reasonable from a Christian point of view.[105] Frank Lovett contends that Rawls's overlapping consensus at first seemed like a tactical retreat from his claims that comprehensive doctrines harm society.[106] But from another point of view, it represents a flanking move, insofar as justice as fairness does not depend on a single comprehensive doctrine being shared by all community members—it merely needs to agree that certain claims to goods are publicly

---

102. Graham, *Rawls*, 97.
103. Graham, *Rawls*, 97.
104. Lovett, *Rawls' A Theory of Justice*, 145.
105. Lovett, *Rawls' A Theory of Justice*, 145.
106. Lovett, *Rawls' A Theory of Justice*, 149.

reasonable.[107] Robert George notes that Rawls's idea of "public reason" was an attempt to establish a substantive principle of justice.[108] George argues that Rawls intended to provide a "wide criterion of reciprocity" for social cooperation.[109] Therefore, Rawls's attempt to create a comprehensive doctrine whereby religious and non-religious citizens could agree was the *overlapping consensus.*

Nevertheless, overlapping consensus narrows religious freedom. Rawlsian thought constrains religious belief so only "publicly reasonable" claims are permissible in discussions of justice.[110] Hunter Baker notes that Rawls's overlapping consensus pretends to be neutral, but it disadvantages people of faith in two ways. First, many principles that would benefit the common good are left unheard. Baker posits that comprehensive doctrines vary in the degree to which they can demonstrate the correctness of a view; therefore, those with highly convincing and strong cases are forbidden from contributing to public debates simply because their origins emerge from faith.[111]

Similarly, Robert George believes that overlapping consensus is significantly biased against Roman Catholic natural law. Because Roman Catholic natural law integrates faith and public reason, it must be excluded from political debate.[112] Natural law offers many convincing and cogent arguments on abortion, homosexuality, and euthanasia. Subsequently, in Rawls's framework, these arguments are relegated to the sideline simply because they emerge from a comprehensive doctrine that includes faith, and this wrongly disadvantages Catholic political philosophers.

Second, Baker contends that people of faith lose the chance to compete in the public square while their competitors refuse to admit that they are even playing in the game.[113] If one's argument relies on special knowledge or one's moral convictions, then it is outside the bounds of public reason. One can be a religious believer in God, but only privately and not in one's public capacity.[114] But Rom 1:18–32 reveals that faith and

---

107. Lovett, *Rawls' A Theory of Justice*, 149.
108. George, *Clash of Orthodoxies*, 55.
109. George, *Clash of Orthodoxies*, 50.
110. George, *Clash of Orthodoxies*, 50.
111. Baker, "The Secularist Biases of Rawls's 'Neutral' Rules," 91.
112. George, *Clash of Orthodoxies*, 51.
113. Baker, "The Secularist Biases of Rawls's 'Neutral' Rules," 101.
114. Foss, "John Rawls," 9.

The Superiority of an Evangelical Model of Religious Liberty

reason are symbiotic; every truth claim contains basic assumptions about the metaphysical world. Rawls's entire theory is grounded on suppositions about the metaphysical world, which is an expression of faith itself. Rawls's overlapping consensus is a pretender to the throne of objectivity and sham referee among orthodoxies.[115] Therefore, one who restricts a claim because it originates in faith only pretends to be neutral.

Moreover, Rawls's overlapping consensus claims to provide religious people an opportunity for public debate. He contends (1) religious concepts are or can be shared by citizens regarded as free and equal, and (2) they do not presuppose any particular fully (or partially) comprehensive doctrine.[116] So, overlapping consensus means that intersecting truth claims are permissible so long as one does not reference an overarching religious doctrine. For instance, Christians, Muslims, Jews, and secularists all agree that the law should forbid stealing. But in Rawlsian thought, one cannot mention why stealing is wrong for reasons other than utility. Overlapping consensus bars religious people from providing a public witness, and this cuts them off from missiological convictions. Evangelicals find themselves uniquely constrained because they are not allowed to witness in public political spaces, which infringes on their calling to provide prophetic witness to the state. Additionally, Os Guinness points out that the principles found in overlapping consensus make religious people lie.[117] Guinness says, "Thus unintentionally but no less dramatically, liberals demean human personhood when they invite people freely into the public square, but only on the condition that they leave their faith behind—in other words, when liberals ask religious believers to jettison the deepest source that makes them who they are."[118] In Rawls's economy, the apostle Paul would have had to remain silent before Agrippa. Therefore, overlapping consensus restricts evangelism to the personal realm, and this is a limitation on religious freedom.

Overlapping consensus was a thoughtful attempt to provide space for religious views in the public square. But ultimately, it neuters religious beliefs and asks religious people to lie about their identity. Robert George is right when he states, "The good should not necessarily yield to a particular form of rights-based discourse, that government need not be neutral with regard to the good, and that governments inevitably embrace some concept

---

115. Baker, "The Secularist Biases of Rawls's 'Neutral' Rules," 101.
116. Rawls, *Political Liberalism*, 176.
117. Guinness, *The Case for Civility*, 122.
118. Guinness, *The Case for Civility*, 122.

Justice as Fairness

of the good."[119] Consequently, overlapping consensus suppresses one's religious convictions and restricts one's freedom of speech.

Good Prior to the Right

The priority of good before the right is established in the creation order. God declared his world was good before the creation of man and woman. O'Donovan argues that the good of God's creation fixed humans within a moral framework.[120] He says, "Our existence is framed within an order of things that stands behind and before it. The world was a reality before I was a reality, an object of attention to God, angels, and men before it was an object of my attention."[121] God's declaration of "good" establishes he is the source and authority of good. Therefore, the announcement of good was before the creation of man and woman, which suggests that humans are stewards of good but not originators.

Moreover, Gen 1:28 reveals that God commanded his representatives to "be fruitful and multiply and fill the earth and subdue it." God blesses his creatures at the same time he imparts a command. Hoekema notes, "Though these words are called a blessing, they also contain a commandment or mandate. Because the cultural mandate applies to all humans, it provides the universal and public principles that Rawls diligently desired."[122] Therefore, because the cultural mandate is an imperative that applies to all humankind, it establishes the first principles of law and establishes the order of good prior to the right.

Rawls was wrong to prioritize right before good, and his error fundamentally changes how one conceives the state's role in society. Martin Luther is helpful to understand the danger in the right before good theory. Luther argued that the state is not an order of creation but an emergency order evoked by the fall. Before the fall, the state was not needed.[123] Because humans were initially created good, they related rightly to God, the world (others), themselves, and time. It was only after the fall did humanity require institutionalized rules of justice.[124] Thielicke noted, "Hence the state

119. George, *Making Men Moral*, 161–62.
120. O'Donovan, *Self, World, and Time*, 10.
121. O'Donovan, *Self, World, and Time*, 10.
122. Hoekema, *Created in God's Image*, 14.
123. Thielicke, *Theological Ethics*, 2:17.
124. Luther, *Luther's Works*, 45:590–93.

is simply the institutionalized form of God's call to order. It is a 'remedy' required by our corrupted nature. For it is necessary that lust be held in check by the bonds of the laws and by the penalties lest it riots in freedom."[125] Thus, the role of the state is to restrain sin. The state is called to promote good only as far as it serves to check sin. Rawls's ordering of right prior to good empowers the state to declare and implement its own definition of good. A state empowered to enforce arbitrary concepts of good forsakes its role in Rom 13 and becomes the monster of Rev 13. Consequently, to reorder good before right becomes a subtle attempt to overthrow the authoritative structure of God.

Biblical Justice

The Western mind envisages justice as fairness.[126] Modern notions of justice are far removed from the traditional ideas of justice found in the Old Testament and Plato's and Aristotle's works. Today's concept of justice is distinctly symmetrical and measured in terms of arithmetic. But biblical justice is teleologic and geometric. Biblical justice is defined as proper alignment with God. Paul, in his letters, refers to justice in terms of one's condition before God. Romans 3:25 reveals that justice is measured by one's alignment to God. Augustine is also helpful in defining biblical justice. He says justice is "the disposition of all things, equal and unequal, in their appropriate positions."[127] Simply stated, justice is equal treatment for equal things. Matthew B. Arbo contends that the etymology of the word "justice" supports the right-alignment concept, in contrast to modern notions of fairness.[128] Arbo says, "This identification of justice with an objective right is likewise assumed throughout the New Testament. The words 'right' and 'righteousness,' 'just' and 'justify' stand out starkly from the above definitions. In this context (the NT) 'right' always refers to an objective relationship in reality."[129] When one recognizes that biblical justice is proper alignment toward the ultimate good (God), one realizes how vital it is to understand the priority of good before the right correctly. If one does not comprehend that justice is first measured in one's proper relationship to

125. Thielicke, *Theological Ethics*, 2:17.
126. Arbo, "Much More than Fairness," 50.
127. Augustine, *The City of God*, 427.
128. Arbo, "Much More than Fairness," 57.
129. Arbo, "Much More than Fairness," 57.

God, then one will not properly understand one's relation to self, others, and the rest of creation. Therefore, Rawls's ordering of right over good distorts one's relationships in the personal, civil, and spiritual realms.

Privatized Religion

John Rawls is to be applauded for his desire to preserve social cohesion and protect religious freedom. And it seems he sincerely believed that political structures that prioritize good before right lessen religious freedom.[130] Also, Rawls's humility was laudable. His work *Political Liberalism* was an honest attempt to rework legitimate problems from *TJ*. Therefore, although Rawls rejected his Christian faith, it would be wrong to portray Rawls as a man hostile to religious people's rights.

Nevertheless, Rawls's justice as fairness narrowed religious freedom. Rawls did not believe religious freedom was intrinsically valuable. He argued for religious liberty because it is the product of autonomous choice.[131] But assimilating religious freedom into one of many autonomous choices diminishes its values.[132] First, religion loses its transcendent quality. Religion is reduced to merely another option alongside a myriad of other alternatives. Religious beliefs become commercialized as consumers choose what fits them. Second, when religious liberty is reduced to autonomous choice, it loses its prophetic witness. Religious claims are viewed with no authority when they are merely products of one's individual preference. Michael Sandel notes, in his critique of Rawls,

> To place religious convictions on a par with the various interests and ends an independent self may choose makes it difficult to distinguish between claims of conscience, on the one hand, and mere preferences, on the other. Once this distinction is lost, the right to demand of the state a special justification for laws that burden the free exercise of religion is bound to appear as nothing weightier than a private right to ignore generally applicable laws.[133]

Sandel rightly recognizes that numbering religious beliefs among other autonomous choices diminishes the power of conviction. Third, when

---

130. Rawls, *A Theory of Justice*, 288.
131. Sandel, *Liberalism and the Limits of Justice*, xii.
132. Sandel, *Liberalism and the Limits of Justice*, xii.
133. Sandel, *Liberalism and the Limits of Justice*, xii.

religious liberty is reduced to individual choice, it is privatized. Individuals are allowed to worship according to their beliefs. But personal worship is different from the right of free exercise—free exercise makes no distinction between public and private. Consequently, Rawls's justice as fairness sets out to protect the rights of diverse people in a democracy, but it ultimately decreases religious freedom.

Conclusion

This chapter argued that Rawls's framework for religious freedom falls on two anthropological assumptions. First, I tried to explain that Rawls believed humanity's most significant problems are sociological and not spiritual. Second, I attempted to clarify that Rawls's answers for social discord are purely political. He does not try to consider the inner concerns of the human soul. Therefore, Rawls's theory assumes the perfectibility of humans through the political process.

I then set out to explain Rawls's concept of human agency. Rawls believed that human agency consists of two powers of reason: empathy and self-authentication. According to Rawls, the power of reason establishes the principles of good.[134] But Rawls's concept of human agency breaks down in relationship to the agent and time, and the agent and self. Consequently, Rawlsian conceptions of human agency fail to be coherent.

Finally, I attempted to explain how Rawls's ordering of values diminishes religious freedom. Rawls prioritized right before good, and this limited the rights of religious people. Rawls recognized his error but did not change the view that right is prior to good. Instead, he developed a political instrument called "overlapping consensus." Here I explained how this instrument diminishes religious people's rights because it restricts them in the public square. Rawls is to be applauded for his attempt to preserve religious freedom in a pluralistic culture, but his model proves inconsistent and unstable; therefore, justice as fairness is inferior to the model established in Scripture's foundational claims.

---

134. Rawls, *A Theory of Justice*, 324.

CHAPTER 4

Natural Law Philosophy
John Courtney Murray's Contribution to Modern Religious Liberty

IN DECEMBER 1960, FATHER John Courtney Murray appeared on the cover of *Time* magazine. The cover read, "U.S. Catholics and the State."[1] Father Murray received this distinguished honor because of his relentless fight to alter the Roman Catholic Church's opposition to religious freedom. Before John Courtney Murray's work, the Catholic Church opposed religious liberty based on two abstract principles: that error has no rights, and, its correlate, that the government should repress error whenever possible and tolerate it whenever necessary.[2] But American Catholic theologians struggled with the Church's position. American priests sought to reconcile the universal and immutable truths found within Catholic doctrine and the practical principles of American democracy.[3] As an American scholar and a Roman Catholic priest, John Courtney Murray was committed to tradition and modernity.[4] He sought to explain how faithful Catholics could affirm the American political system while holding to Catholic doctrine's universal truths. John Courtney Murray laid the intellectual groundwork for the Church to embrace religious freedom as a moral ideal. And he wrote the official text that marked that embrace, the Vatican II *Declaration on*

1. Murray, *We Hold These Truths*, vii.
2. Pelotte, *John Courtney Murray*, 120.
3. Ferguson, *Catholic and American*, x.
4. Murray and Hooper, *Religious Liberty*, 11.

Religious Freedom.⁵ Murray wrote thirty-eight articles on religious freedom before Vatican II and another thirty during the council.⁶ This chapter will begin with a brief biography of John Courtney Murray. I will present a short historical sketch of the Roman Catholic Church's struggle with religious freedom before Vatican II. Next, I will present Father Murray's argument against the Roman Catholic Church's official teaching on religious freedom. I will examine Murray's method and his use of natural law philosophy. I will then show the critical elements of his theory focusing on his concept of consensus. Finally, I will offer a summary explaining some of the weaknesses in Murray's argument.

John Courtney Murray (1904–67)

John Courtney Murray was committed to the Roman Catholic Church throughout his entire life. He was born in New York City on September 12, 1904. His father, a Scottish-born lawyer, and his Irish mother were strict Roman Catholics.⁷ He attended a Jesuit high school and entered the Society of Jesus in 1920.⁸ Murray majored in theology and philosophy at Woodstock College in Woodstock, Maryland.⁹ After his ordination to the priesthood, he continued his graduate studies at the Roman Gregorian University in Rome.¹⁰ He spent most of his career studying and working in mainly Jesuit institutions. Consequently, Murray was raised and lived within an insulated Roman Catholic culture.

John Courtney Murray came of age in an era shaken by Pope Leo XIII's (1878–1903) encyclical *Testem Benvolentiae*.¹¹ Leo's encyclical warned the American church of the danger associated with modernism. Leo argued that modernization dehumanized the lower class. Therefore, Leo believed, modernization, left unchecked, would ultimately lead to social unrest. Leo's encyclical also reaffirmed Pope Pius IX's (1856–78) endorsement of intolerance toward religious pluralism. Following the European religious wars, the Roman Catholic Church adopted a policy of religious toleration. The Treaty

---

5. Berg, "John Courtney Murray and Reinhold Niebuhr," 4.
6. Murray and Hooper, *Religious Liberty*, 12.
7. Pelotte, *John Courtney Murray*, 3.
8. Hooper, "John Courtney Murray, SJ (1904–67)," 342.
9. Pelotte, *John Courtney Murray*, 3.
10. Hooper, "John Courtney Murray, SJ (1904–67)," 342.
11. Pelotte, *John Courtney Murray*, 3.

of Westphalia (1648) allowed Catholics and Protestants to live in relative peace. But Roman Catholic leaders did not believe toleration was the ideal condition. Catholics continued to contend that Catholicism offered the best set of principles for ordering a just society.[12]

Catholic teaching claims that truth resides in the church. Thus, a Roman Catholic state was considered the ideal structure for civil society. Pope Pius later blamed religious toleration for the bloody revolutions of the late eighteenth and early nineteenth centuries. And Leo said in his 1888 encyclical, "It is absurd to say that all opinions have equal rights. Heretical teachings are a source of injury to the deepest welfare of true believers."[13] Both Pius and Leo argued that the state ought to suppress the public expression of heretical and atheistic beliefs.[14] Therefore, in traditional Catholic thought, religious freedom was considered merely a "hypothesis" or a prudent strategy, but not an ideal state.

John Courtney Murray adopted a tradition opposed to religious freedom and ecumenical cooperation. When one studies Murray's early work, one finds that Murray first agreed with the historic teaching against toleration. While he was a student at Woodstock, he published an article entitled "A Crisis in the History of Trent."[15] Here Murray argued that Charles of Guise, the French Cardinal who sought compromise with Protestants, failed to understand the severity of the rupture between the reformers and the Catholic Church.[16] Murray affirmed Pope Pius IV's (1559–65) declaration that tolerating theological and ecclesiological issues was impossible.[17] Consequently, Murray initially believed that religious toleration was an imperfect reality and not something to be championed.

Nevertheless, by the end of the nineteenth century, the Roman Church had boxed itself into a corner. The Catholic Church's doctrine against religious freedom saw the suppression of heresy as a permanent condition, which caused several problems for Roman Catholics in America.[18] First, the early years of the twentieth century saw an increase in Roman Catholic immigration. Leo's anti-American encyclical created suspicion among

12. Murray and Hooper, *Religious Liberty*, 26.
13. Burns, "John Courtney Murray, Religious Liberty, and Modernity," 18.
14. Murray and Hooper, *Religious Liberty*, 13.
15. Hooper, "John Courtney Murray, SJ (1904–67)," 344.
16. Murray, *Bridging the Sacred and the Secular*, 285.
17. Murray, *Bridging the Sacred and the Secular*, 285.
18. Murray and Hooper, *Religious Liberty*, 16.

The Superiority of an Evangelical Model of Religious Liberty

American Protestants. Donald Pelotte noted that the Church's defensive posture and withdrawal from secular academia increased hostility toward Roman Catholics.[19]

Second, the Great Depression, the New Deal, and World War II disrupted the American social order, which led to an increase in Catholic civil concern. Francesca Cadeddu recognized that rapid demographic changes and disruption to social order placed Roman Catholics in the mainstream for the first time.[20] Roman Catholic civil engagement rose steadily in the first half of the twentieth century.

Third, post-war America saw a rise in secularism. Leon Hooper posits that post-war reconstruction championed utilitarian principles, not eternal truths.[21] John Courtney Murray began to fear that America would lose its soul if it settled into secular monism.[22] He was concerned that if Roman Catholics did not contribute to America's political philosophy, the nation would drown in a tidal wave of secularism. Consequently, Murray realized that the Catholic Church needed to revisit its opposition to religious freedom for the sake of the common good.[23]

John Courtney Murray maintained his commitment to Roman Catholic doctrine. But he desired to move Catholic social ethics beyond the walls of parochialism. Murray sought to engage a non-Catholic world using the power of autonomous reason—and he did. His expertise earned him admiration beyond the Roman Catholic world. In September 1951, Murray was invited to work as a visiting professor at Yale University. Emmet John Hughes notes, "As the first Catholic priest to be so honored, he shattered all precedent—and some prejudice—by spending a year at Yale University."[24] Murray settled in at Woodstock College for the remainder of his career, where he trained Jesuits for the priesthood until his death in 1967.[25] Consequently, John Courtney Murray was among the first American priests able to bridge the gap between religious scholarship and secular academia.

---

19. Pelotte, *John Courtney Murray*, 4.
20. Cadeddu, "A Call to Action," 533.
21. Hooper, "John Courtney Murray, SJ (1904–67)," 346.
22. Murray, *We Hold These Truths*, 271.
23. Hooper, "John Courtney Murray, SJ (1904–67)," 336.
24. Pelotte, *John Courtney Murray*, 31.
25. Hooper, "John Courtney Murray, SJ (1904–67)," 342.

Natural Law Philosophy

Murray's Purpose

Murray set out to prove that Catholicism and Americanism need not fear each other. For Murray, the common good included an environment shaped by public trust, not public suspicion.[26] He realized that the common good required more than Leo's and Pius's realpolitik strategy; therefore, his goal was twofold. First, Murray sought to convince the Roman Catholic Church that American constitutionalism was consistent with its tradition. Murray argued that non-Catholics were guided by providence to discover new truths concerning human dignity. Murray used natural law philosophy to support his claim that America's founders built a system of government "better than they knew."[27] He contended that the framers "built better than they knew" because they were influenced by a "vigorous but decaying" natural law tradition.[28]

Second, Murray sought to convince American Protestants and atheists that the First Amendment was compatible with Roman Catholic social doctrine. Murray created a careful and nuanced position that synchronized historical Catholic thought with the American concept of religious liberty. To achieve his task, Murray relied upon the work of Pope Gelasius I (492–96), Thomas Aquinas (1225–75), and John of Paris (1250–1306). Consequently, Murray directed his first goal toward the church's mission in the temporal order. And his second goal was directed toward establishing Roman Catholic credibility in a pluralistic society.

Justification to the Church

Murray defended American constitutionalism with a focus on the Declaration of Independence. He argued that within the Declaration, "there is a truth that lies beyond politics; it imparts fundamental human meaning to politics. I mean the sovereignty of God over nations as well as over individual men."[29] Murray used the Declaration's affirmation of God (albeit a deist version) to distinguish America's tradition from the European Jacobin tradition. Jacobinism celebrated the virtues of individual autonomous reason. The Continental European states codified the philosophical principles

---

26. Murray and Hooper, *Religious Liberty*, 16.
27. Murray, *We Hold These Truths*, 46.
28. Murray, *We Hold These Truths*, 11.
29. Murray, *We Hold These Truths*, 44.

The Superiority of an Evangelical Model of Religious Liberty

of *conscientia ex lex* (law is by conscience) and *principatus sine modo sine lege* (without the government no law) in their statutory law.[30] European constitutionalism forced separation of church and state, but it afforded the power to the state to regulate the public existence of the church. Therefore, the Roman Catholic Church strongly rejected the Jacobin tradition.

In contrast, Murray contended that the American Constitution recognized the sovereignty of God as its first organizing principle.[31] The founders' acknowledgment of God's sovereignty was consistent with traditional Roman Catholic social thought. But this is not to say that Murray thought the American Constitution was primarily a product of evangelical theology or the Enlightenment's secular philosophy. He believed the genius of the American Constitution was simply a matter of God's providence working through the "self-evident" principle of natural law.[32] Murray wrote, "We consider the establishment of our country's independence, the shaping of its liberties and laws, as a work of special providence, its framers building better than they knew the Almighty's hand guiding them."[33] For Murray, God's guiding hand revealed "self-evident" principles of human dignity to non-Catholics. Although the Founding Fathers were not Catholic, Murray believed God's providence led them to discover transcendent principles. Therefore, Murray credited God's providence as the ultimate source of the US Constitution.

Nevertheless, Murray believed that apart from Roman Catholic insight, the Constitution was incomplete. He argued that the Founding Fathers derived their natural law insights from John Locke's individualistic concept of natural law.[34] Because Locke did not use Roman Catholic natural law, Murray argued that Locke's idea of natural rights could not fully comprehend metaphysical realities.[35] Like Rawls, Murray posited that Locke's egoism led America toward radical individualism and atomization. He claimed three failures characterized Locke's natural rights

---

30. Ferguson, *Catholic and American*, 95.
31. Murray, *We Hold These Truths*, 44.
32. Murray, *We Hold These Truths*, 23.
33. Murray, *We Hold These Truths*, 46.
34. John Locke's natural rights theory was a form of natural law philosophy. Locke's natural rights theory was based on reason apart from divine revelation. But Locke's theory of natural rights was not completely cut off from Scripture. Locke's concept of the State of Nature was influenced by the Bible's Genesis account.
35. Murray, *We Hold These Truths*, 276.

philosophy—its rationalism, individualism, and its nominalism.[36] Murray sought to win over opponents of religious freedom in the Roman Catholic Church by replacing Locke's natural right theory with Roman Catholic natural law. Consequently, Murray contended that Roman Catholic theology filled in the gaps and strengthened Locke's partial truths.

Justification to Non-Catholics

Simultaneously, Murray sought to calm the fears of non-Catholic Americans. He contended that religious freedom could be derived from reason apart from Catholic doctrine.[37] Murray understood that Protestants derived religious liberty from their doctrines. But he also understood that Protestants and atheists would be suspicious of religious freedom derived from Roman Catholic theology. So, Murray worked to justify a view of religious freedom based on the power of autonomous reason apart from the church. Leon Hooper notes that Murray wanted to ensure that all people of goodwill could arrive at the same premises for religious freedom. For Murray, if non-Catholics develop a theological argument for religious freedom from their doctrines, so be it.[38] But his goal was to justify religious liberty from the powers of autonomous reason apart from any religious doctrine. Therefore, Murray used natural law philosophy to establish his principles of religious freedom.

Throughout the 1950s, John Courtney Murray wrote extensively on religious freedom. His articles on church-state relations frequently appeared in scholarly journals. But when *Theological Studies* published Murray's four critiques of Pope Leo XIII's encyclical, Murray found himself out of favor with Rome. Donald Pelotte notes that these writings brought severe rebukes from such conservative centers as the Holy Office in Rome, the Apostolic Delegation in Washington, and the Catholic University in America.[39] Consequently, by 1955, Murray was officially censored from writing further about church-state matters.

Nevertheless, the Vatican softened toward Father Murray as the 1950s closed. Father Murray's work became unexpectedly favorable among Catholic scholars at the end of the decade. John F. Kennedy's nomination

---

36. Murray, *We Hold These Truths*, 276.
37. Hooper, "John Courtney Murray, SJ (1904–67)," 347.
38. Murray and Hooper, *Religious Liberty*, 28.
39. Pelotte, *John Courtney Murray*, 34.

for president caused the Roman Catholic Church to reconsider its official position on church-state relations. Pelotte contends that Alfred Smith and John F. Kennedy brought Roman Catholic political thought to the forefront of American politics. But John Courtney Murray was the "back-room" man who influenced the elites and won over Catholic intellectuals.[40] Following Kennedy's election, the publishers of *Time* magazine placed John Courtney Murray on their cover for his work, *We Hold These Truths: Catholic Reflections on the American Proposition*.[41] Consequently, the Roman Catholic Church endorsed Murray's principles of religious freedom and codified them at Vatican II.

Natural Law Philosophy

Murray believed that natural law philosophy established the first principles for religious liberty. But it is essential to recognize that natural law takes on several variants in social ethics. Daniel Heimbach notes,

> Natural law tradition through history divides into profoundly irreconcilable streams over whether the power by which one determines what is normative in nature is itself part of nature, or is located beyond nature and only reflected in nature. That is, whether the morally normative in nature involves nothing more than what occurs in nature, or reflects rationally discernable purposes and plans for how natural things should work even when they do not, and in reference to which human beings can evaluate natural occurrences as morally good or bad.[42]

Natural law theology posits that humans participate in God's governance of creation through their inclinations and actions toward the end that is proper to them by nature.[43] But there is a distinction between natural law theology and natural law philosophy based on naturalism. Natural law theology assumes God's existence and divine illumination. Natural law philosophy assumes that one can derive social ethics by observing nature using one's autonomous reason. Consequently, Murray used natural law philosophy rooted in one's ability to discern social ethics through reason apart from divine revelation.

40. Pelotte, *John Courtney Murray*, ix.
41. Pelotte, *John Courtney Murray*, vii.
42. Heimbach, "Natural Law in the Public Square," 689.
43. Ferguson, *Catholic and American*, 15.

Natural Law Philosophy

John Courtney Murray thought any religious liberty concept based on theology would not win a broad appeal. He vehemently argued that claims to religious liberty must not be "rooted in religion itself."[44] Thus, he relied on the ancient and medieval natural law philosophy tradition. Murray believed that a blend of Aristotelian-Thomistic philosophy offered the best basis for establishing broad appeal.[45] While atheists may reject Thomistic arguments, Murray thought they could accept Aristotle's rationale found within St. Thomas. And while Protestants may reject the substance of Thomistic natural law, they could receive a theory that was established on divine providence. Also, whereas Catholics may reject Protestant calls to theology, they could accept Thomistic philosophy. Consequently, Murray sought to establish religious liberty principles using a method that syncretized theology and philosophy.

Roman Catholic Precedent

Murray found precedent for his method in the works of Pope Gelasius (492–96). In his letter to Emperor Anastasius, Pope Gelasius argued there are two great societies upon the earth—the religious and the civil.[46] Gelasius contended that only Christ held the ability to be priest-king. Thus, the roles of priest and king were to be considered separate. Yet, both roles were under the authority of God. Gelasius's concept of duality between priest and king helped establish how he would understand Christian citizens' role. Pope Gelasius, like Augustine, believed Christians were both spiritual citizens and temporal citizens. As spiritual citizens, Christians were accountable to the church. But in the civil realm, Christians fulfill their nature as political animals. Consequently, in Pope Gelasius, John Courtney Murray found source material to support Aristotle's philosophy of citizen.[47] Therefore, in Gelasius, Murray saw a precedent for applying Aristotle's political thought into Catholic theology.[48]

---

44. Murray, *We Hold These Truths*, 64.
45. Ferguson, *Catholic and American*, xi.
46. O'Donovan and O'Donovan, *From Irenaeus to Grotius*, 179.
47. Murray, "Contemporary Orientations of Catholic Thought," 177.
48. Aquinas would eventually combine Aristotle's political philosophy with Catholic theology. But because Gelasius predated Aquinas, Murray appealed to the former. Murray believed Gelasius provided a more direct link to Aristotle, and this would be more palatable to non-Catholics.

The Superiority of an Evangelical Model of Religious Liberty

Moreover, Aristotle's political philosophy was foundational to John Courtney Murray's social ethic.[49] Aristotle believed that humans are political animals by nature.[50] According to Aristotle, humans naturally form associations for the purpose of flourishing. Aristotle said,

> Just as an individual man is the natural end of the process of human coming-to-be, so too the state is the natural end and culmination of the other and the earlier associations, which were themselves natural; the state therefore exists by nature. It provides all man's needs (material, social, religious, etc.), and it offers them the fulfillment not only of living but of living "well," in accordance with those virtues that are particularly human.[51]

Aristotle believed that by observing human interaction, one rationally discerns that humans form natural associations. And these associations are directed toward the purpose of human flourishing. Aristotle defined human flourishing as the internal state of happiness or *eudaimonia*.[52] The philosopher argued that humans fulfill their natural purpose when they seek happiness, and happiness is achieved through the practice of four chief virtues: prudence, courage, temperance, and justice.[53] Therefore, Aristotelian political philosophy posits that humans instinctively form a consensus around principles of the common good.

Principle of Consensus

Murray's anthropology was rooted in Aristotle's philosophy blended with Catholic theology. But Thomas P. Ferguson contends that Murray firmly established himself in the Aristotelian concept.[54] Aristotle conceived of humans as "natural political animals."[55] Murray used Aristotle's theory of human nature to develop his claim that humanity's goal in the temporal realm was to establish justice, peace, and prosperity. Murray posited that human society naturally formed for the purpose of cultivating virtue. Therefore,

---

49. Murray, "Contemporary Orientations of Catholic Thought," 177.
50. Aristotle, *The Politics*, 55.
51. Aristotle, *The Politics*, 55.
52. Aristotle, *The Nicomachean Ethics*, 3.
53. Aristotle, *The Nicomachean Ethics*, 6.
54. Ferguson, *Catholic and American*, 8.
55. Ferguson, *Catholic and American*, 8.

humanity's end in the temporal realm can be said to be the perfection and realization of these common goods.[56]

Father Murray contended that the cultivation of virtue formed a public consensus. He argued that through the power of observation and reason one can perceive consensus as the ultimate aim of social life simply by observing kinship relationships.[57] Although kinship relationships may be argumentative from time to time, kinship relationships form a union based on more than a common opinion. Husband and wives may disagree, and parents and children may quarrel, but the relationship's nature binds them together. In like manner, the political community forms a union with more than the majority opinion; their commitment to dialogue binds the community.[58] Consequently, the public consensus witnessed in nature established the foundation for Murray's political thought.

Murray believed that the First Amendment of the US Constitution reflected humanity's natural inclination toward consensus. He believed that political association was the result of rational beings engaging in the process of deliberation.[59] Similar to John Stuart Mill, Murray thought the activity of argument created cohesiveness among men. This is not to say that consensus is an agreement to disagree. Murray contended that societies must maintain an agreement based upon substantive beliefs, and democratic societies especially must possess a shared philosophy.[60] By blending natural law philosophy and natural law theology, Murray sought to establish a set of universal beliefs. It is important to note that for Murray, public consensus did not mean the same as "majority opinion." The majority opinion is the agreement in matters of views, tenets, and testimonies by the majority of the population. Murray claimed a technical use of the word "public consensus" whereby he applied the term in a constitutional sense:

> Public opinion is a shorthanded phrase expressing the fact that a large body of the community has reached or may reach specific conclusions in some particular situation. These conclusions are spontaneous, perhaps emotionally, reached, usually from some unstated but very real premises. The "public" consensus is the body of these general, unstated premises which has come to be

56. Ferguson, *Catholic and American*, 9.
57. Murray, *We Hold These Truths*, 48.
58. Murray, *We Hold These Truths*, 12.
59. Murray, *We Hold These Truths*, 24.
60. Murray, *We Hold These Truths*, 91.

> accepted. It furnishes the basis for public opinion. Public opinion is the specific application of tenets embodied in the public consensus to some situation which has come into general consciousness.[61]

Public consensus emphasizes the subjectivity of persuasion and the ultimate values of the democratic process. Murray understood public consensus as the set of ideas widely held by the community; therefore, the concept of consensus forms a body of doctrine that becomes the accepted authority over said people. In his mind, American society established a consensus based on the virtue of freedom. Murray did not believe it mattered how diverse people came to believe in freedom, so long as they arrived at the same conclusion. For Murray, a consensus was not an agreement on the premises and the purposes; it is solely an agreement regarding the method of making decisions.[62] Therefore, the American consensus is purely procedural.

In Aristotelian fashion, Murray argued that a government established upon consensus would necessarily progress toward the common good. Murray's definition of government simply denoted the idea of "the ruler-in-relationship-to-the-ruled . . . [and] the ruled-in-relation-to-the-ruler."[63] Because government is relational, and all people naturally seek their own good, one can conclude that the government's role is to promote the common good. Thus, Father Murray believed that collective humanity has the power to achieve much good in society. Therefore, Murray's theory of religious freedom emerged from his belief that humans naturally seek the good for one another.

Murray specifically thought America served the common good because it embodied the principles of social cooperation. Religious freedom in America was not an attempt to make people agree on theology. Murray understood that diverse people might never agree on theological issues, but they can agree on procedural premises. According to Murray, the American proposition of "freedom" is a self-evident proposition that all rational people can affirm as good. Consequently, Murray's natural law methodology maintained an optimistic view of human nature and social cooperation.

---

61. Murray, *We Hold These Truths*, 106.
62. Murray, *We Hold These Truths*, 91.
63. Ferguson, *Catholic and American*, 30.

Natural Law Philosophy

Weakness in Relationship to the World

John Courtney Murray was a careful scholar and a meticulous student of Roman Catholic history. His work was thoughtful and timely. And Christians of all denominations can applaud his efforts to stave off aggressive secularism. His work on *Dignitatis Humanae* helped Roman Catholics reimagine the church-state relationship and establish their public square voice. John Courtney Murray came along at the right moment, and his efforts helped create a new era of cooperation between Catholics and Evangelicals. Therefore, John Courtney Murray deserved his place on the cover of *Time* magazine.

Nevertheless, Murray was too sanguine in his judgment about human engagement in the world. Murray's assumptions about human consensus were overly optimistic in three ways. First, his Aristotelian foundations overemphasized the power of the political process over human pride. Murray exaggerated humanity's capacity to maintain a positive consensus. Murray rightly recognized that humans naturally form a consensus, but he did not give an account for the character of a consensus if common values erode. In his book *The Madness of Crowds*, Douglas Murray argues that when a society loses its grand narrative, a vacuum arises.[64] And this vacuum is inevitably filled by the micro-narratives of atomized tribes. Douglas Murray contends that each tribe forms a consensus over niche demands, resulting in constant war among differing groups.[65] Also, one can observe that the presence of sin in the collective often reduces logic and reason to gratuitous insults.[66] But Murray presented no solutions for the kind of consensus that occurred in the Jacobin Revolution. He naïvely assumed that the Founding Fathers' appeal to divine transcendence was enough to stave off the pride inherent in autonomous reason. Murray thought that Jacobinism would not occur in America because, in God's providence, Americans have progressed past mob rule.[67] But John Courtney Murray's foundation for religious freedom has no answer for the negative consensus that often galvanizes a collective once transcendent authority is rejected. Consequently, because Murray's theory only presents a positive vision of consensus, it is not realistic.

---

64. Murray, *The Madness of Crowds*, 1.
65. Murray, *The Madness of Crowds*, 2.
66. D'Abrera, "Farce from the Madding Crowd," 56–61.
67. Murray, *We Hold These Truths*, 16.

The Superiority of an Evangelical Model of Religious Liberty

Moreover, Roman Catholic author Michael Baxter notes that a breakdown of consensus has occurred within the Roman Catholic Church itself.[68] Baxter says,

> He believed that the United States was exceptional among modern states. Unlike France, it was founded on principles inherited from Catholic political theory. This meant that Catholics could carry out the crucial task of transforming public discourse with the principles of natural law and returning the nation to the consensus on which it was founded . . . What he did not foresee, however, is how this consensus would fall apart even among American Catholics; how, in attempting to transform the nation, Catholics would become politically divided and therefore incapable of performing their pivotal role as, in his words, "guardians of the American consensus." Without that role, his story of Catholicism and the United States falls apart.[69]

Murray's method is unstable because it does not directly appeal to an authority beyond that which is observable in nature. Apart from divine revelation, his reliance on natural law philosophy cannot establish a consensus within his own church. Consequently, Murray failed to fully appreciate the reality of sin and its influence on all social interaction.

Roman Catholic ethicist Charles E. Curran foresaw Murray's flaw. Curran criticized Murray for failing to recognize the reality of sin and its influence on human existence in the temporal sphere.[70] Curran contended that Murray held the political, social, cultural, and economic aspects of society univocally in light of the natural, which was too narrow.[71] Curran argued that sin affects all aspects of the natural sphere. This is not to say that Murray did not maintain a sense of realism.[72] He claimed that only virtuous people could self-govern; thus, if people fail to be virtuous, they will not be able to maintain public consensus.[73] But his political philosophy lacked any theoretical power to account for the presence of sin.[74] Because Murray

---

68. Baxter, "Murray's Mistake."
69. Baxter, "Murray's Mistake."
70. Curran, *American Catholic Social Ethics*, 225.
71. Curran, *American Catholic Social Ethics*, 225.
72. Curran, *American Catholic Social Ethics*, 225.
73. Murray, *We Hold These Truths*, 50.
74. Curran, *American Catholic Social Ethics*, 225.

founded his political theory on reason apart from divine revelation, he had no categories to explain the phenomenon of collective sin.

The Individual and Society

Second, Murray's failure to recognize sin clouded how he understood the relationship between the individual and society. Murray's theory applied what he observed in the individual (a desire for virtue) to the whole of society. But Reinhold Niebuhr argued there is a distinction between individual ethics and collective morality. Niebuhr's *Moral Man and Immoral Society* recognized a notable difference between individuals' moral behavior and the collective's behavior.[75] Niebuhr argued that the individual does have a real possibility to act altruistically. But when individuals gather in families, clans, classes, states, or nations, they cannot dislodge from their will to power.[76] Niebuhr rightly recognized that in communities, the group's self-interest is inevitably the predominant factor. Many things an individual will not do, a group will do together to further its fortunes.[77] Murray's foundation for religious liberty rested upon the premise of social consensus. But again, social consensus based solely on reason does not account for the presence of collective sin. Consequently, Murray's foundation for religious liberty was naïve.

Perfectionism and Social Vision

Third, Murray's unwillingness to appeal to divine transcendence left his foundation unstable. Murray emphasized the role of structures and institutions in the formation of consensus. But he did not call for personal conversion.[78] Curran notes that Murray formed his theory of religious freedom based on the distinction between the spiritual and temporal world. However, because he interprets the difference primarily based on the distinction between natural and supernatural, he fails to see how the gospel affects the Christian's relationship to the world.[79] Murray contended

---

75. Niebuhr, *Moral Man and Immoral Society*, xviii.
76. Niebuhr, *Moral Man and Immoral Society*, 13.
77. Niebuhr, *Moral Man and Immoral Society*, xviii.
78. Curran, *American Catholic Social Ethics*, 225.
79. Curran, *American Catholic Social Ethics*, 225.

that humans form consensus for virtue, but he did not seriously take the need for a change of heart. Consequently, Murray's foundation for religious freedom was unstable.

Murray's ethical foundation promoted perfectionist principles. He argued that using only teleological philosophy, and teleological philosophy cut off from divine revelation, assumes natural power is needed to form virtue. John Rawls recognizes the instability of such perfectionist principles.[80] Rawls argues that teleological theories seek to promote human excellence along two poles. At one extreme is Nietzsche's emphasis on striving to produce great men—the virtue of strength.[81] And on the other pole stands Aristotle's view that culture forms excellence among humans. But if culture determines social values, then it is necessary to override individual liberty if one's view of the good differs from the collective's. Rawls contends that coercion was needed to form society's vision of the good.[82] He says, "In order to arrive at the ethic of perfectionism, we should have to attribute to the parties a prior acceptance of some natural duty, say the duty to develop human persons of a certain style and aesthetic grace, and to advance the pursuit of knowledge and the civilization of the arts."[83] Rawls realizes that perfectionism presupposes a shared vision of the good. Thus, because John Courtney Murray relied on Aristotle's perfectionism, his theory could not fully answer the claims put forth in Rawls's *TJ*. If human excellence is good and achievable, then what stops institutions from coercing the good? According to Murray's theory, it would seem that social institutions maintain a moral responsibility to suppress religious beliefs that are judged to be socially harmful. If society's purpose is the perfection of humans, then it seems immoral not to enforce virtue. Murray's theory cannot fully explain why social institutions should not coerce the good. Consequently, Murray's foundation for religious liberty was unstable because he assumed Aristotle's perfectibility of humanity.

Weakness in Relationship to Time

The Roman Catholic Church's history opposing religious freedom presented a problem for Murray. He found himself confronted with the doctrine of

80. Graham, *Rawls*, 49.
81. Rawls, *A Theory of Justice*, 286.
82. Rawls, *A Theory of Justice*, 286.
83. Rawls, *A Theory of Justice*, 289.

Natural Law Philosophy

papal infallibility. Murray could not outrightly declare Rome to be in error. Therefore, he crafted an argument that consisted of two principles.

Murray's first principle was ontological. He argued that every human person is endowed with a dignity that surpasses the rest of creation because the human person is in charge of themselves—autonomous.[84] Human dignity consists of a person's responsibility to themselves and their responsibility as a moral agent.[85] His second principle was a social principle. The social principle states that the human person is the subject, foundation, and end of the entire social life.[86] The connection of these two principles was vital to Murray's argument. The ontological principle set each person as a moral subject, each owning responsibilities and duties toward the moral order. And the social principles recognized that each person exists with others and is subject to the historical order which unfolds throughout time.[87]

Moreover, Murray contended that the principle of human dignity was a matter of natural law. According to Murray, natural law principles are permanent and unchanging. But the application of natural law principles may change to fit unique circumstances in time. He argued that as political philosophers grow in their understanding of human dignity, they adjusted civil law accordingly.[88] Murray said,

> While history cannot alter the natural law, in so far as the natural law is constituted by the ethical a priori, by the primary principles of the moral reason, and by their immediate derivatives . . . But history, as any history book shows, does change what I have called the human reality. It evokes situations that never happened before. It calls into being relationships that had not existed. It involves human life in an increasing multitude of institutions of all kinds, which proliferate in response to new human needs and desires, as well as in consequence of the creative possibilities that are inexhaustibly resident in human freedom.[89]

Murray believed it was the progressive knowledge of human dignity that ultimately birthed the American proposition. Consequently, for Murray,

---

84. Murray and Hooper, *Religious Liberty*, 238.
85. Murray and Hooper, *Religious Liberty*, 238.
86. Murray and Hooper, *Religious Liberty*, 238.
87. Murray, *We Hold These Truths*, 114.
88. Murray, *We Hold These Truths*, 46.
89. Murray, *We Hold These Truths*, 114.

The Superiority of an Evangelical Model of Religious Liberty

natural law principles are permanent, but the theoretical application of principles is a matter of historical consciousness.

However, Murray's dependence on historicism presented problems. He maintained that religious freedom "was the demand of the natural law at the present moment of history."[90] According to Murray, a state, over time, grows in its social consciousness so that it comes to realize its role in promoting religious freedom.[91] But this presents a practical problem. If religious liberty is a consequence of time, then it is not fixed on ontological realities. And if not set on ontological realities, then religious liberty becomes relativistic. Murray's argument for religious freedom was based on the contingencies of history; therefore, not only was it formulated on Aristotelian philosophy, but it also relied on Hegelian principles regarding time. Consequently, because Murray only used principles of reason, his argument for religious liberty collapses under relativism.

Murray recognized his polemic for religious freedom was contingent. In a significant work titled *The Problem of Religious Freedom*, Murray stated, "The institution of intolerance and establishment must be judged *in situ* and might well be valid *in situ*, for the function of law is to be useful to the people."[92] In his essay "The Vatican Declaration on Religious Freedom," he admitted that a "sacred society" could come into existence again if the circumstances dictate.[93] Charles Curran was notably concerned about Murray's historicism. Curran says, "Murray's position means that circumstances could arise in which religious liberty would not be required."[94] Murray implied that what has happened in the past could happen again in the future. He did not rule out a return to a restrictive church-state if circumstances arose. E. A. Goerner strongly criticizes Murray's polemic in his work titled *Peter and Caesar*.[95] Goerner argues that Murray relativized political forms, which reduced political theology to nothing more than situationism.[96] Goerner, a Roman Catholic, also levels similar criticism at Protestant political theology. But his critique of Murray is significant because he undermines Murray's application

---

90. Murray, *The Problem of Religious Freedom*, 11.
91. Murray, *The Problem of Religious Freedom*, 41.
92. Murray, *The Problem of Religious Freedom*, 102.
93. Murray, "The Vatican Declaration on Religious Freedom," 8.
94. Curran, *American Catholic Social Ethics*, 227.
95. Goerner, *Peter and Caesar*, 190.
96. Goerner, *Peter and Caesar*, 190.

Natural Law Philosophy

of natural law. Consequently, because Murray's application of natural law was essentially Hegelian, it weakened his argument.

Weakness in Relationship to Self

Murray boldly asserted that American constitutionalism is essentially a natural law philosophy. The articles featured in his book *We Hold These Truths* claim that the only viable basis for civil unity is "traditional reason" or, under another name, "natural law philosophy."[97] Murray argued that natural reason, unaided by grace, could arrive at an understanding that might unite people who otherwise could not agree theologically.[98] He insisted that the correct use of reason was sufficient for the creation of social consensus. But his appeal to natural law philosophy contained two weaknesses about the human conscience. First, Murray presented the human conscience as a matter of reason and not one's capacity to hear the voice of God. Second, Murray's appeal to natural law philosophy alone assumed epistemological and metaphysical unity. But without divine revelation, epistemological unity is limited. Subsequently, Murray's appeal to natural law philosophy lacks a substantive bridge.

Conscience and Natural Law

The Roman Catholic Church conceived of the conscience in terms of Thomistic natural law philosophy. Pope Leo contended that non-Catholic concepts of the conscience lead to *conscienta ex lex*.[99] *Conscienta ex lex* is the idea that a conscience pursues an end that it has chosen for itself without reference to any objective standard. Leo argued that the "lawless conscience" gave rise to radical autonomy, laicism, and ultimately secular monism. Leo condemned any voluntarist concepts of conscience.

Moreover, the notion of "outlaw conscience" permeated Murray's analysis of religious freedom.[100] Murray maintained that the conscience is a function of natural law and not an autonomous, subjective experience. He understood conscience as that power of reason that allows one to recognize

---

97. Murray, *Bridging the Sacred and the Secular*, xi.
98. Murray, *Bridging the Sacred and the Secular*, xii.
99. Ferguson, *Catholic and American*, 37.
100. Murray and Hooper, *Religious Liberty*, 118.

The Superiority of an Evangelical Model of Religious Liberty

and apply the moral law to social life properly.[101] Murray argued that the proposition "We the People" found within the American Constitution affirms the Catholic understanding that conscience is applied within a social order. In this sense, conscience is a power of reason that manifests itself in social engagement. Therefore, Murray's concept of conscience is a social function that staves off the radical autonomy found in Jacobinism.

Furthermore, as social animals, individuals can reach consensus for the common good through the power of conscience. Murray contended that creatures of the spiritual and temporal realm used the power of conscience to bridge the gap between spiritual beliefs and their application to the temporal. Therefore, conscience in Murray's analysis can guide society positively because it is the application of spiritual beliefs in the social realm.

Additionally, for Murray, human dignity is the ability to live undivided between the two realms; dignity is the ability to apply spiritual beliefs to the temporal world. Commenting on Murray's concept of conscience, J. Leon Hopper notes, "A man's religious decisions, however personal, are made in the social context of man's existence."[102] Therefore, the human conscience is that power of reason that allows one to live as spiritual and temporal beings, which implies that the conscience is essentially a social function.[103]

Nevertheless, Murray's understanding of conscience deemphasizes individual accountability before God. Murray was not necessarily wrong to understand the conscience as a social function. But his claim that the human conscience leads in a positive moral direction and the civic consensus was too optimistic. Scripture does present the conscience as having a social component, but its social function is first and foremost between God and humans. Romans 1:19–20 argues that all humans know intuitively by the witness of nature that God exists and must be absolutely powerful.[104]

Moreover, Rom 2:14–15 teaches that everyone also has a conscience, an imperfect-but-accurate version of God's will, as common knowledge in the human heart.[105] But verse 16 clarifies that the conscience serves a judicial function in that it renders humans accountable before God. J. D. Crowley argues that the conscience functions as an inner sense that allows one to know that they will someday be judged before a tremendous and

---

101. Murray, *Bridging the Sacred and the Secular*, 14.
102. Murray and Hooper, *Religious Liberty*, 141.
103. Murray and Hooper, *Religious Liberty*, 141.
104. Naselli and Crowley, *Conscience*, 24.
105. Naselli and Crowley, *Conscience*, 24.

terrifying tribunal.[106] The conscience is not reasoned as a syllogism but an intuition that makes one aware of strong accountability to an all-powerful, all-knowing God, even if we suppress that intuition, as Rom 1:18 claims.[107] Therefore, it seems that Murray's understanding of conscience contradicts the scriptural role of conscience and misunderstands the individual relationship between God and self.

Moreover, Murray's concept of conscience assumes a power toward positive moral direction. But this also seems contrary to Scripture and history. The word "conscience" is used thirty-one times in the New Testament, and it is primarily found in the writings of the apostle Paul.[108] Claude Anthony Pierce notes that Paul used the word συνείδησις sparingly in the New Testament.[109] Where Paul does use συνείδησις, it was in the popular form, which most commonly referred to the feeling of guilt one has from past actions.[110] Pierce argues that popular Greek culture understood conscience as the pain of guilt that occurred once an act had already been committed. Because guilt occurs after a specific action, the standard Greek citizen did not consider συνείδησις as a reliable guide for moral behavior. Pierce argues that when Paul used the concept of συνείδησις, it was not because he was particularly impressed by the power of conscience as a guiding agent. Nevertheless, Paul used the word because it appealed to the local context of his first-century audience.[111] Pierce notes that on the limited occasions where the New Testament used the word "conscience," it is most commonly referred to as a feeling of guilt after an action.

> As it is, however, we have examined abundant evidence which unanimously indicates the overwhelming probability that "*conscience*" in the New Testament is the individual's conscious record of his *past acts*. We were not able to discover in Greek usage a single case of the reference of any of the συνείδησις group of words to the future. This alone should be enough: but besides that, St. Paul in this passage (I Cor. 8) is unquestionably referring to the conscience as the pain (or its seat) consequent upon the inception of an act believed to be wrong.[112]

106. Naselli and Crowley, *Conscience*, 24.
107. Naselli and Crowley, *Conscience*, 24.
108. Beitzel, "Conscience," 510.
109. Pierce, *Conscience in the New Testament*, 16.
110. Pierce, *Conscience in the New Testament*, 49.
111. Pierce, *Conscience in the New Testament*, 66.
112. Pierce, *Conscience in the New Testament*, 82.

The Superiority of an Evangelical Model of Religious Liberty

Mark Liederbach suggests that if Pierce is correct, then the Pauline notion of conscience is vital to understanding moral guidance.[113] Therefore, Pierce's argument presents a compelling counter-claim to Murray's assertion that the unregenerate conscience creates a positive social consensus aimed toward the good.

Additionally, Murray's view of conscience underestimates the power of ego. Again, Niebuhr's realism seems to understand the power of sin and its effect on human relationships. Niebuhr contended that the human conscience is a moral resource and was not powerful enough to cultivate a sense of duty among collective groups.[114] The human conscience, by nature, pursues self-interest, often at the expense of others. Niebuhr believed that when individuals form into collective communities, the power of social impulse takes over. And when social impulse takes over, the individual conscience is completely overrun. Niebuhr affirmed the limitation of public consensus when he said the following about the collective communities: "They do not see the limitations of the human imagination, the easy subservience of reason to prejudice and passion, and the consequent persistence of irrational egoism, particularly in group behavior, make social conflict an inevitability in human history probably to its very end."[115] Niebuhr's realism may appear to be dark; nevertheless, Niebuhr is accurate. Autonomous reason only allows a person to gain a partial perspective; therefore, majority opinions take on a power that apes the individual conscience. This fact was realized in Nazi Germany, when thousands of Lutherans violated their conscience to commit atrocities. Niebuhr rightly identified the Achilles' heel of John Courtney Murray's argument. Therefore, sin prohibits the conscience's ability to create large-scale and lasting harmony.

Conscience and Epistemology

Murray believed that autonomous reason is powerful enough to maintain civil unity while balancing religious pluralism. He assumed that men and women could agree to a common good based on an unilluminated conscience. But Murray's thesis presupposed a shared epistemology. Natural law only has the power to form a consensus if all parties work from a shared epistemology. But in a pluralistic society, this is seldom the case. Charles

---

113. Liederbach, "The Religious and Moral Conscience," 28.
114. Niebuhr, *Moral Man and Immoral Society*, 39.
115. Niebuhr, *Moral Man and Immoral Society*, xxxiv.

Curran recognizes Murray's weakness.[116] Curran realizes that Murray based his civic unity on epistemological and metaphysical unity. He argues that one has to accept the natural law with its philosophical underpinning to accept Murray's theory of consensus logically.[117] But pluralistic societies not only maintain diverse religious convictions, but they also have different philosophical foundations. Murray's argument for religious liberty falls short without a shared philosophy. Therefore, Murray's thesis weakens as societies become more philosophically diverse.

John Courtney Murray worked and lived in the era of American Christendom. In 1952, at the apex of Murray's career, the United States Supreme Court affirmed, "We are a religious people whose institutions presuppose a supreme being." Three times prior—1815, 1892, and 1931—the court had espoused the same principle.[118] Father Murray's appeal to public consensus only worked when most Americans shared a similar set of philosophical assumptions. Americans may not have been religious "Christians," but the Judeo-Christian faith's influence shaped the nation's theory of knowledge. The concept of *E Pluribus Unum* was broadly understood under a Judeo-Christian framework. Father Murray's conception of American religious pluralism was composed of four distinct "conspiracies" according to Thomas P. Ferguson. The four conspiracies that made the most significant contribution to public life in America were Catholicism, Protestantism, Judaism, and secularism.[119] These "conspiracies" seldom agreed with one another, but they all shared a common belief that absolute objective truth was available to humanity. The debate was never about "knowledge" itself; the debate concerned itself with the source of knowledge and the whole truth. Today there are approximately two thousand identifiable religions and sects in America, and many do not share the same epistemological assumptions.[120] Consequently, the exponential increase of religious pluralism has changed how Americans conceive of religious liberty and how Americans understand knowledge itself.

Protestant theologian Helmut Thielicke warned that natural law detached from faith withers away.[121] Thielicke saw natural law philosophy

---

116. Curran, *American Catholic Social Ethics*, 225.
117. Curran, *American Catholic Social Ethics*, 226.
118. Murray, *We Hold These Truths*, 46.
119. Ferguson, *Catholic and American*, 96.
120. Kemeny, *Church, State, and Public Justice*, 114.
121. Thielicke, *Theological Ethics*, 2:67.

The Superiority of an Evangelical Model of Religious Liberty

cut off from the supernatural collapses along two poles. First, natural law stripped of transcendent principles only has practical value. Thus, natural law follows along the same path as the Social Gospel Movement.[122] Second, natural law cut off from faith results in relativism. Commenting on the Declaration for Human Rights, Thielicke said, "These fundamental rights will have shrunk to the power where it no longer endows them with any binding authority; when the door will have been open wide to a rudderless capriciousness of action, which may well take the form of the capriciousness of motive in respect of good and moral action."[123] Daniel Heimbach warns that natural law philosophy deteriorates once society rejects the supernatural.[124] Heimbach affirms that so long as a majority of people believe that moral standards observable in nature depend on some notion of supernatural reality, there is hope of reaching some basic agreement on moral standards justified through appeal to natural law.[125] But once society rejects the idea of transcendent truth, natural law philosophy cannot establish the kind of consensus necessary for religious freedom. Murray used a philosophy that would appeal to both secular and religious minds. But once a large segment of society rejects transcendent realities, there is little hope of establishing a lasting consensus. This point is evidenced in the arguments of conservative political philosophy Andrew Sullivan.

Sullivan addresses natural law arguments using natural law terms. In his book *Conservative Soul*, he uses natural law philosophy to argue for homosexuality and biological evolution.[126] Sullivan argues that natural law philosophy is indeed relational, but it is not necessarily self-evident. He contends that rational people arrive at various conclusions. Sullivan writes, "The basic assertion of natural law philosophers is that their argument is self-evidently true to any reasonable person. But quite obviously, the vast majority of human beings who have ever lived, and even the vast majority of Catholics, seem to have a different idea. Are these people being completely irrational?"[127] Sullivan recognizes that natural law philosophy is not strong enough to create social consensus. Consequently, Murray's appeal to natural law philosophy was weakened because he did not appeal to supernatural authority.

---

122. Thielicke, *Theological Ethics*, 2:68.
123. Thielicke, *Theological Ethics*, 2:68.
124. Heimbach, "Natural Law in the Public Square," 697.
125. Heimbach, "Natural Law in the Public Square," 697.
126. Sullivan, *The Conservative Soul*, 90.
127. Sullivan, *The Conservative Soul*, 90.

Conclusion

In this chapter, I argue that John Courtney Murray's work in religious liberty is commendable. Murray's brilliant analysis of Catholic theology and American democracy is stunning.[128] But his unwillingness to rely on Scripture leaves his argument susceptible to the ever-changing world of human philosophy. Natural law philosophy does have a place in the debate over religious freedom. But natural law philosophy untethered from biblical revelation inevitably becomes nothing more than pragmatism.

Next, I argued that Father Murray's public consensus concept also failed to realize the power of sin. James 4:1 is transcendent truth: "What causes quarrels and what causes fights among you? Is it not this that your passions are at war within you?" John Courtney Murray's optimism for consensus is not consistent with what we see in Scripture or human nature. His argument that kindred relationships provide a consensus model failed to recognize the violent record of family relationships throughout time. Cain and Abel, Jacob and Esau, and Joseph are only a few of the ancient records, but one does not need to look any further than the American family's current state for more. Murray's appeal to natural law is simply not consistent with what human nature has proven to be. Then I argued that Murray's natural law disintegrates as society grows more diverse. Natural law philosophy cut off from transcendent principles contains no epistemological bridge; therefore, it cannot hold together a society of diverse values. In the next chapter, I will argue that the evangelical paradigm for religious liberty is superior to those found in secular rationalism or Roman Catholic natural law.

---

128. Regan, *American Pluralism and the Catholic Conscience*, 10.

CHAPTER 5

The Evangelical Paradigm for Religious Liberty

The evangelical paradigm for religious liberty is anthropologically, cosmologically, and teleologically superior to competing frameworks. John Stuart Mill's utilitarianism is unstable because it lacks a substantive anthropological foundation. Also, Mill's ethic is idealistic because its teleology is overly progressive. John Rawls's theory provides an impressive framework for procedural justice in a pluralistic world. But because Rawls denied metaphysical realities, he could not explain the epistemological presuppositions that supported his theory of justice. Rawls's original position assumes that humans have shared intuitions, but he cannot explain what animates these intuitions. Consequently, Rawls provides no justification to explain what or why humans share certain intuitions, which renders his theory unstable.

Rawls also supported a utopian teleology. Rawlsian thought assumes that humans are progressing toward greater principles of justice. But his conception of time creates an exaggerated expectation of equality, and this results in unrealistic visions of obtainable justice in this age. Therefore, both nineteenth- and twentieth-century utilitarian philosophies do not provide the best paradigm for addressing modern challenges to religious freedom.

John Courtney Murray's natural law framework contains a substantive anthropological foundation. But his teleology and cosmology do not fully account for the reality of human sin. Murray's paradigm lacks a sufficient epistemological link with unbelievers, which leaves his cosmology unstable.

The Evangelical Paradigm for Religious Liberty

Murray's natural law assumes divine transcendence; therefore, he might as well go ahead and cite the Scriptures as the source of metaphysical authority.[1] This is not to say Murray's natural law approach is not helpful for modern conversations regarding religious liberty. Roman Catholic natural law provides an impressive framework for the advancement of religious liberty. But because Murray veiled his scriptural foundations, he undermined his own argument. God's word is powerful enough to shock and awaken even the most hardened human psyche. Therefore, one can use God's word in public debate regardless of one's opponent's willingness to accept or deny its validity.[2]

In contrast, the evangelical framework for religious liberty is superior because its anthropology, cosmology, and teleology provide reasonable philosophical answers while it unapologetically relies upon the power of Scripture. In this chapter I will first define what it means to be evangelical in the classic sense. Second, I will present the essential elements historically present in an evangelical framework for religious freedom. Third, I will argue that the evangelical perspective of the human person is superior to secular anthropology. Because the evangelical perspective rests upon the faculty of human conscience, it has a stable ontological foundation. Fourth, I will examine evangelical cosmology and its explanation of the surrounding world. Evangelical cosmology is accessible to all because God willed that humanity can know the innate orderliness in objective truth; therefore, Christians can use Scripture boldly in the public square. Finally, this chapter will present the evangelical teleology. The evangelical framework for religious freedom argues that the goal of history is submission to Christ (Col 1:15–20). Because Jesus Christ is judge over all creatures, one's ultimate freedom is only found in surrender to Christ. Therefore, the evangelical understanding of time provides a critical foundation for religious liberty.

Evangelicalism Rediscovered

The word "evangelical" seems to be in trouble in recent years.[3] Since Donald Trump's election to the White House, the term appears to be identified more as a voting constituency than a theological movement. Historian Mark Noll notes that American pollsters and pundits have fixated on the overwhelming support Donald Trump received from "white Evangelicals"

---

1. Thornbury, *Recovering Classic Evangelicalism*, 190.
2. Thornbury, *Recovering Classic Evangelicalism*, 68.
3. Noll et al., *Evangelicals*, 16.

The Superiority of an Evangelical Model of Religious Liberty

in his 2016 presidential election.[4] Although Evangelicals include more than just white people, the American media and the political class seem to understand Evangelicalism exclusively as a voting bloc. Subsequently, the media's misunderstanding of Evangelicalism further confuses the term in the minds of many.

Additionally, the word "evangelical" does not define one denomination or church, so the term is often confusing. George Marsden notes that "Evangelicalism" does not simply refer to a broad grouping of Christians who happen to believe some of the same doctrines. "Evangelicalism" can also mean a self-conscious interdenominational movement, with leaders, publications, and institutions whereby many subgroups exist.[5] Additionally, scholar Gregory Thornbury argues that Evangelicals are people who are constantly reimagining and critiquing themselves.[6] Thornbury contends that continuous self-criticism also adds to the confusion of defining modern Evangelicalism. Therefore, any argument contending for the superiority of Evangelicalism must provide a clear definition.

Simply stated, "Evangelicalism" is a belief that the Bible is a supernatural revelation from God and its central message is the saving work of God through Jesus Christ. "Evangelical" comes from the Greek word for "gospel"; therefore, it presupposes the declaration of good news.[7] In 1944, Max Warren, the general secretary of the Church Missionary Society, argued that Evangelicalism prioritizes evangelism over everything else, including worship.[8] But John Stott argued for a broader definition. Stott contended that Evangelicalism stands on two convictions: First, Evangelicals are Bible people. Second, Evangelicals possess a gospel to proclaim. The cross, conversion, and effort for its spread are all under its comprehensive heading.[9] Thus, Evangelicalism includes more than evangelism alone. Marsden offers a more thorough description based on five critical beliefs, including (1) the Reformation doctrine of the final authority of the Bible, (2) the real historical character of God's saving work recorded in Scripture, (3) salvation to eternal life based on the redemptive work of Christ, (4) the importance

---

4. Noll et al., *Evangelicals*, 17.
5. Marsden, *Understanding Fundamentalism and Evangelicalism*, 5.
6. Thornbury, *Recovering Classic Evangelicalism*, 17.
7. Marsden, *Understanding Fundamentalism and Evangelicalism*, 4.
8. Noll et al. *Evangelicals*, 93.
9. Noll et al., *Evangelicals*, 94.

The Evangelical Paradigm for Religious Liberty

of evangelism and missions, and (5) the importance of a spiritually transformed life.[10] Thus, what seems essential to the definition of "Evangelical" is the core belief that the Bible is the authoritative word of God, and from it all other beliefs proceed. Therefore, Evangelicalism necessarily demands that one affirms the authority of Scripture as its final source for all truth.

If religious freedom is to survive and flourish, it must draw upon the most stable ethical foundations available. Because evangelical ethics rely on special revelation as their source, evangelical ethics can account for seen and unseen realities. Thus, evangelical ethics are more stable than other ethical frameworks. As previously argued, secular ethics are incomplete because they are founded exclusively on internal powers such as intuition or reason. Secular ethics are devoid of transcendence, so they cannot offer complete answers regarding the visible world, nor can they fully explain the internal complexities of humans. And secular ethics cannot establish absolute universal truths. Natural law ethics are far better than secular paradigms. Subsequently, natural law ethics, apart from divine revelation, are limited because they do not directly call individuals into account before a personal divine creator.

However, evangelical ethics offer humans the fullest access to moral truth. Evangelical ethics exist on propositional truth claims derived from Scripture. Scripture reveals the propositional truths that shape the world (John 1:1–3); therefore, they make rational sense of the world (Heb 11:3). Simply stated, Scripture forms the world and informs how one knows the world. Consequently, individuals have the fullest access to reality through Scripture.

Moreover, secular ethics and natural law ethics only provide partial truth to individuals, limiting their ability to make fully informed decisions. John Calvin made the point that only through divine revelation derived from Scripture does the human mind have access to knowledge of God, oneself, and the surrounding world.[11] Scriptural revelation is the only source that provides rationally consistent propositions concerning both material and immaterial realities. Thus, individuals can make decisions with the fullest information possible. Therefore, the Evangelical's commitment to supernatural revelation allows individuals to exercise the fullest power of human agency.

---

10. Marsden, *Understanding Fundamentalism and Evangelicalism*, 4.
11. Calvin, *Institutes of the Christian Religion*, 15.

The Superiority of an Evangelical Model of Religious Liberty

Ethicist Carl F. H. Henry made a similar point in his Rutherford House lectures. Henry contended that only the power of Scripture could provide humans full access to their agency because they have the fullest access to truth.[12] He argued that modern ethical frameworks are based almost exclusively on existential or consequential theory.[13] But existential and consequentialist approaches ignore the individual's capacity for discerning objective patterns of nature, leaving individuals with only partial knowledge. Subsequently, humans left to make decisions based on partial knowledge ultimately view human agency as mechanical determinism or anarchical chaos.[14]

In contrast, Scripture reveals God's mind to humans. Scripture reveals the possibilities of both the material and immaterial world, and this conception provides the most extensive set of data for decision making. Individuals that work from an evangelical ethical framework have access to transcendent propositions, including those relating to unseen realities. And because individuals can objectively test Scripture's revelatory propositions against the surrounding world, they engage the power of reason more fully. Therefore, because evangelical social ethics rest on divine revelation, they provide complete information concerning oneself, the surrounding world, and time.

Evangelical Structure for Religious Freedom

The comprehensive nature of evangelical ethics provides the best structure to ground religious liberty. The evangelical metanarrative of creation, fall, redemption, and restoration secures religious freedom within a framework that is consistent with objective reality and provides an overarching purpose of truth. Ethicist Andrew Walker notes that unless religious liberty is understood from the storyline of Scripture, it will devolve under the pressure of unstable political philosophies.[15] Political philosophy apart from Scripture only recognizes partial truths. Individuals working with partial truths ultimately deify certain ideologies and demonize others, and both extremes pose a threat to religious freedom.[16] But the evangelical metanarrative

12. Henry, *Toward a Recovery of Christian Belief*, 22.
13. Henry, *Toward a Recovery of Christian Belief*, 22.
14. Henry, *Toward a Recovery of Christian Belief*, 23.
15. Walker and George, *Liberty for All*, 49.
16. Henry, *God, Revelation and Authority*, 6:192.

provides solid ontological, epistemological, and teleological foundations from within its doctrines of anthropology, cosmology, and eschatology. Evangelical anthropology offers a theory of the human self that realizes humanity's rational and spiritual self. Evangelical cosmology explains the proper ordering of creation including the unseen realities that support visible realities. Evangelical cosmology provides individuals a structural order that allows them to make sense of themselves and the surrounding world. Evangelical eschatology also provides an overarching teleological purpose, which directs how one understands the course of time. Therefore, the doctrines found within the evangelical metanarrative offer a stable framework for religious liberty.

Evangelical Historical Framework

While the Bible does not explicitly command religious freedom, the principles of religious freedom are found throughout.[17] Evangelical scholars, pastors, and activists have a long history of applying Christian anthropology, cosmology, and teleology to establish religious freedom.

Tertullian

Tertullian was the first in the history of Western civilization to use the phrase "freedom of religion."[18] Tertullian's *Apology* was one of the most substantive works to argue for religious freedom. In his appeal to the Roman government, he argued that religion posed no threat to civil governments. Tertullian said,

> Let one man worship God, another Jupiter; let one lift suppliant hands to the heavens, another to the altar of Fides; let one—if you choose to take this view of it—count in prayer the clouds, and another the ceiling panels; let one consecrate his own life to his God, and another that of a goat. For see that you do not give a further ground for the charge of irreligion, by taking away religious liberty, and forbidding free choice of deity, so that I may no longer worship according to my inclination, but am compelled to

---

17. Duesing et al., *First Freedom*, 15.
18. Wilken, *Liberty in the Things of God*, 11.

worship against it. Not even a human being would care to have unwilling homage rendered him.[19]

Tertullian's argument for religious liberty was founded on the evangelical belief that humans are moral agents that act according to their beliefs.[20] Tertullian recognized that humans are not only rational creatures but creatures of will. The human will is a self-governing domain; therefore, it must be respected.[21] Tertullian founded his argument for religious freedom on the nature of a belief itself. He argued that the nature of belief requires an exercise of the will for it to be genuinely a belief. Robert Louis Wilken notes that Tertullian's argument centered on the nature of religious belief and its relationship to the human will, whereas the Roman point of focus was religious practice.[22] Simply stated, one may coerce a religious practice, but one must freely choose a religious belief if it is to be a belief at all. Therefore, Tertullian understood that human agency is what gives a belief its ontology.

Additionally, Tertullian argued that the doctrine of sanctification informed how Christians understood themselves in the world.[23] In part one of his *The Apology*, Tertullian contended that Christianity's ethical separation for the culture allowed Christians to contribute to the commonwealth fully. He said,

> I shall at once go on, then, to exhibit the peculiarities of the Christian society, that, as I have refuted the evil charged against it, I may point out its positive good. We are a body knit together as such by a common religious profession, by unity of discipline, and by the bond of a common hope. We meet together as an assembly and congregation, that, offering up prayer to God as with united force, we may wrestle with Him in our supplications. This violence God delights in. We pray, too, for the emperors, for their ministers and for all in authority, for the welfare of the world, for the prevalence of peace, for the delay of the final consummation.[24]

---

19. Tertullian, *The Apology*, 3:339.

20. While Tertullian does not explicitly cite Scripture in this section of *The Apology*, earlier in chapter XV he established his doctrine of human agency from the *imago Dei*. In chapter XV regarding Idolatry, Tertullian cites Gen 1:26–27; 9:6; 1 Cor 11:7; therefore, Tertullian's argument was fixed in the divine revelation through Scripture.

21. Wilken, *Liberty in the Things of God*, 11.

22. Wilken, *Liberty in the Things of God*, 12.

23. Tertullian, *The Apology*, 3:336.

24. Tertullian, *The Apology*, 3:336.

The Evangelical Paradigm for Religious Liberty

Tertullian contended that Christians were distinct in their conduct and, in this regard, separate from the commonwealth. The early Christians understood their new life against the backdrop of a hostile society; Christians are in the world but not of the world (John 15:9). But ethical separation did not mean they were a seditious faction seeking to overthrow civil authority, as was often claimed. Instead, Christians were a body within the commonwealth that sought good for the emperor and his servants. Tertullian contended that Christian beliefs made individuals more conscientious citizens as they fervently prayed for the emperor's good. Therefore, Christians belong to a community that is distinct from society ethically but part of society functionally.

Tertullian also argued that the presence of Christians in the world helps to preserve society. Tertullian contended that sin harmed the entire community and brought about God's judgment. But the Christian message of repentance served to warn of coming judgment. The gospel message offered society a chance to turn from the sin that caused present judgment and future judgment. Tertullian wrote,

> The truth is, the human race has always deserved ill at God's hand. First of all, as undutiful to Him, because when it knew Him in part, it not only did not seek after Him, but even invented other gods of its own to worship; and further, because, as the result of their willing ignorance of the Teacher of righteousness, the Judge and Avenger of sin, all vices and crimes grew and flourished. But had men sought, they would have come to know the glorious object of their seeking; and knowledge would have produced obedience, and obedience would have found a gracious instead of an angry God. They ought then to see that the very same God is angry with them now as in ancient times, before Christians were so much as spoken of. It was *His* blessings they enjoyed—created before they made any of their deities: and why can they not take it in, that their evils come from the Being whose goodness they have failed to recognize? They suffer at the hands of Him to whom they have been ungrateful. And, for all that is said, if we compare the calamities of former times, they fall on us more lightly now, since God gave Christians to the world; for from that time virtue put some restraint on the world's wickedness, and men began to pray for the averting of God's wrath.[25]

---

25. Tertullian, *The Apology*, 3:348.

The Superiority of an Evangelical Model of Religious Liberty

Tertullian argued that Christians should be free to worship because their faithfulness affected the present common good. And Christian witness not only altered the world's current condition but also warned of future judgment. His argument for religious freedom recognizes that God engages his creation in and throughout time. Tertullian believed that Christianity's message of coming judgment was a gift because it gave structure and meaning to time.[26] Therefore, a careful reading of the ancient apologist reveals that his argument for religious liberty emerged from the evangelical doctrines of anthropology, cosmology, and eschatology.

John Calvin

John Calvin is not often considered a religious liberty advocate. But in his seminal work *The Institutes of Christian Religion*, he argued that no man could be forced to faith.[27] In Calvin's reflections concerning excommunication from the church, he stated that neither Turks, Saracens, nor any other "enemy of religion" ought to be coerced to faith.[28] Calvin understood that faith is only genuine when it is freely chosen. Although his opponents often misrepresented his theology, Calvin maintained that the powers of human agency were essential for salvation.[29] He argued that the image of God in humans included both the powers of intellect and the powers of will. Calvin said,

> Let us, therefore, hold, for the purpose of the present work, that the soul consists of two parts, the intellect and the will, the office of the intellect being to distinguish between objects, according as they seem deserving of being approved or disapproved; and the office of the will, to choose and follow what the intellect declares to be good, to reject and shun what it declares to be bad.[30]

Calvin argued that only the supernatural power of God's word could free the mind and the will to desire God (John 6:63); therefore, any attempt to coerce faith is pointless. But this is not to say that Calvin was always consistent with his own theology; Calvin, at times, employed the power of the

---

26. Tertullian, *The Apology*, 3:348.
27. Calvin, *Institutes of the Christian Religion 1536 Edition*, 62.
28. Calvin, *Institutes of the Christian Religion 1536 Edition*, 62.
29. Calvin, *Institutes of the Christian Religion 1536 Edition*, 3.
30. Calvin, *Institutes of the Christian Religion*, 227.

The Evangelical Paradigm for Religious Liberty

Genevan authorities to punish heretics. But his theology of human agency did provide principles essential for religious freedom. Consequently, Calvin understood that it must be unfettered from external constraints for a belief to be genuine.

Additionally, Calvin argued that humans understood themselves in relation to the surrounding world.[31] He said,

> Still, none who have the use of their eyes can be ignorant of the divine skill manifested so conspicuously in the endless variety, yet distinct and well-ordered array, of the heavenly host; and, therefore, it is plain that the Lord has furnished every man with abundant proofs of his wisdom. The same is true in regard to the structure of the human frame. To determine the connection of its parts, its symmetry and beauty, with the skill of a Galen, requires singular acuteness; and yet all men acknowledge that the human body bears on its face such proofs of ingenious contrivance as are sufficient to proclaim the admirable wisdom of its Maker.[32]

He formulated his theory of social structure based on the well-ordered design of the human body. The human body not only testifies of God's wisdom but also provides a form for church-state relationships. Calvin postulated the distinction between spiritual and political government, which paralleled the difference between soul and body.[33] Therefore, Calvin's structure of church-state relationship emerged from his theology of the human self and its relationship to the surrounding world.

Calvin's belief in liberty of conscience emerged from his evangelical theology regarding the human self, the objective order of creation, and the purpose of time. While Calvin's *Institutes* may seem relatively scant concerning the eschaton, the theme of kingdom is ubiquitous throughout his work. J. H. van Wyk argues that Calvin's kingdom theology not only animates the present age but stimulates and directs human activity toward the age to come.[34] For Calvin, the purpose of time in this age was to gather God's elect and sanctify them through the preaching of his word. Calvin's commentary on Matt 28:19 contends that the track of history is to bring all nations to the obedience of the faith.[35] But this obedience would not be

---

31. Calvin, *Institutes of the Christian Religion*, 62.
32. Calvin, *Institutes of the Christian Religion*, 67.
33. Calvin, *Institutes of the Christian Religion 1536 Edition*, iv.
34. Van Wyk, "John Calvin on the Kingdom of God and Eschatology," 191.
35. Calvin, *Commentary on a Harmony of the Evangelists*, 3:383.

coerced; it is the work of the Spirit that confirmed the power of the gospel. Calvin understood the purpose of time was to establish God's kingdom in the heart of humans, and the kingdom's final consummation would result in the rewarding or condemning of the just and unjust.[36] Therefore, the purpose of history was the consummation of God's rule over the hearts of humanity on earth.

Roger Williams

Baptist theologian Roger Williams built upon John Calvin's anthropology, cosmology, and eschatology to advocate for religious freedom. Williams contended that the incarnation of Christ radically changed how the individual related to God.[37] He argued that before the incarnation, the individual communed with God through the covenant made with Israel. The Old Testament covenant was a national covenant. Individuals participated constructively in the kingdom of God through the institutions of religion and public law.[38] But after the incarnation, humans related to God individually through the faculty of the conscience. James Calvin Davis notes, "For Williams, the incarnation was the starting point for both Christian theology and Christian morality because, in the person of Christ, God had initiated a relationship with God's chosen people that was starkly dissimilar to the divine relationship with Israel prior to Christ's birth."[39] Williams's theology altered the way individual persons related to God and understood their moral obligation in the world. The incarnation meant that God not only expected a personal response to Christ, but God also empowered the individual to act in accord with an upright and moral life.[40] Williams's incarnation theology changed anthropology in two ways: First, it changed the inner self, so the individual could now respond to the inner call of Christ. Second, it provided a moral pattern through the life of Christ. In the earthly life of Christ, individuals now have a design for upright living. Williams believed that each person was responsible for responding to Christ in an initial act of faith and then living according to the dictates of conscience informed by Scripture. For Williams, the incarnation necessarily implied

36. Calvin, *Institutes of the Christian Religion*, 208.
37. Williams, *On Religious Liberty*, 246.
38. Williams and Miller, *The Complete Writings of Roger Williams*, 7:279.
39. Davis, *The Moral Theology of Roger Williams*, 23.
40. Davis, *The Moral Theology of Roger Williams*, 25.

The Evangelical Paradigm for Religious Liberty

religious freedom for individuals. Therefore, Williams's foundation for religious liberty emerged from Christ's work in the incarnation.

Moreover, Williams believed that the incarnation changed how individuals related to the world. Before the incarnation, God related to human beings through the political entity of Israel. But after the incarnation, God connected to people based on one's individual faith. In his work *The Bloody Tenent of Persecution*, Williams argued that genuine Christians are only those who fear God in their conscience; therefore, the church consists of believers only.[41] Williams posited that Christ's incarnation established a dichotomy between the church and the world. The church was to be viewed separately from the world. But the church is called to engage the world using the spiritual means of persuasion and discipline.[42] Williams's incarnational theology set a structure for how the church engages the surrounding world. Consequently, for Williams, the incarnation established a radical opposition between worldly values and Christian values, but it also created an essential relational bridge between opposing belief structures.

Furthermore, Williams's zeal for religious freedom emerged from his theology of time. Williams's theology of incarnation resulted in a unique reformulation of eschatology.[43] Puritan eschatology was largely premillennial; it interpreted history largely through the lens of Christ's return.[44] Thus, Puritan theology taught that the church and the state were both given the task to work symbiotically to sow seeds for Christ's return. Because church and the state worked together, Puritan theology affirmed civil coercion as a viable instrument for spiritual reform. Therefore, the Puritans viewed time instrumentally because they believed the purpose of time was to prepare the earth for the coming kingdom.

However, Roger Williams understood the millennial reign of Christ differently. Williams agreed with his Puritan peers that the telos of history was Christ's return. But he viewed Christ's return as the restoration of the true church on the earth. Williams argued the true church was lost in the Middle Ages and no longer followed in the line of apostolic succession.[45] Williams contended that upon Christ's return, the church would recover its spiritual ministry and ultimately be perfected as the elect spiritual

---

41. Williams, *On Religious Liberty*, 124.
42. Davis, *The Moral Theology of Roger Williams*, 27.
43. Davis, *The Moral Theology of Roger Williams*, 42.
44. Davis, *The Moral Theology of Roger Williams*, 42.
45. Williams, *On Religious Liberty*, 209–10.

The Superiority of an Evangelical Model of Religious Liberty

community of God.⁴⁶ Thus, until Christ's return, the best that Christians can hope for is a "scattered witness" that provides a prophetic warning against the world's corruption.⁴⁷ Williams understood the purpose of time as a preparatory state directed toward Christ's return through the prophetic preaching of his word. For Williams, religious freedom was essential so that individual believers could fulfill their mission by preaching judgment and reconciliation. Consequently, Williams's paradigm of religious liberty emerged from the evangelical proposition that time is a temporary state in which Christians prepare for Christ's imminent eschatological reign.

Eighteenth-Century Baptists

Baptist preachers were among the most ardent religious liberty advocates in eighteenth-century America. Isaac Backus and John Leland both formed their argument for religious freedom from the evangelical categories of self, world, and time. Like Roger Williams, John Leland saw the incarnation as essential to religious freedom.⁴⁸ Leland argued God foreknew that Christ would assume a human nature at the dawn of creation.⁴⁹ Thus, Christ's willingness to take a human nature carried two implications: First, the incarnation endows all humans with dignity. Leland reasoned that because Christ was willing to become human, all humans reflect his glory. Leland believed that human dignity did not emerge merely from humanity's power of reason. Human dignity resulted from Christ's willingness to become human. So, the incarnation fixed human dignity in transcendence, and this makes dignity irrevocable. Second, because Christ willingly assumed human nature, all humans are endowed with the power of agency. Christ was not coerced into the incarnation; he freely chose to come in a human form. Thus, creatures bearing his image also possess the powers of agency. Therefore, to impede upon one's religious freedom is to strike against the image of Christ himself.

Isaac Backus contended that religious freedom was the natural implication of living as social creatures. He argued that humans were made to fit within a rational system.⁵⁰ And he believed that as creatures imprinted

---

46. Davis, *The Moral Theology of Roger Williams*, 44.
47. Davis, *The Moral Theology of Roger Williams*, 44.
48. Leland, *The Writings of the Late Elder John Leland*, 144.
49. Leland, *The Writings of the Late Elder John Leland*, 144.
50. Backus, *A History of New England*, 6.

The Evangelical Paradigm for Religious Liberty

with God's love, all humans were obligated to love God and neighbor. Thus, Backus argued, "Each rational soul, as he is part of the whole system of rational beings, so it was and is, both his duty and his liberty to regard the good of the whole in all his actions."[51] For Backus, freedom aimed to obey God and to love one's neighbor. Therefore, religious freedom was a necessary component for humans to realize their place in the social ecology.

Moreover, Backus realized that sin disrupted the social order. He contended that humans were often inclined to use their liberty in ways that harmed one's neighbor.[52] Thus, God provided governments to restrain sin. But because government was also infected with sin, it could not correctly order liberty apart from divine wisdom. Backus believed God's wisdom was essential for creating just laws and protecting everyone's right to experience the "high pleasure" of loving God.[53] Therefore, religious freedom was necessary to ensure a government maintains its responsibility to order freedom. Subsequently, Backus's framework for religious liberty emerged from his evangelical convictions regarding sin and its effect on social order.

Isaac Backus's concept of time also helped shape his argument for religious liberty. Backus contended that humans are constrained by time; therefore, humans cannot fully know the future.[54] But because God is eternal and infinite, only he holds full knowledge of the past and the future. Thus, God's infinite understanding of time demanded that humans fear him above all else. Backus said,

> God's being is eternal, he knows all things, future as well as past, and inspires those that love them to undertake what is most expedient for them; which is a favor and protection they owe to no man, and grant only to those that invoke and consult them. And we are told by the same author, of another wise heathen, who said, "Tis observable, that those that fear the Deity most, are least afraid of man."[55]

Backus maintained that a society that feared God was a courageous society. He reasoned that one would have the fortitude to face an uncertain future when one fears the all-knowing God. Therefore, a society free to worship according to conscience was a society secure amid any threat.

51. Backus, *A History of New England*, 7.
52. Backus, *A History of New England*, 11.
53. Backus, *A History of New England*, 11.
54. Backus, *A History of New England*, 67.
55. Backus, *A History of New England*, 67.

The Superiority of an Evangelical Model of Religious Liberty

Twentieth Century to Present

In the twentieth century, evangelical theologians and pastors continued to promote religious liberty from theological foundations. Carl F. H. Henry contended that the doctrine of *imago Dei* afforded all people the ability to apprehend transcendent truths.[56] Contra Karl Barth, Henry claimed that sin did not annihilate the image of God in humans.[57] Like the Reformers before him, Henry maintained that all humans retain the ability to discern certain axiomatic principles through general revelation. But because of sin, unbelievers explain these principles according to their rebellious desires (Rom 1:18). Henry contended that believers and unbelievers could not agree on theological truths. But the *imago Dei* in all humans allows for "common ground" regarding functional cooperation.[58] Henry said, "There is indeed a sound basis for interreligious dialogue and, within carefully defined limits, for cooperation also, e.g., the pursuit of religious freedom or protest against dictatorial rulers; neither pursuit provides any ground, however, for softening the biblical claim to special divine disclosure."[59] Henry did not believe it was wise to champion interfaith cooperation regarding theological issues. But he thought cooperation was possible on problems common to all *imago Dei*-bearing people. Consequently, Henry believed that religious freedom was an axiom accessible to all people by nature of the *imago Dei*.

Baptist scholar James E. Wood Jr. argued that the *imago Dei* also provided the theological foundation and structure for human rights.[60] Wood believed that "God-given personhood" was the foundation of religious liberty.[61] He posited that image-bearing inherently implies certain rights, and these rights define the relationship between the individual and the state. Thus, religious freedom serves to regulate the domain and degree of state power. Wood said, "The limited state is not only a derivative of the sacredness of man's rights but also the sovereignty of God, which together constitute an irremovable limit of the State which it cannot with impunity

---

56. Henry, *God, Revelation and Authority*, 1:398.
57. Henry, *God, Revelation and Authority*, 1:397.
58. Henry, *God, Revelation and Authority*, 1:401.
59. Henry, *God, Revelation and Authority*, 1:406.
60. Wood, "Theological and Historical Foundations of Religious Liberty," 243.
61. Wood, "Theological and Historical Foundations of Religious Liberty," 246.

The Evangelical Paradigm for Religious Liberty

transgress."[62] Wood used Acts 4:19 and 5:29 to establish the boundaries of state power—Peter and John affirmed they must obey God rather than men. Thus, the state is excluded from ruling over religious affairs because God's sovereignty excludes an absolute human power.[63] Wood saw that evangelical anthropology necessarily informed evangelical cosmology. Therefore, his framework for religious freedom provided axiomatic principles to understand oneself and one's relationship to the state.

Andrew Walker considers religious liberty within the missiological vision of evangelical theology.[64] Walker's 2018 doctoral dissertation synthesizes a Christological framework for religious freedom using the motifs of the kingdom of God, the image of God, and the mission of God.[65] Because the mission of God recognizes God's future judgment, the mission of God possesses a uniquely eschatological texture. Walker notes,

> Eschatology is central to an understanding of religious liberty because it provides a promise of future judgment without confusing the role of the church with the role of the state. Also, because it brings creation to its final state under the kingship of Christ. This is where ultimate freedom thrives. Because the kingdom of God is given witness through the church, the church can never be coterminous with the operations of the state or nation.[66]

Walker correctly recognizes that religious liberty is a limited right, one that will eventually disappear at Christ's final judgment. But until that time, religious liberty serves as an essential component for spreading the gospel message. Walker's framework for religious liberty uses the themes of the kingdom of God, the image of God, and the mission of God. But these motifs also include vital propositions that give shape to understanding oneself, one's relationship to the world, and one's connection to time. Therefore, as one considers the categories of biblical anthropology, cosmology, and eschatology across the horizon of history, it is clear that evangelical theology gives shape to religious freedom.

---

62. Wood, "Theological and Historical Foundations of Religious Liberty," 251.
63. Wood, "Theological and Historical Foundations of Religious Liberty," 251.
64. Walker and George, *Liberty for All*, 15.
65. Walker, "Religious Liberty in Contemporary Evangelical Social Ethics, 33.
66. Walker and George, *Liberty for All*, 26.

The Superiority of Evangelical Anthropology

The human conscience plays a foundational role in both secular and evangelical frameworks for religious liberty. Rex Ahdar and Ian Leigh contend in their book *Religious Freedom in the Liberal State* that one's attitude regarding the conscience indubitably shapes modern notions of religious freedom.[67] Both John Stuart Mill and John Rawls saw that the human conscience was essential for religious freedom.[68] But because Mill and Rawls rejected the supernatural world, both their theories of conscience are inconsistent. Secular philosophies that reject a personal transcendent being have no stable ground for establishing the origin and purpose of the individual conscience. Therefore, secular theories can only rely on naturalism for answers.

Secular theories posit that the human conscience is a mixture of socially constructed impressions emerging from sources outside oneself. But because the secular concept of conscience rejects a personal transcendent being, it is unbalanced. First, secular theories are inconsistent because they reduce humans to merely a series of naturalistic causes. Second, secular ideas cannot maintain an equilibrium between the individual self and the surrounding world. Individuals in secular philosophy have no basis for uniqueness, which erodes any argument from hierarchy among other creatures. Third, secular theory ultimately sees the individual as a product of an evolutionary cycle, and this means the aim of time is merely self-preservation.[69] Fourth, individuals cut off from divine transcendence have no objective basis for establishing universal absolute moral values; thus, morals are determined according to naturalistic benefits. Thus, the content of moral values is determined only by their contribution toward self-preservation. Morals become only a word for a sociological framework.[70] Therefore, apart from divine transcendence, the human conscience is reduced to a reflexive instinct aimed toward evolutionary survival.

Nevertheless, if the human conscience is merely a faculty of natural reflex, then free choice is an illusion—one's decisions are merely predetermined instincts aimed toward survival. Francis Schaeffer argued that if humanity is reduced to simply naturalistic causes, then morals have no

---

67. Ahdar and Leigh, *Religious Freedom in the Liberal State*, 38.
68. Rawls, *A Theory of Justice*, 180.
69. Henry, *Christian Personal Ethics*, 510.
70. Schaeffer et al., *The Francis A. Schaeffer Trilogy*, 231.

boundaries, and human choice is merely instinct.[71] Thus, one has nothing to regulate between what one *can* do from what one *ought* to do.[72] Schaeffer persuasively argued that values are up for grabs, and humans have no limits other than what is limited by human circumstances. Therefore, the secular conscience offers only chimeras, not genuine free choice.

Moreover, secular theory rejects the view of conscience as a communicative link between creation and creator. Instead, the secular mind treats the conscience as an evolving apparatus that emerges from one's survival instincts. But because the secular conscience is constantly evolving, it contains no coherent ontological principles. One's conscience is worthy of protection only so far as it contributes to the overall progress of human advancement. Thus, secular theories cannot provide a consistent reason to protect a conservative conscience.[73] One's religious conscience can be tolerated only so far as it maintains the survival of the species. But if a conscience is judged harmful, there is no substantive reason for protecting it. Consequently, the secular concept of conscience offers no logical reason for preserving a conscience that does not advance so-called "human advancement."

Furthermore, if the human conscience is only a product of chemical phenomena and social imprinting, then there is no distinctive difference between humans and other creatures of the natural world. Apart from divine revelation, the conscience is degraded into simply a feeling of pleasure or pain, a volition impulse, or a mere faculty of subjective judgment.[74] But Carl. F. H. Henry rightly noted that the evangelical conscience provides a distinctive break between humanity and otherworldly creatures.[75] Henry argued that the conscience is the faculty that provides humans with direct knowledge of God, oneself, and one's standing against the surrounding world. He contended that the doctrine of creation supplied a safeguard against ontological monism and made possible the distinction between thought and things.[76] But secular theories of conscience cannot provide this needed break. If the human conscience is merely the result of

---

71. Schaeffer, *Back to Freedom and Dignity*, 26.

72. Schaeffer, *Back to Freedom and Dignity*, 26.

73. "Conservative" in this sense is not used in reference to political affiliations or theological movements. "Conservative" is used in the sense of holding to principles of the past or principles deemed contrary to human progress.

74. Henry, *Christian Personal Ethics*, 509.

75. Henry, *God, Revelation and Authority*, 1:303.

76. Henry, *God, Revelation and Authority*, 1:304.

naturalistic evolution, there is no distinct separation from the surrounding world. When the conscience is reduced to a cultural imprint, then it cannot separate itself from the natural environment in which it was created; thus, no substantive reason for human dignity exists.[77] Religious choices are no different from choices made within the animal kingdom. Secular ethicist Peter Singer makes this point when he says, "The ethical principle on which human equality rests requires us to extend equal consideration to animals too."[78] Singer's statement confirms Francis Schaeffer's assertion that modern man cannot hold on to the dignity of humans once they lose the doctrine of *imago Dei*.[79] Thus, secular theories of conscience logically collapse into a pantheistic abyss. Therefore, secular ideas of conscience provide no justifiable boundary for the protection of human rights.

Moreover, culturally conditioned theories of conscience cannot sustain liberal democracy. Liberal democracy requires self-restraint, and self-restraint necessarily assumes absolute universal values exist. But cut off from divine transcendence, absolute morals disintegrate, and the individual conscience becomes an idolatrous law unto itself.[80] Carl F. H. Henry noted, "A generation that elevates the essentiality of human rights to intellectual priority yet simultaneously contends that all philosophical affirmations are culture-conditioned sooner or later will engulf those very rights in moral relativism."[81] A theory of conscience that holds no accountability beyond culture itself will ultimately implode. Consequently, the human conscience untethered from divine transcendence proves unstable and lacks the necessary objective boundaries to justify free choice, human dignity, and a stable society.

Moreover, secular theories of conscience contain a second fault line. Secular views cannot explain why individuals would break from the collective. Mill and Rawls correctly recognized the social influence upon one's moral vision. Humans are relational creatures, and one's relationships certainly influence one's values. But if the conscience is merely a socially constructed phenomenon, how does one explain objections to social norms? For instance, secular theories can have no explanation for the tremendous reformers of history. If the human conscience is merely the

---

77. Henry, *God, Revelation and Authority*, 1:303–4.
78. Singer, *Animal Liberation*, 3.
79. Schaeffer et al., *The Francis A. Schaeffer Trilogy*, 220.
80. Pierce, *Conscience in the New Testament*, 121.
81. Henry, *Has Democracy Had Its Day?*, 9.

The Evangelical Paradigm for Religious Liberty

result of collective will, how does one explain individual deviations from social norms? Ethicist Wayne Grudem rightly recognizes that the power of collective thought often coarsens and hardens the conscience.[82] Thus, secular theories of conscience provide no substantive reason for individuals to speak out against collective injustice. Secular views leave one unable to explain the abolition of slavery and the advancement of women's rights—both movements opposed collective conscience in their day. Both Mill and Rawls argued for the rights of conscience, but apart from divine transcendence there is no coherent ontological principle to support the protection of individual conscience.

The Roman Catholic concept of conscience is more stable than secular theories. Roman Catholic moral theology recognizes the conscience as a faculty that empowers free will and reason in all humans.[83] Irenaeus was among the first to argue that the conscience was fundamental to the doctrine of *imago Dei*.[84] He contended that the conscience was an essential component of image-bearing; therefore, the conscience has a fixed ontology within all humans. And while Roman Catholic theologians properly recognize that the fall wounded the conscience, they argue that a high degree of functionality remains. Roman Catholic theology maintains that the conscience, in its post-fallen state, possesses the power to direct humans toward God's eternal law.[85] But as Roman Catholic moral theology evolved, it imported concepts alien to Scripture. The apostle Paul indicated in Romans 2 that the conscience served only as a faculty of judgment after actions, and this implies that the conscience does not serve as a directional guide *a priori*. Martin Luther said the following in a lecture on Romans:

> What the conscience is which bears witness, *their thoughts* by which they interpret themselves to themselves, what sort of people they are, *accuse*, in the things they have done wrong, *or also defend them*, in the things they have done well. *On the day*, against the day, that is, these things all are done now and take place now so that they may be judged then according to them, *when God will judge the secrets of men*, the sins which are not known to men, that is, even their innermost thoughts, *according to my Gospel*, that is,

---

82. Grudem, *Systematic Theology*, 660.
83. Liederbach, "The Religious and Moral Conscience," 32.
84. Irenaeus of Lyons, *Irenaeus against Heresies*, 1518.
85. Aquinas, *A Summa of the Summa*, 297.

that which is preached by me, *by Jesus Christ*. For He will be the judge because of His likeness of men, that He may be seen by all.[86]

Similarly, Carl F. H. Henry recognized the conscience functioning subsequent to moral acts. Henry said, "Conscience is identified as an adverse moral judgment passed upon acts begun in the past and completed or in process. Its operation is subsequent; its cause, the specific antecedent act or acts; its verdict, normally condemnatory."[87] Thus, while the Roman Catholic concept of conscience does provide a universal and stable ontology, it is overly optimistic regarding humanity's ability to perform God's will. Subsequently, the Roman Catholic theory of conscience does provide a substantive foundation for human dignity. Still, Roman Catholic political views fail to appreciate the effects of sin fully, and they over-realize humanity's capacity for moral discernment.

Evangelical theory of conscience maintains a robust ontology in its doctrine of the *imago Dei*. But unlike Roman Catholic and secular theories, the evangelical concept fully recognizes the effect of sin on the entire person. Evangelical theory understands the conscience as a power of the flesh. Thus, the conscience and all the powers of the flesh are severely wounded from the fall.[88] The wounded conscience can both ignore true teaching and be bound by false teaching; therefore, the conscience is not an infallible guide for moral decision-making.[89] Oliver O'Donovan persuasively argues that the conscience's ability to reason and its power to will have been torn apart by the absurdity of sin.[90] O'Donovan recognizes that the doctrine of sin effectively explains why individuals often commit moral acts that are illogical and contrary to reason. Carl F. H. Henry contended only the doctrine of the fall could adequately explain the diversity of moral claims among individuals.[91] Henry argued,

> A major problem faced by every high view of conscience is the diverse claims which conscience seems to impose upon men in different cultures. Apart from the Christian conception of the fall, as well as of the unique moral dignity of man, the intuitional view has no adequate and satisfactory explanation of this difficulty.

86. Luther, *Luther's Works*, 25:20.
87. Henry, *Christian Personal Ethics*, 515.
88. Zachman, *The Assurance of Faith*, 21.
89. Zachman, *The Assurance of Faith*, 28.
90. O'Donovan, *Resurrection and Moral Order*, 114.
91. Henry, *Christian Personal Ethics*, 511.

The Evangelical Paradigm for Religious Liberty

> Speculative Theism or Idealism, which revolt against the biblical doctrine of the fall, often attack the attachment of any objective significance to conscience. Contemporary studies more and more despair of tracing the origin of conscience because they lack a secure account of the origin of man.[92]

The evangelical doctrine of human dignity and the fall's effect help explain why moral reform emerges, and this stands distinctly different from secular theory. Consequently, the evangelical doctrine of *imago Dei* and the fall put forth the most consistent explanation for observable human behavior.

However, the evangelical doctrine of sin recognizes the need for conscience to stand alongside the absolute objective moral standard of Scripture.[93] Secular theories do not offer a fence to stave off moral relativism. But evangelical theology posits that the Holy Spirit awakens the conscience at the moment of regeneration, allowing the believer to bear witness to moral truth (Rom 9:1). The awakened conscience gives image-bearers not only the ability to know the will of God but the power to obey it. Because all image-bearers maintain the potential for an awakened conscience, all people maintain dignity. Consequently, the evangelical conscience is superior because it supports humanity's universal dignity while acknowledging its dependence on a transcendent source of authority.

Moreover, evangelical anthropology is superior because it recognizes the communicative link between God and humans. Secular theories reduce the conscience to decision-making power. Ahdar and Leigh convincingly argue that secular approaches consider religious conscience a matter of autonomous choice.[94] Thus, religious conscience is essentially the ability to choose among a multitude of other competing choices. But if the conscience is merely a decision-making faculty, then it loses its special value. One's religious choices are no different than other choices such as music, food, or sexual partner; thus, religion needs no special protections. But evangelical anthropology understands the conscience as the communicative link between a transcendent person and humans. God's willingness to speak directly to his creatures through conscience not only imparts dignity, it also establishes specific requirements. The evangelical conscience may be conceived not so much in terms of choice but more in terms of duty; therefore, religious freedom is a freedom given to fulfill a duty and to respond

---

92. Henry, *Christian Personal Ethics*, 511.
93. Henry, *Christian Personal Ethics*, 510.
94. Ahdar and Leigh, *Religious Freedom in the Liberal State*, 60.

The Superiority of an Evangelical Model of Religious Liberty

to a divine command.[95] Thus, the evangelical notion of conscience is not primarily about autonomous choice. Rather, religious freedom requires one to fulfill their duty before a transcendent, living person. To violate one's religious duty is to undermine human dignity and do violence to the soul. Roger Williams vehemently argued that to sin against one's conscience was to be cut off from Christ, the head of his church.[96] For Williams, any authority that prevents, coerces, or ignores one's "secret checks and whispers" emerging from conscience has committed the sin of "soul rape."[97] Isaac Backus argued that to forsake one's religious duty for the doctrines of men was to force an implicit faith on the human soul, which destroys not only one's faith but reason.[98] Consequently, evangelical anthropology provides a superior explanation of the human conscience.

The evangelical conscience is superior in three distinct ways. First, it is established on the firm ontological principle of the *imago Dei*, which respects the conscience as a communicative link between individuals and a transcendent person. Second, the evangelical conscience acknowledges humanity's finitude and fallenness. Third, the evangelical conscience establishes an absolute universal principle that protects the dignity of all humans. Therefore, the evangelical doctrine of conscience provides logical answers for religious freedom for all persons.

Evangelical Self and Freedom

As previously stated, secular theories cannot provide absolute universal moral boundaries; therefore, secular theories contain no content for ordering individual freedoms. Liberal philosophies place autonomous freedom as the highest value. But apart from divine revelation, autonomous freedom means the individual is the center of the universe; therefore, individual freedom becomes freedom without restraints. Schaeffer noted that once freedom is cut off from transcendent authority, autonomous freedom is stripped of meaning.[99] Thus, freedom becomes contentless. Freedom stripped of content meaning has no boundaries to provide order. Therefore, the concept of enumerated rights and ordered liberty becomes logically impossible.

---

95. Ahdar and Leigh, *Religious Freedom in the Liberal State*, 32.
96. Williams, *On Religious Liberty*, 104.
97. Williams, *On Religious Liberty*, 78.
98. Backus, *A History of New England*, 71.
99. Schaeffer et al., *The Francis A. Schaeffer Trilogy*, 228.

The Evangelical Paradigm for Religious Liberty

Moreover, creatures made in the image of God cannot function in a meaningless world. Francis Schaeffer put forth a compelling proposition when he stated, "Humans will use autonomous freedom to create meaning where meaning is absent."[100] Schaeffer contended that apart from God, humans will inevitably use autonomous freedom to create self-authenticating experiences. And one's self-authenticating experience, regardless of rationality or absurdity, becomes one's value system whereby they interpret the world. But if self-authentication becomes the content of freedom, then every autonomous act must be given equal value—no one act can claim moral superiority over another. Thus, freedom takes on a distinctly egalitarian texture. As a result, society loses its ability to rank individual freedom, which makes civic duty challenging to enforce. Rex Ahdar argues that egalitarian concepts of freedom present especially unique problems for maintaining religious liberty.[101] He posits that almost any set of self-authenticating experiences could conceivably count as a religious belief.[102] Thus, citizens may object to any civil duty that conflicts with one's own self-authenticating experience. Therefore, freedom stripped from transcendent authority loses its moral content and orderability, which diminishes social responsibility.

Nevertheless, the evangelical concept of freedom contains objective moral content and a basic structure. First, the evangelical understanding of freedom finds objective moral content in Jesus Christ. Millard Erickson contends that Jesus's sinless life serves as the universal standard of moral purity.[103] Erickson says, "Jesus is not only as human as we are; he is more human. Our humanity is not a standard by which we are to measure his. His humanity, true and unadulterated, is the standard by which we are to be measured."[104] And Christ's resurrection affirmed Jesus's life as the moral standard whereby all humans are judged (John 5:22–23). Yet, apart from divine help, no human can conform to the full content of his moral standard (Rom 7:7–8). Thus, the evangelical ethic argues that supernatural power is required for moral living. Christ's resurrection not only affirms the objective moral content of his life, but it also becomes the source whereby moral energy flows. Oliver O'Donovan convincingly argues that the apostolic

---

100. Schaeffer et al., *The Francis A. Schaeffer Trilogy*, 238.
101. Ahdar and Leigh, *Religious Freedom in the Liberal State*, 116.
102. Ahdar and Leigh, *Religious Freedom in the Liberal State*, 117.
103. Erickson and Hustad, *Introducing Christian Doctrine*, 231.
104. Erickson and Hustad, *Introducing Christian Doctrine*, 231.

The Superiority of an Evangelical Model of Religious Liberty

message of resurrection included the proclamation of the Holy Spirit.[105] O'Donovan argues that the Holy Spirit not only makes the reality of moral content knowable, but the Spirit also gives individuals the power to obey it. O'Donovan explains,

> To do this he does not take over our subjecthood; he enables us to realize it. In a sentence of critical importance for theological ethics Saint Paul wrote: "God is at work in you, both to will and to work for His good pleasure" (Phil 2:13). This sentence, too, may sometimes be misunderstood, as though the apostle were speaking of an absorption of man's work into God's virtue of a qualitative inwardness. But the willing and the working are man's willing and working. Human willing and working are made possible by the defined work "within," which brings the free human agency to expression. God is present to man-as-subject, God, the Holy Spirit, attesting God the Son and evoking human attestation of him in human will and deed.[106]

Thus, the content of freedom is not a self-authenticating experience but rather submission to the will of God. Autonomous freedom is unstable because it alienates itself and produces non-freedom, and this cuts individuals off from the possibility of more freedom.[107] The apostle Paul stresses the problem of freedom apart from Christ in his letter to the Galatians. Paul asserts the content of freedom is submission to Christ (Gal 5:1). But when fallen humans make choices contrary to the will of God, they find themselves under the yoke of slavery—and slavery is a condition of less freedom. Paul stresses that those who refuse to submit to the will of Christ inevitably experience diminished freedom.[108] So, if the content of freedom is submission to Christ, then any act that impedes or forbids submission harms the individuals greatly by cutting them off from potentially more freedom. It is no wonder the apostle Peter declared, "We must obey God rather than men" (Acts 5:29). Consequently, the evangelical concept of freedom is superior because its content is secure in the person of Christ, and it promises to expand freedom under his authority.

Second, the evangelical concept of freedom has a structure found within the Great Commandment. Once the Holy Spirit makes a person

---

105. O'Donovan, *Resurrection and Moral Order*, 102.
106. O'Donovan, *Resurrection and Moral Order*, 106.
107. Schaeffer et al., *The Francis A. Schaeffer Trilogy*, 232.
108. O'Donovan, *Resurrection and Moral Order*, 109.

free, that freedom is immediately demonstrated in self-binding service to God and others (Gal 5:13).[109] Whereas secular theories of freedom turn toward self-authentication, evangelical freedom turns away from self. The Great Commandment sets the order for how humans are to use individual freedom. Humans are to use freedom to love God by keeping his commandments (John 14:15). And one's love of God is confirmed by loving others (Matt 22:36–39). Yet, the command to love God and others is not a command that demolishes individual dignity. One who loves God necessarily must know his love (1 John 4:19). It is impossible for one who loves God not to love oneself because God's love grounds all other loves.[110] And one who knows God's love rightly will love oneself and seek the same kind of love for one's neighbor.[111] In their classic book *Christian Ethics*, Waldo Beach and H. Richard Niebuhr argue that true love of God balances love of self and others.[112] The ethicists note,

> Within the variables of Christian ethical theories, there is a constant *triadic* relation—the "vertical" relation of the believing and acting self to God, and the "horizontal" relation of the self to otherselves—a relation in which God is, so to speak, the "middle term." How and why the neighbor is loved depends on how and why God is loved. Thus, in Jesus' summary of the law, the Second Command, to love the neighbor, is described as like or part of the First.[113]

The Great Commandment balances one's duty to God, others, and self. Thus, the Great Commandment provides a structure and order to freedom in general and religious freedom in particular. The evangelical concept of freedom is bounded by love; therefore, the Evangelical does not use religious freedom to denigrate, abuse, or physically harm one's neighbor. Because the evangelical concept of freedom is established in love, it allows people of competing values to live peaceably. Therefore, the evangelical idea of freedom allows for a superior vision of liberty for all people.

---

109. O'Donovan, *Resurrection and Moral Order*, 108.
110. Beach and Niebuhr, *Christian Ethics*, 117.
111. Augustine, *On the Morals of the Catholic Church*, 4:443.
112. Beach and Niebuhr, *Christian Ethics*, 117.
113. Beach and Niebuhr, *Christian Ethics*, 5.

The Superiority of Evangelical Cosmology

Evangelical anthropology possesses a superior foundation. Evangelical cosmology recognizes that seen and unseen realities provide order to the world. Utilitarian cosmology depends entirely on empiricism. But empiricism alone cannot maintain a full-orbed justice system. Utilitarian justice can only imagine punishments and rewards in terms of good results; therefore, it does not consider the punishment or reward as good within itself.[114] Utilitarian cosmology flattens justice because it does not consider aspects of motive and intent, and this makes justice distinctively one-dimensional. Natural law provides an ordered structure to the world. Roman Catholic natural law rightly recognizes that the objective order interacts with unseen realities. But because Catholic natural law does not call upon Scripture in the public square, at best, the unregenerate are left with a vague sense of moral realism. Evangelical cosmology is superior because it acknowledges that humans exist within an intelligibly-ordered world. Evangelical cosmology realizes that unseen realities influence visible realities. O'Donovan notes that Scripture always presents humanity as living within a framed order of things that stand before and behind it.[115] He argues that the objective realities of the visible world press upon the subjective realities of the inner self, making all humans aware of their place in an ordered structure.[116] And because God created humans in his image, both the regenerate and unregenerate know they exist within an ordered universe (Rom 1:18–19). While the unregenerate mind cannot apprehend the fullness of truth, the unbeliever does bump into truth. But because the unregenerate mind is limited, it can only explain these partial truths through a flawed imagination. Thus, the unregenerate mind creates totalizing ideologies or false religions to describe its encounter with truth.[117] Consequently, these ideologies and false religions eventually erode the boundaries needed to maintain a free and civil social order.

Nevertheless, evangelical cosmology acknowledges the fullness of an objectively ordered world. Evangelical cosmology posits that God created the world with boundaries, and God willed that all people know these boundaries. Evangelical cosmology stresses absolute dependence on God

---

114. O'Donovan, *The Ways of Judgment*, 114.
115. O'Donovan, *Self, World, and Time*, 1:10.
116. O'Donovan, *Self, World, and Time*, 1:10.
117. Henry, *God, Revelation and Authority*, 1:402.

The Evangelical Paradigm for Religious Liberty

for all knowledge, whether objective or subjective. In other words, we know what we know because God wills both the possibility and the content of knowledge.[118] And this means God wills that all humans can logically discern natural and supernatural boundaries.[119] The evangelical doctrine of creation offers a transcendent guarantee of unity, orderliness, intelligibility, and stability of natural process; it also provides a basis for the belief that some rational overlap exists between explanatory images and the objects of experimentation.[120] This is not to confuse general revelation with natural theology. Humans have an absolute dependence upon special revelation for *true understanding* of the created order.[121] But God's general revelation makes the world's order knowable to all humans; the world as we know it is so because God declares it to be so.[122] Consequently, while general revelation is not salvific, it does communicate the boundaries of an ordered world.

Religious freedom serves as means to maintain boundaries in an ordered world. The evangelical paradigm understands religious liberty as a gracious instrument ordained by God to maintain proper separation between the natural and supernatural, individual and collective, and the sacred and secular worlds. The evangelical paradigm upholds an orderly world in three ways. First, evangelical religious freedom respects both believers and unbelievers as truth-seekers, and this allows all people to explore natural and transcendent realities. Second, evangelical religious freedom respects the distinction between spheres of authority. God created different jurisdictions to adjudicate civil and spiritual matters. Third, evangelical religious freedom spans both objective and philosophical boundaries.

First, the evangelical paradigm of religious freedom recognizes all humans as truth-seekers. But the doctrine of general revelation is insufficient for gaining specific knowledge about salvation. Yet, general revelation is sufficient to inform humans that transcendent realities exist. General revelation compels the individual conscience to seek answers to transcendent questions (Job 12:7–25). The apostle Paul noted that the men of Athens acknowledged transcendent realities, but he vigorously debated their conclusions (Acts 17:22–23). While Evangelicals will disagree with how the unregenerate explain transcendent realities, Evangelicals realize that each

---

118. Thornbury, *Recovering Classic Evangelicalism*, 52.
119. Henry, *God, Revelation and Authority*, 1:402.
120. Henry, *Toward a Recovery of Christian Belief*, 51.
121. Thornbury, *Recovering Classic Evangelicalism*, 49.
122. Thornbury, *Recovering Classic Evangelicalism*, 49.

The Superiority of an Evangelical Model of Religious Liberty

person must be freed to form their conclusions. The evangelical framework of religious liberty extends to everyone because everyone is on a quest to pursue transcendent truth, even if incorrectly.[123] Therefore, because Christians and non-Christians both perceive transcendent realities, a point of mutual overlap exists. And this overlap allows for common respect and civility while individuals seek and explore the truth.

Moreover, one's quest to explain transcendent truth also serves as an acknowledgment that one lives within an ordered universe. Reinhold Niebuhr suggested that humanity's realization of finitude while living under a sense of transcendence is "the basic paradox of human existence."[124] Evangelical religious liberty maintains that all humans are not only capable but necessarily engage with transcendent realities. And at the same time, the evangelical paradigm maintains a boundary between true salvific religion and false religion. While Evangelicals can applaud each individual's quest for truth, they do so without affirming all values as equally true. Therefore, the evangelical framework can maintain the boundaries between creature and creator, truth and non-truth.

Utilitarian paradigms also recognize humans as truth-seekers. But apart from special revelation, utilitarian theories cannot maintain objective boundaries. John Stuart Mill could not fix truth in anything more significant than empiricism. Thus, Mill's theory metastasizes into the ideology of pragmatism. Pragmatism ultimately destroys the boundaries needed for democracy because it dignifies every kind of cultural pattern as a form of "creativity"—it cannot maintain boundaries between truth and non-truth.[125] Carl F. H. Henry noted,

> Pragmatism in any event contains the seeds of its own undoing. It professes to be tolerant of all views, but its concealed intolerance becomes clear when, confronted and seriously challenged by the Christian absolute, it dogmatically refuses to reconsider any return to universally valid truth and objective principle.[126]

Henry understood that democratic government could not be predicated simply on the will of the majority.[127] Instead, democratic governments require firm boundaries to restrain power and protect the dignity of

---

123. Walker and George, *Liberty for All*, 4.
124. Niebuhr, *The Nature and Destiny of Man*, 175.
125. Henry, *God, Revelation and Authority*, 1:43.
126. Henry, *God, Revelation and Authority*, 1:41.
127. Henry, *Has Democracy Had Its Day?*, xi.

minorities. Consequently, the ideology of pragmatism cannot sustain the necessary limits as are required for democracies' long-term flourishing.

Moreover, Rawls also recognized humans as truth-seekers, but apart from special revelation, his theory creates an ideology of equity. The ideology of equity not only erodes the boundaries created by institutions; the ideology of equity destroys the institutions themselves. Rawls's veil of ignorance diminishes the role of family, church, and economics in shaping and instilling values. His veil of ignorance requires that individuals cast off values instilled by social institutions, even as many of those values are necessary for sustaining social boundaries. Therefore, while Rawls correctly recognized that all humans are truth-seekers, his theory created an ideology that works against the ordered limits established by family and religion.

However, evangelical religious freedom serves to protect ordered boundaries. The evangelical paradigm recognizes the role that families and religious institutions play in forming and instilling values. Religious institutions are necessary for instilling the principles and the boundaries needed to sustain democratic principles. Democracy requires the principles of individual self-restraint, accountability, and service to someone or something beyond oneself. Henry noted that democracies must look to transcendent truth to provide the boundaries needed to preserve the delicate order between individuals and majority groups.[128] Western democracies require the protection of solid boundaries, especially between family, religion, the press, and the state. But utilitarian theories cannot maintain the proper boundaries because they have no fixed foundation for balancing competing value systems. Therefore, because evangelical epistemology recognizes seen and unseen realities, its paradigm for religious liberty can establish objective boundaries, allowing individuals to respond to transcendent realities.

Spheres of Authority

Evangelical religious freedom also establishes a specific order between prosecutorial spheres of authority. Jesus's declaration "render to Caesar the things that are Caesar's, and to God, the things that are God's" (Mark 12:13) is significant for understanding the earthly orders of authority. Theologian Don Carson contends that some interpreters have understood Mark 12:13 as a powerful way of saying that *nothing* belongs to Caesar, so nothing is

---

128. Henry, *Has Democracy Had Its Day?*, 14.

The Superiority of an Evangelical Model of Religious Liberty

owed to him.[129] But that interpretation does not stand with the traditional understanding.[130] The conventional interpretation of Mark 12 balances the adjudicating power between civil and church authorities. Yet, Carson notes that against the backdrop of Matthew 28 and Romans 13, Jesus's command does not establish a rigid separation between earthly kingdoms, for Christ sovereignly rules over both the church and the state (Col 1:16). But Christ delegates authority to prosecute crimes appropriate to each sphere's domain. Therefore, it is best not to understand Christ's command to "give unto Caesar" as two distinct kingdoms or realms but one kingdom with two prosecutorial authorities.

Theologian Jonathan Leeman argues that the order established in Mark 12 follows from the order of the Noachian covenant. The Noachian covenant distinguishes between secular crimes and sacred beliefs. Drawing upon the work of Baptist theologian Jonathan Leeman, ethicist Andrew Walker argues that the structure for evangelical religious freedom emerges from Genesis 9.[131] Walker says,

> The Noahic Covenant preserves a common social order in which humans interact with one another. This covenant assumes the reality of sin and braces for it by constraining it through the establishment of justice and right order (Gen 9:5–6). More important, the Noahic Covenant still operates and will continue on until future judgment—or "while the earth remains" (Gen 8:22). This means that all of the earth's inhabitants share in the blessing of common grace established by the Noahic Covenant.[132]

The Noachian covenant is significant for religious freedom because it creates an ongoing, objectively ordered structure for adjudicating justice. God authorized humans to execute judgment on crimes that are destructive to civil order. He gives civil authorities coercive power to execute judgment for civil crimes (Rom 13:1–4). But God does not authorize humans to use coercive power to prosecute crimes against himself.[133] Rex Ahdar and Ian Leigh refer to this order as the *dual authority principle*.[134] Ahdar and Leigh say,

---

129. Carson, *Christ and Culture Revisited*, 160.
130. Carson, *Christ and Culture Revisited*, 160.
131. Walker and George, *Liberty for All*, 53.
132. Walker and George, *Liberty for All*, 52.
133. Leeman, *Political Church*, 201.
134. Ahdar and Leigh, *Religious Freedom in the Liberal State*, 34.

The Evangelical Paradigm for Religious Liberty

> The state's delegated authority stops short of directing citizens' souls. Its proper concerns and jurisdiction involve earthly, temporal matters. There is another authority which is prior both chronologically and in the degree of obligation humankind owes to it. Temporal government must defer to this eternal spiritual Governor.[135]

The evangelical paradigm recognizes that objective spheres of authority exist. Therefore, crimes against society are adjudicated by humans, and God is the judge of crimes of belief—humans are not tasked with criminalizing wrong beliefs.[136]

Nonetheless, this does not mean that spiritual crimes are not judged on earth. God gave the keys to the kingdom to judge spiritual crimes in the present age (Matt 18:18–20). Carson contends that the distinction between governing authorities sets believers as a separate and distinguishable community set within a common culture.[137] Christians understand themselves as part of the objective social order, even when they stand uniquely against the culture's prevailing beliefs. Christians fall under a common civil law authority even where there is no common spiritual belief. But this is not to say that the civil authority is an autonomous authority. Matthew 28 is clear that all authority in heaven and on earth is given to Jesus. All earthly authority exists by Jesus's permission, and Jesus will judge all nations and governments.[138] Walker notes that the distinction in prosecutorial authority shows that society cannot function without a common morality, but it can function without a common religion.[139] Consequently, the evangelical distinction between civil and spiritual power provides ordered boundaries, allowing for religious pluralism.

The World and Mission

The evangelical concept of an ordered world necessarily establishes insider-outsider boundaries. Those who profess faith in Christ reside inside the church, and they receive the benefits of living in this world and the world to come. Those who do not know Christ reside outside the church. Non-Christians are cut off from full knowledge in this world and are condemned

---

135. Ahdar and Leigh, *Religious Freedom in the Liberal State*, 37.
136. Walker and George, *Liberty for All*, 53.
137. Carson, *Christ and Culture Revisited*, 165.
138. Leeman, *How the Nations Rage*, 12.
139. Walker and George, *Liberty for All*, 54.

The Superiority of an Evangelical Model of Religious Liberty

in the world to come. But the insider-outsider boundary is not impassable; the goal of Christian evangelism is to span the gap between the insider-outsider boundaries. Therefore, the clear distinction between insider-outsider boundaries is significant for religious freedom because it establishes a foundation for the Christian mission.

Jesus commanded his followers to make disciples and baptize them in the name of the Father, Son, and Holy Spirit (Matt 28:19–20). Baptism serves as an objective boundary between insiders and outsiders. And while Christian sects may differ on the mode of baptism and meaning of baptism, every Christian denomination understands baptism as inclusion into the visible church. Religious freedom assists the Great Commission by removing objective barriers that may impede one's entry into the church. And while the Great Commission does not need legal assistance to advance the gospel, religious freedom does offer significant support for its expansion.[140] Evangelical religious freedom cultivates a pathway so one can cross the objective insider-outsider boundary. Consequently, evangelical religious freedom promotes an overall culture whereby outsiders may freely move toward the gospel.[141]

The objective boundaries of insider-outsider move in both directions. Religious freedom allows individuals to enter faith and permits an individual to leave the faith. The principle of *unrestricted conscience* means that all people, at any time, may leave their faith commitments.[142] Because the evangelical concept of the world maintains boundaries, one does not lose one's individuality when one joins the church. Therefore, because one never forgoes one's identity, one may cross the insider-outsider boundary at any given time.

Moreover, evangelical religious freedom spans philosophical boundaries. The motive of religious liberty comes from the command to love one's neighbor.[143] The command to love assumes the underlying philosophical propositions that love is not love if coerced. Ethicist Philip Wogaman notes, "Applied to the question of religious liberty, the approach would be to consider all political philosophies and legal structures relative to the underlying drama of love seeking response, but it would also assume that love cannot coerce response. Love has no motive to coerce, but only to seek the good of

---

140. Leland, *The Writings of the Late Elder John Leland*, 112.
141. Walker and George, *Liberty for All*, 192.
142. Ahdar and Leigh, *Religious Freedom in the Liberal State*, 37.
143. Walker and George, *Liberty for All*, 192.

The Evangelical Paradigm for Religious Liberty

the other."[144] Evangelical religious liberty is an act of love because one's response to the gospel does not determine whether or not one is loved. Also, because faith is a voluntary matter, one's decision to accept or reject Christ does not alter the Christian's duty regarding charity. Therefore, Christian love crosses philosophical barriers and allows for disagreement.

Furthermore, evangelical religious liberty applies to the Christian mission and extends to all people and all faiths. Barrett Duke notes,

> But religious liberty does not apply only to Christianity. Religious liberty extends to all people at all faiths or no faiths. Jesus sent his disciples into all the world to make disciples, but their method was to make disciples by teaching others to observe all that he had taught them (Matt 28:19–20). There is no hint in the Great Commission that Jesus expected his disciples to coerce true faith or to stop people from practicing their false religion.[145]

The evangelical framework recognizes all people's right to proselytize. Walker notes that religious freedom creates a moral ecology and social tranquility because it respects every person's right to pursue truth.[146] Christians can love their neighbors by listening to their beliefs and thoughtfully asking questions. Because Evangelicals claim to possess absolute truth, there is no fear in giving a hearing to competing truths of claims. Subsequently, the evangelical paradigm for religious freedom is superior because it assists the Great Commission while respecting the boundaries of individuals.

The Superiority of Evangelical Eschatology

Evangelical eschatology is superior to other teleological visions because it recognizes the personal nature of time. Time is personal in the evangelical paradigm because it acknowledges a personal God is guiding history toward the goal of a new heaven and earth. Utilitarian ethics maintain an impersonal concept of time. The utilitarian theory assumes that history is merely the accumulative process of calculated consequences. But because the utilitarian ethic is the result of consequence, it contains no guide to direct future acts. Also, utilitarianism's belief in the perfectibility of humans is inconsistent. Utilitarianism cannot provide a vision of a "future good"

---

144. Wogaman, *Protestant Faith and Religious Liberty*, 74.
145. Duke, "The Christian Doctrine of Religious Liberty," 25.
146. Walker, *Liberty for All*, 189.

The Superiority of an Evangelical Model of Religious Liberty

because of its *a posteriori* nature. Roman Catholic natural law rightly recognizes that time moves toward the ultimate goal of happiness. And Roman Catholic natural law provides an absolute universal standard for judging the future good. Roman Catholic natural law also assumes that Christ is the ultimate arbiter of good and evil. But Roman Catholic natural law hides its presuppositions in the public square; thus, unbelievers are not challenged to consider final judgment. Roman Catholic natural law assumes the same preposition as unbelievers—namely, that time is an impersonal consequence of natural causation. But evangelical teleology contends that a crucified, resurrected, and enthroned Messiah guides all history toward ultimate judgment.[147] The evangelical concept of time appeals to an objective record of history—history in space and time moving toward an ultimate moment.[148] Evangelical teleology fits within an eschatological vision of Christ's present and active role in time. Evangelical eschatology posits that time is moving toward a moment where Jesus will personally judge good and evil. Thus, religious freedom is a spiritual and instrumental good because it provides a consistent and cohesive vision of justice. All humans will stand before Christ in judgment with a universal standard of good and evil. Consequently, evangelical teleology is superior because it understands that time belongs to a redemptive narrative whereby all humans are judged by the same moral normal.

Evangelical eschatology influences religious freedom in two ways. First, Jesus Christ is understood to rule both the current and coming ages. Second, Christ is personally guiding redemptive history toward final judgment. Evangelical eschatology recognizes that Jesus Christ is the Alpha and the Omega (Rev 22:13), and this gives history a deeply personal texture. Time is not the record of random cause and effect, as the utilitarian philosophy posits. Instead, history is relational and moving toward humanity's ultimate redemption. In his commentary on Revelation, theologian G. K. Beale argues that the title Alpha and Omega serves to show Christ's presence at, and sovereignty over, the beginning of creation and over the end of creation, and his present reign over all events in between.[149] Consequently, Christ's reign over the past, present, and future sets the stage for how Evangelicals understand their role in the public square.

---

147. Moore, *The Kingdom of Christ*, 12.
148. Schaeffer et al., *The Francis A. Schaeffer Trilogy*, 269.
149. Beale, *The Book of Revelation*, 1138.

Inaugurated Eschatology

Traditional Protestant eschatology understood Christ's kingdom in light of Luther's two kingdoms theology. Martin Luther contended that God divided humankind into two kingdoms. The first kingdom belonged to God, and the second kingdom belonged to the world.[150] But Luther's divisions caused some writers to imagine different authorities ruling over each kingdom.[151] Evangelical eschatology has more recently adopted an Augustinian hue of the kingdom.[152] Theologians such as George Ladd posit that the kingdom arrived "already" in the person of Christ and yet possesses a "not yet" aspect reserved for the millennial reign and eternal state.[153] Oliver O'Donovan argues that the kingdom of God is experienced differently in light of the resurrection.[154] O'Donovan states, "The kingly rule of Christ is God's ownership exercised over the whole world. It is visible in the life of the church but not there only."[155] And Jonathan Leeman says, "We don't live in two kingdoms; we simultaneously live in two ages, the age of the fall and the age of the new creation."[156] The evangelical concept of one kingdom / two experiences posits that all humans live in Christ's kingdom, but his rule is experienced differently throughout the ages. Subsequently, evangelical eschatology has primarily adopted a view of time that recognizes Christ's reign over one kingdom (Col 2:10) with the experience of believers and unbelievers differing according to the timetable of redemptive history.

The evangelical doctrine of two ages or inaugurated eschatology has become popular among New Testament theologians for characterizing Christ's kingdom.[157] Baptist theologian Russell Moore contends that inaugurated kingdom theology provides a theological framework for evangelical social engagement.[158] Moore argues that Christ's present kingly role rules the Christian church, allowing the church to scrutinize current

---

150. Luther and Calvin, *Luther and Calvin on Secular Authority*, 8.
151. Leeman, *How the Nations Rage*, 64.
152. Moore, *The Kingdom of Christ*, 50.
153. Ladd, *The Gospel of the Kingdom*, 16.
154. O'Donovan, *The Desire of the Nations*, 146.
155. O'Donovan, *The Desire of the Nations*, 146.
156. Leeman, *How the Nations Rage*, 64.
157. Leeman, *Political Church*, 274.
158. Moore, *The Kingdom of Christ*, 24.

The Superiority of an Evangelical Model of Religious Liberty

political relationships.[159] But inaugurated kingdom theology also recognizes that utopian ideals will not materialize until final consummation.[160] This distinction between the "now" and "not yet" allows Christians to boldly proclaim Christ's righteous requirements while realizing that perfect justice will not be achieved in the present age. Therefore, Christians living in between the current and future age understand themselves as ambassadors of Christ's kingdom, ambassadors proclaiming apocalyptic and prophetic messages (2 Cor 5:20).

Nevertheless, not all evangelical theologians accept inaugurated kingdom theology. Evangelicals are not monolithic; therefore, many eschatological visions exist within Evangelicalism. Dispensational fundamentalists believe that Christ's Davidic rule awaits a future millennial kingdom. So many dispensational Evangelicals avoid current social concerns.[161] Amillennialists emphasize the kingdom in entirely present, spiritual terms; therefore, they may also avoid social engagement. However, dispensational fundamentalist, amillennialist, and inaugurated theologians all agree that the current role of Christ's people is one of ambassador. Therefore, Christians are emissaries delivering a message that is both apocalyptic and prophetic in the present age.[162]

While Evangelicals maintain diverse views of eschatology, Evangelicals also maintain unity regarding the current role of believers. Christians in this age announce the content of Christ's righteous requirements (prophetic). And Christians in the current age declare a future judgment awaits (apocalyptic). Consequently, the kingdom of God influences religious liberty because it allows Christians to declare Christ's current righteous standard against the backdrop of future judgment.

Ultimate Consummation

The evangelical concept of time recognizes that Christ sovereignly moves all of life toward its final goal. The message of coming judgment for all humanity, with Jesus Christ completing the work of his kingdom by acting as judge on his Father's behalf, runs throughout the New Testament.[163]

---

159. Moore, *The Kingdom of Christ*, 68.
160. Moore, *The Kingdom of Christ*, 71.
161. Henry, *The Uneasy Conscience of Modern Fundamentalism*, 7.
162. Henry, "Dare We Renew the Controversy?," 23.
163. Packer, *Concise Theology*, 238.

The Evangelical Paradigm for Religious Liberty

The evangelical belief in divine judgment is significant for religious liberty in two ways. First, divine judgment ensures that perfect justice is coming. Second, divine judgment encourages patience in the current age. Therefore, the evangelical concept of time can balance a public square of competing beliefs because Christ will ultimately punish evil and reward the good.

Secular social ethics imagine perfect justice in the current age. But because secular social ethics hold no theory of divine justice, secular ethics must attempt perfect justice immediately. Jonathan Leeman persuasively argues,

> Utopianism is the belief that perfect justice is possible in this world and that we can bring heaven to earth now . . . yet utopianism, whether of the Christian or non-Christian variety, often produces injustice. The utopian mindset relies on its own strength instead of God's, it overestimates what can be done in this world and so forces its way. Utopianism exploits and abuses people in the name of the greater good.[164]

But evangelical theology holds a high view of divine retribution, ensuring that ultimate justice will come in the next life (Rom 12:19). Because evangelical ethics look toward ultimate justice in the future, evangelical social policy serves to restrain vengeance in the present age. With its retribution theology, Evangelicalism allows "wheat and tares" (Matt 13:24–30) to live together, peaceable in the current age because ultimate judgment is promised in the future. Therefore, evangelical religious freedom serves as a bulwark against utopianism and vengeance and instead promotes a culture of civility.

Moreover, divine retribution provides an important distinction between religious freedom and sexual freedom. Ethicist Daniel Heimbach argues that pagans believe spiritual and material life are not different things but one thing, and so they reduce spiritual life to experiencing physical and emotional sensations in the material world.[165] But when the spiritual is reduced to merely the material world, one may argue that one's erotic liberty is the same as religious liberty. After all, sex in the pagan world is a religion. But a theology of coming judgment maintains a distinction between erotic liberty and religious liberty. One may argue that one's sexual expression is religious. But it is hardly convincing to say that one fears divine judgment for sexual restraint. Therefore, the promise of divine punishment is significant for religious freedom because it provides an important distinction between material and spiritual liberties.

---

164. Leeman, *How the Nations Rage*, 164.
165. Heimbach, *True Sexual Morality*, 52.

The Superiority of an Evangelical Model of Religious Liberty

Second, the evangelical vision of future judgment encourages patience and urgency in the present age. The evangelical paradigm understands that the current age is one of coexistence. Thus, the public square is a contested space in this age; therefore, patience is demanded for erring consciences.[166] Additionally, the promise of future judgment also creates an urgency for debate. Individuals under the possibility of divine retribution must receive warning. Andrew Walker argues convincingly that "religious liberty exists because it issues from a place of sincere urgency, emanating from sober conviction about the future judgment awaiting humanity."[167] The Scripture's clarity concerning future judgment means that religious liberty is a temporary condition (Phil 2:9–11). Therefore, the evangelical paradigm for religious freedom is superior because its purpose is fixed in a sincere belief to warn one's neighbor of future judgment.

Nevertheless, judgment is two-sided; divine justice is both retributive and distributive. The evangelical concept of the future also includes the possibility of heavenly reward. Jesus encouraged his disciples to seek treasures in heaven (Matt 6:19–20). And Paul commanded individual believers to seek imperishable rewards (1 Cor 9:25). The Scripture's vision of distributive justice serves to balance the relationship between individualism and collectivism. Individuals are encouraged to seek their good through obedience to Christ, promoting a healthy egoism. But the evangelical idea of individual obedience is never cut off from one's motive to love God and others, which prevents a collapse into radical individualism or excessive collectivism.

Moreover, the evangelical promise of future reward promotes emotional flourishing in this age. Christian psychologist Gary Collins correctly recognizes that feelings of hopelessness often contribute to social breakdown.[168] Collins notes that hopelessness is often the cause of excessive drinking, impulsivity, and anti-social behavior.[169] Ethical theories that deny individuals the opportunity to better one's eternal condition cause psychological distress, resulting in diminished social flourishing. But the evangelical vision of divine rewards promotes a sense of hope that positively influences all people. Consequently, an evangelical paradigm of religious freedom with its vision of future divine rewards promotes general social flourishing and purpose in this age.

---

166. Walker and George, *Liberty for All*, 25.
167. Walker, "Religious Liberty in Contemporary Evangelical Social Ethics," 158.
168. Collins, *Christian Counseling*, 460.
169. Collins, *Christian Counseling*, 460.

Conclusion

This chapter argues that the evangelical paradigm of religious freedom is superior to other frameworks. First, I tried to explain the historical definition of Evangelicalism. Our current American political discourse has confused the term, leading to misrepresentations and unnecessary self-deprecation. Second, I showed that historically Evangelicalism maintained a cohesive and comprehensive framework. Religious freedom was not the result of modern Enlightenment philosophy. Instead, religious freedom's roots are found in classic evangelical theology. Third, I argued that evangelical anthropology is superior to secular anthropology because it maintains a substantive ontology fixed in the doctrine of *imago Dei*. John Courtney Murray's argument from natural law also upholds a substantive ontology. But Murray suppresses Scripture, and this strips his argument of prophetic power. Fourth, I showed that evangelical epistemology is superior because it gives shape and order to the world. Evangelical epistemology is superior because it is accessible to all humans through its doctrine of general revelation. Through general revelation, all humans can intuitively know that seen and unseen realities exist. But secular social ethics only recognize visible realities, and this means it has no ethical foundation to balance authority. The evangelical ethical structure recognizes that both seen and unseen realities exist. And these unseen realities provide authoritative boundaries to balance individual and collective power. Finally, the evangelical paradigm of religious freedom is superior because its teleology aims toward an ultimate purpose of humility and freedom. Secular social ethics aim toward an unrealistic utopianism that ultimately reduces individual freedom. Roman Catholic social ethics progress toward human happiness and flourishing. But without a clear call to repentance and faith, Roman Catholic social ethics lack apocalyptic and prophetic urgency. The evangelical paradigm for religious freedom is superior because it calls individuals to consider final justice.

CHAPTER 6

Summary Thoughts and Conclusion

THIS BOOK ASSUMES RELIGIOUS freedom is an essential good and is necessary for human flourishing. For the better part of 250 years, both religious and non-religious people have agreed that religious freedom is necessary for democracy to thrive. This is because religious freedom maintains civil order and respects individual freedoms while creating an overall culture of civility. And because religious freedom is essential for human flourishing, religious freedom must rest upon the highest set of principles. Therefore, this book maintains that religious freedom is most secure when established on principles that acknowledge a transcendent personal being.

Another underlying assumption within this book is that principled pluralism is the best structure to foster religious freedom. While the Bible does not prescribe an exact political structure, principled pluralism supports essential doctrines found within the pattern of creation, fall, redemption, and restoration. Principled pluralism rests upon several key ideas. First, God created the world with a basic structure and order. Second, God's sovereign hand maintains structure and order through various institutions such as marriage, family, church, and school. Third, ordered institutions were established prior to the fall. Thus, God delegated the power of coercion to civil magisters only after the fall. But the doctrine of the fall does not negate the existence of ordered institutions prior to sin. Fourth, God established human beings to serve as officeholders in various spheres of

Summary Thoughts and Conclusion

life.[1] Humanity's role as an image-bearer is one of royal viceregent; thus, humanity is given the immense responsibility to govern and develop creation.[2] Fifth, God's creation of institutions results in a *structural pluralism*; therefore, no one institution can properly usurp another institution's power or functions.[3] Gary Smith says, "God has created each of these structures to be independent from the others; this sphere sovereignty means that no one sphere can properly usurp the function of or dominate others. These various structures however should work together (sphere universality) to promote righteousness and cooperation in society."[4] While other government structures are acceptable within Evangelicalism, this book has assumed the form found within principled pluralism.

Moreover, I have also assumed the growing complexity of civil society. Contemporary civilization is growing more diverse and complex. And the increase in diversity presents constant challenges for religious liberty and liberal democracy in general. According to Pew Research, Americans are growing less religiously affiliated year after year.[5] Ryan P. Burge's book titled *The Nones: Where They Came From, Who They Are, and Where They Are Going* notes that since 2018 those claiming no official religious belief are equal in size to Roman Catholics and evangelical Protestants.[6] Philosophers Jocelyn Maclure and Charles Taylor believe that increasing moral pluralism is one of the central concerns of modern society.[7] He posits that disagreements concerning scientific advancement in genetics, state intervention in economics, and moral teaching in schools are rooted in the diversity of value systems.[8] Finally, attorney Luke Goodrich contends that "the conflict between gay rights and religious freedom is the most significant threat to religious freedom in the United States today. If handled poorly, we can expect a variety of painful consequences."[9] Consequently, this book assumes that religious freedom issues will only exacerbate as the nation grows more diverse.

1. Smith, *God and Politics*, 75.
2. Skillen, *The Good of Politics*, xx.
3. Smith, *God and Politics*, 75.
4. Smith, *God and Politics*, 75.
5. Whitehead and Perry, *Taking America Back for God*, 223.
6. Burge, *The Nones*, 2.
7. Maclure and Taylor, *Secularism and Freedom of Conscience*, 10.
8. Maclure and Taylor, *Secularism and Freedom of Conscience*, 11.
9. Goodrich, *Free to Believe*, 117.

The Superiority of an Evangelical Model of Religious Liberty

Additionally, the United States is not the only place where religious freedom faces new challenges. Globalization is further complicating issues of religious freedom. In May 2019, the United Nations Secretary-General António Guterres put forth a global strategy to end hate speech. Guterres's five-page document states, "Hate speech is a menace to democratic values, social stability, and peace. As a matter of principle, the United Nations must confront hate speech at every turn. Silence can signal indifference to bigotry and intolerance, even as a situation escalates, and the vulnerable become victims."[10] While the desire to end hate speech is laudable, there are problems in Guterres's document. First, who defines hate speech? The term "hate speech" is subjective; therefore, it becomes impossible to determine objectively. Second, the term "hate speech" presumes to know people's motives. Os Guinness notes that the assumptions inherent in the term "hate speech" become weapons in the hands of the power wielder, and this poses a constant danger to the rights of minorities or those whose views are out of favor.[11] Third, immorality is not necessarily illegal. While some actions and words may be distasteful, offensive, and depraved, they are not criminal. Fourth, the proposed ban on hate speech creates a threat to religious freedom because any truth claim that is deemed offensive may be declared intolerant and discriminatory, and this creates unique challenges for Christian evangelism. Finally, as contemporary society becomes more diverse, competing visions of morality will challenge religious freedom. Therefore, one must draw from the richest intellectual resources available to maintain religious freedom, including evangelical thought.

Nevertheless, in recent years, some Evangelicals have considered a withdrawal from the public square.[12] In the wake of Donald Trump's presidency, some Evangelicals are questioning the church's political engagement. Researchers Andrew L. Whitehead and Samuel L. Perry note that younger Evangelicals are rejecting the idea of Christian activity in politics altogether.[13] Movements such as "emptythepews.com" and "x-evangelical" encourage a generation of Evangelicals to deconstruct their faith. In addition, theologian Greg Thornbury notes that Evangelicals have a propensity

---

10. Guterres, *United Nations Strategy and Plan of Action on Hate Speech*, lines 1–3.

11. Guinness, *The Case for Civility*, 128.

12. Dalrymple, "If You're Selling Scorn for Conservative Christians, the Market Is Hot." Other examples include Matthew Lee Anderson's article titled "The Christian Right's Democratic Virtues: An Interview with John Shields," and an essay by Frederica Mathewes-Green titled "Loving the Storm-Drenched."

13. Whitehead and Perry, *Taking America Back for God*, 162.

Summary Thoughts and Conclusion

toward self-evaluation and endless critique. But evangelical navel-gazing results in a poor self-image and academic insecurity.[14] Consequently, it seems modern Evangelicals are experiencing an identity crisis, and this contributes to a lack of confidence toward public engagement.

However, Carl F. H. Henry warned that an evangelical withdrawal would be catastrophic for society.[15] He believed that, if left unchecked, secularism alone would shape the moral norms of America. And because secularism does not consider transcendent realities, a society without evangelical theology is a community built on partial truth. And partial truth is insufficient for today's complex moral problems. Secularism's one-sidedness cannot provide a full-orbed view of justice, righteousness, and order. Henry posited that evangelical theology possessed a genius to provide positive answers for today's most pressing social problems.[16] Therefore, an evangelical withdrawal would leave the public square fragmented and cut off from the source of all truth.

But Henry's concern emerged in an era when Americans shared many moral values. American culture generally shared the same ideals concerning morality until the latter part of the twentieth century. This is not to say that Americans were essentially moral, but there was general agreement regarding public morality. Ethicist Russell Moore notes that many of these values in this era were shared by Evangelicals and non-Evangelicals.[17] Moore argues "that most Americans shared common goals with Christianity, if not at the level of metaphysics, then at the level of morality."[18] Consequently, Christian values synchronized well with cultural conservatism.

But America no longer enjoys the benefits of shared morality. Sociologist Gene Veith argues that twenty-first-century America is post-Christian.[19] The term "post-Christian" describes a fractured culture whereby warring tribes seek cultural power. He contends that postmodern thought metastasized following the terror attacks of September 11, 2001.[20] Veith says,

> Before, all religions, in elite opinion, were considered to be equally good. Afterward, all religions were considered to be equally bad.

---

14. Thornbury, *Recovering Classic Evangelicalism*, 14.
15. Henry, *The Uneasy Conscience of Modern Fundamentalism*, xvii.
16. Henry, *The Uneasy Conscience of Modern Fundamentalism*, xvii.
17. Moore, *Onward*, 6.
18. Moore, *Onward*, 6.
19. Veith, *Post-Christian*, 4.
20. Veith, *Post-Christian*, 14.

> Terrorism began to be defined not as a moral transgression but as what you get when a group of people believes that "they have the only truth" and that "theirs is the only valid religion." The terrorists were Islamic "fundamentalists," so not Islam but fundamentalism was to blame, with Christian "fundamentalists" being considered, in many circles, as no better. Religious pluralism used to mean that different beliefs and traditions were allowed to exist side by side. But with the interfaith services that became ubiquitous after 9/11 and the reaction against every kind of fundamentalism, pluralism became something more like polytheism. You must accept all of these deities and religious traditions, but you are not allowed to believe in one of them only.[21]

Still, America's long-standing relationship with Christian morality is not forgotten. Christian values have left a residue upon the American mind. But today, many Americans cannot distinguish between cultural conservatism and genuine evangelical theology, which results in gross misrepresentations of Evangelicalism. For instance, Whitehead and Perry argue that Evangelicalism is a leading contributor to the rise of white Christian nationalism in America.[22] They argue that next to political conservatism, Evangelicalism is the most contributing factor in predicting one's adherence to white nationalism.[23] While Whitehead and Perry stop short of defining Christian nationalism and Evangelicalism as synonymous, they often confuse "white nationalism" and evangelical belief, rendering them almost synonymous.[24] Whereas Carl F. H. Henry feared evangelical withdrawal would lead to greater secularization, today's concern is that evangelical withdrawal will lead to more significant misrepresentation in the surrounding culture. Therefore, evangelical withdrawal in a post-Christian era will result in greater polarization and social discord.

Moreover, the close relationship between Evangelicalism and cultural conservatism threatens to cloud evangelical self-understanding altogether. Intellectuals such as Carl F. H. Henry and Francis Schaeffer understood the theological foundations that upheld evangelical social ethics. But today, many mainstream Evangelicals cannot distinguish between issues of political preference and essential matters of the Christian faith. Ligonier Ministries' 2020 report titled *The State of Theology 2020* revealed that

21. Veith, *Post-Christian*, 15.
22. Whitehead and Perry, *Taking America Back for God*, 10.
23. Whitehead and Perry, *Taking America Back for God*, 13.
24. Whitehead and Perry, *Taking America Back for God*, 17.

Summary Thoughts and Conclusion

evangelical beliefs regarding core doctrine correspond with the same erroneous manner as the broader US culture.[25] Because Christian values and cultural values were once closely tied, Evangelicals debated social ethics without a carefully articulated theology. And this results in two problems: First, many claiming the name "evangelical" are merely pagans covered in a thin veneer of Christian morality. Many calling themselves Evangelicals do not understand the gospel of Jesus Christ. Second, when Evangelicals debate social ethics without a clearly articulated theology, social ethics are reduced to "cultural warring." A church engaged in "culture warring" often presents an incoherent witness at best and counter-Christian witness at worst.[26] Consequently, if authentic Evangelicals withdraw from the public sphere, then many quasi-Evangelicals will define the church's social witness, which is devastating for the church and the culture.

One implication of this book is to encourage evangelical intellectuals toward greater public engagement. Andrew Walker's 2018 dissertation provides a cohesive theological framework for religious liberty. This work builds upon Walker's and encourages Evangelicals to engage the public square confidently. Evangelical intellectuals maintain a superior framework for social ethics; therefore, Evangelicals can boldly fulfill Paul's command to proclaim, warn, and teach everyone with all wisdom (Col 1:28).

However, Evangelicals often engage the public square using the secular world's logic and language, which presents two problems. First, the post-Christian world does not possess a vocabulary to talk about religion. So, when Evangelicals appeal to conscience concerning religious liberty, secularists do not understand the human conscience the same way. Second, when Evangelicals use the logic of the secular world, their argument is turned against them. For instance, the 1992 Supreme Court case *Planned Parenthood v. Casey* said that men and women of good conscience could disagree regarding abortion.[27] The language and logic presented in this argument assume abortion is a matter of conscience, thus rendering it the same as religious freedom. Jonathan Leeman rightly recognizes, "When you define religious freedom apart from the God of Scripture, eventually those terms will be used against the people of that God. That is the paradox of religious freedom."[28] Consequently, this book encourages Evangelicals

---

25. Ligonier Ministries, "The State of Theology."
26. Moore, *Onward*, 139.
27. Leeman, *How the Nations Rage*, 36.
28. Leeman, *How the Nations Rage*, 37.

The Superiority of an Evangelical Model of Religious Liberty

to confidently present theological arguments for religious freedom in the public domain.

Summary of Arguments

Chapter 1 introduced the purpose of this book by showing the philosophical problems in secular and Roman Catholic social ethics. The chapter began by defining religious freedom as the principle that supports the separation of church and state. The conception of separation is essential for a flourishing democracy because it maintains proper order between citizens and institutions. But this does not mean that people of faith cannot draw upon their religious convictions in the public sphere. Chapter 1 also defined the term "secular." Secular social ethics rely primarily upon autonomous reason as a grounding principle for morality. But secular frameworks cannot legitimately establish absolute universal moral norms; thus, secular social ethics are inherently unstable. I also presented Roman Catholic natural law as a better framework. But Roman Catholic natural law is inferior because it does not consider the noetic effects of the fall. Chapter 1 presented a thesis for this book: The evangelical framework for religious liberty is superior to the paradigms provided by secular philosophers John Stuart Mill and John Rawls and the Roman Catholic philosopher John Courtney Murray. The evangelical framework is superior because it recognizes a personal transcendent being, which provides principles that can balance the tensions between individualism and collectivism. Chapter 1 provided a background explaining the problem of classic liberal thought and providing a methodology relying on Oliver O'Donovan's ethical structure of self, world, and time. O'Donovan's categories provide a comprehensive device to critique secular and Christian anthropology, cosmology, and teleology. Finally, Chapter 1 provided additional background information and a general overview of the book's significant chapters.

Chapter 2 argued that John Stuart Mill's utilitarianism is insufficient to sustain religious freedom in a pluralistic society. The chapter first offered a brief biographical sketch of John Stuart Mill. I argued that Mill's atheistic upbringing preconditioned him to reject the possibility of a supernatural world. Next, the chapter offered a general critique of Mill's underlying assumptions. I argued that Mill's rejection of metaphysics resulted in several fallacies that ultimately undermine his argument for religious liberty. Chapter 2 also analyzed Mill's seminal work *On Liberty*. I attempted to

Summary Thoughts and Conclusion

prove that Mill's utilitarianism failed to present a substantive reason for elevating happiness as the highest good. Thus, Mill's framework contributed to excesses in opposite directions—radical individualism at one pole and extreme collectivism at the other. The chapter then evaluated Mill's four premises for religious freedom using the categories of self, world, and time. The chapter concluded that Mill's framework offered a thin structure for religious tolerance but could not provide enduring religious freedom. Chapter 2 also attempted to prove that Mill's harm principle created problems for religious speech, which ultimately gave way to totalitarian authority structures. Chapter 2 ended with an appreciation for Mill's intentions, but in the end, those intentions fell short of establishing an enduring paradigm for religious freedom.

Chapter 3 explored John Rawls's model for religious freedom. First, the chapter offered a brief history of John Rawls's early life. I argued that Rawls's experience in World War II significantly influenced his religious beliefs and conception of justice. Second, chapter 3 offered a critique of Rawls's original position. I attempted to prove that his notion of human agency was limited because he did not fully appreciate the role of religious, cultural, and historical influences in one's life. The chapter also explored the concept of time in one's decision-making. I contended that Rawls's original position did not correctly consider the process of human reflection and deliberation in the process of decision making. While Rawls attempted to offer a framework for procedural justice, procedural justice must work within the reality of how humans make decisions. Third, chapter 3 argued that Rawls's teleology prioritized the right over the good, resulting in restricting publicly expressed faith. Fourth, the chapter admired Rawls's attempt to preserve religious freedom, especially his theory of overlapping consensus. But chapter 3 argued that Rawls's rejection of special revelation resulted in a framework that only allows for privatized religious belief.

Chapter 4 offered a critique of John Courtney Murray's natural law framework. The chapter reflected on the Roman Catholic problem of religious freedom prior to Vatican II. It analyzed Murray's argument to his church and his argument to the broader American culture. Next, the chapter explored the epistemology and the teleology of his natural law philosophy. I attempted to prove that Roman Catholic natural law is a sound framework for religious freedom when illuminated by Scripture. But natural law cut off from divine revelation descends into naturalism. The chapter applauded Murray's desire to support religious freedom, but his epistemology and

The Superiority of an Evangelical Model of Religious Liberty

teleology were overly optimistic. Chapter 4 concluded that Murray presupposed transcendence; therefore, he should have publicly used Scripture to contend for religious freedom.

Chapter 5 presented the evangelical paradigm for religious freedom. The chapter attempted to reclaim a narrow conception by noting five essential elements of Evangelicalism. First, chapter 5 traced religious freedom throughout church history. While the term "religious freedom" is not explicitly used in Scripture, I attempted to prove that the principles supporting religious freedom were present. Second, the chapter argued that evangelical anthropology is superior because it offers a stable ontology through its doctrine of *imago Dei*. Third, chapter 5 also attempted to prove that evangelical epistemology is superior because the truths found in Scripture are accessible to all people. The regenerate and unregenerate can discern that Scripture is both reasonable and coherent. Fourth, the chapter also contended that evangelical religious freedom is teleologically superior because it provides structure and order to history. Finally, I sought to demonstrate that evangelical eschatology supports religious freedom for both the religious and irreligious because all will stand before Christ in judgment.

Lastly, chapter 6 has examined the implications of evangelical theology in the public square. The chapter calls for evangelical intellectuals to engage the public square boldly. Chapter 6 contends that an evangelical withdrawal from public engagement will only lead to further polarization on the political right and left. Chapter 6 concludes by considering further areas of research regarding religious liberty.

Further Research

On July 18, 2019, the US State Department released a statement of concern regarding technology and religious freedom.[29] The report argues that social media platforms are often used to promote hate speech, encourage radicalizing ideologies, and spread disinformation campaigns targeting religious minorities. While the State Department supports an open and secure internet, it is unclear how to maintain one's right to share sincere religious ideas without suppressing others. Evangelicals claim a particular concern regarding policing thoughts online because the internet and social media are powerful tools for world evangelism. But the internet's ubiquitous influence

---

29. Ministerial to Advance Religious Freedom, "Statement on the Use of Technology and Religious Freedom."

Summary Thoughts and Conclusion

and the rapid development of social media have surpassed much of the current research in religious liberty. Also, the removal of religious materials from distribution platforms such as Amazon targets certain religious minorities. Further exploration of how to promote the free exchange of religious ideas and prevent disinformation campaigns that harm religious minorities seems necessary.

Second, the Arab Awakening that began in 2011 is changing the face of the Middle East and North Africa.[30] James Skillen notes that Christian minorities living in these countries have not challenged the discrimination they experience from the Muslim majority until recently.[31] But now, younger Christians are rejecting passivity and are engaging in debate in the public square. Third, while religious freedom is still a contested human right within Islam, there are efforts to broaden religious freedom in Muslim nations. Abdullah Saeed argues that modernist Muslim interpreters increasingly advocate an approach toward the Qur'an and Islamic jurisprudence that would place Islam on a path toward a broader appreciation of religious freedom, including equality under the law for all religious individuals and groups.[32] Without coming to grips with the freedom of conscience, Islam cannot modernize peacefully.[33] Also, the recent influx of Muslim refugees into European democracies will not advance peacefully if Islam does not establish a framework for religious freedom. Perhaps evangelical scholarship can help to influence religious freedom within Islamic communities. But evangelical research regarding Islam's capacity for religious freedom seems limited. Interaction with the Islamic proposal for religious freedom juxtaposed with an evangelical proposal may prove helpful for Muslim refugees and evangelical missionaries.

Third, a critique of theonomy and reconstructionism may also prove helpful for Evangelicals. Pastor and scholar Greg Bahnsen uses the terms "theonomy" and "reconstruction" this way: Theonomists are committed to the *transformation* (or reconstruction) of every area of life, including the institutions and affairs of the socio-political realm, according to holy principles of God's revealed word.[34] Thus, theonomists repudiate the distinction between sacred and secular authorities. But reconstructionism presents

---

30. Skillen, *The Good of Politics*, ix.
31. Skillen, *The Good of Politics*, xi.
32. Abdullah Saeed, "Development of Religious Freedom in Islamic Thought," 5.
33. Guinness, *A Free People's Suicide*, 126.
34. Skillen, *The Scattered Voice*, 164.

The Superiority of an Evangelical Model of Religious Liberty

certain challenges and opportunities within Evangelicalism. Further scholarship critiquing principled pluralism and theonomy proposals may help protect Evangelicalism from perverted forms of Christian nationalism.

Conclusion

On January 6, 2021, Americans watched in horror as a mob of angry protestors stormed the United States Capitol Building. Many protestors carried Christian symbols and offered public prayers. Rioters smashed windows and broke down doors, and by day's end five people lost their lives. The media was quick to label the rioters as "white Evangelicals." Unfortunately, the tragedy of January 6 only served to confuse both those in and outside the evangelical world.

But the riot of January 6 was indicative of more complex problems facing our nation. At the time of this writing, America finds herself in a fragile state. Americans are increasingly polarized. Public trust in institutions has eroded, and increasingly razor-thin margins decide our elections—the middle is deteriorating. Many American Christians not only fear the loss of religious freedom, but they sense a growing hatred and contempt for their way of life.[35] And those on the political left fear the enforcement of religious liberty will close off opportunities for non-religious people.[36] Those on the political left and political right fear the nation may soon be lost if something is not done. Some Americans believe the threat of civil war is not only possible but likely if we do not turn course.[37] The riot of January 6 was driven by similar fears that sparked urban uprisings in the summer of 2020. Americans seem to have a looming sense that we are in the final days of a collapsing empire. Consequently, both sides fear we are losing our country.

Arthur John Hubbard set out to solve a significant problem: "What makes empires rise or fall?"[38] Hubbard argued that certain distinctive forces, both constructive or destructive, contributed to the rise or fall of empires.[39] He argued that it was superficial to say that the fall of empires results exclusively from luxury or decadence. Thus, Hubbard sought to discover if underlying powers lead to a nation's growth or decline. Hubbard said, "If we

---

35. French, *Divided We Fall*, 58.
36. French, *Divided We Fall*, 55.
37. French, *Divided We Fall*, 7.
38. Hubbard, *The Fate of Empires*, 40.
39. Hubbard, *The Fate of Empires*, 16.

Summary Thoughts and Conclusion

can do this successfully, we shall possess nothing less than the knowledge of good and evil in the State, and we shall be provided with an understanding of the conditions that decide between future loss of the civilization that is our heritage, and its unlimited expansion."[40] Hubbard studied the empires of Greece, Rome, and China and discovered that one animating principle was common to all. Put shortly, Hubbard found that the permanence of a civilization is based on religious motives. He contended that neither reason nor enlightened self-interest were sufficient to restrain the corrosive forces that devour social bonds. Hubbard found that only religion was adequate to encourage the positive birth rates needed to sustain a civilization. And only the power of religion was strident enough to restrain libertinism. This is not to say Hubbard contended for theonomy. But he did realize that only the power of religion can maintain a cohesive society. Therefore, he found that luxury and decadence were not the ultimate cause of a social implosion; instead, empires fall because they move away from unifying moral convictions.

I chose to write this book on religious freedom because our nation is at a crossroads. As I finish this work, I am watching the painful and humiliating withdrawal of American troops from Afghanistan. The aftermath of our retreat will likely cause further division and confusion across our nation. One would be naïve not to think that Hubbard's descriptions of collapsing empires do not define America's current state. But this does not need to be the case. A crossroad necessarily implies that we still have time to take a different path.

I wrote this book because I wanted to test the principles found within Evangelicalism. I wanted to see if one could prove Evangelicalism is the answer for our eroding republic. I wrote this book because I wanted to encourage Evangelicals to exercise boldness in defending their philosophical assumptions. I wrote to show that Evangelicalism is the best chance for America to recapture the principles that led to our ascendance. And I wrote this as a project of love. The title of this book is not meant to imply arrogance or pride. Instead, the title merely seeks to show that the evangelical framework for religious freedom is complete. The doctrines found in evangelism fill in the many gaps left by competing doctrines. Therefore, the term "superiority" is intended to describe a complete and coherent set of principles that can support freedom for all peoples.

---

40. Hubbard, *The Fate of Empires*, 17.

The Superiority of an Evangelical Model of Religious Liberty

Augustine argued that a nation is bound together by its common love. He said, "A nation is judged superior or inferior in proportion to its highest interests."[41] Modern America is an increasingly diverse nation; thus, we encounter people with many loves. Yet one love that has historically bonded Americans—the love of freedom. Americans may hold different opinions regarding the permissions allowed by freedom, but Americans have generally agreed regarding the virtue of freedom itself. Therefore, I wrote this book as an attempt to love my neighbor as myself (Lev 19:18). Because only the principles found within evangelical theology are principles that can support the freedom of all Americans; therefore, I have taken it as my task to share the tenets of Evangelicalism for the good of my neighbors and the glory of Christ.

---

41. Augustine, *The City of God*, 2:418.

Bibliography

Ahdar, Rex, and Ian Leigh. *Religious Freedom in the Liberal State*. New York: Oxford University Press, 2005.
Ahn, Ilsup. "John Stuart Mill on Utilitarianism." In *Beyond the Pale: Reading Ethics from the Margins*, edited by Stacey M. Floyd-Thomas and Miguel A. De La Torre, 81–89. Louisville: Westminster John Knox, 2011.
Alexander, Frank S., and John Witte. *Christianity and Human Rights: An Introduction*. Cambridge, UK: Cambridge University Press, 2010.
American Civil Liberties Union. "Religious Liberty." https://www.aclu.org/issues/religious-liberty.
Anderson, Matthew Lee. "The Christian Right's Democratic Virtues: An Interview with John Shields." *Mere Orthodoxy*, June 5, 2012. https://mereorthodoxy.com/democratic-virtues-christian-right-interview-jon-shields.
Anderson, Ryan T. *Truth Overruled: The Future of Marriage and Religious Freedom*. Washington, DC: Regnery Publishing, 2015.
Aquinas, Thomas. *A Summa of the Summa: The Essential Philosophical Passages of St. Thomas Aquinas' Summa Theologica*. Edited by Peter Kreeft. San Francisco: Ignatius, 1990.
———. *Summa Theologica*. Translated by Fathers of the English Dominican Province. London: Burns Oates & Washbourne, 1912.
Arbo, Matthew B. "Much More than Fairness: The Shape of Justice in the New Testament." In *John Rawls and Christian Social Engagement*, edited by Anthony B. Bradley and Greg Forster, 49–60. Lanham, MD: Lexington, 2015.
Aristotle. *The Nicomachean Ethics*. Edited by Lesley Brown and W. D. Ross. Oxford: Oxford University Press, 2009.
———. *The Politics*. Edited by Trevor J. Saunders, translated by Thomas A. Sinclair. Rev. ed. New York: Penguin Classics, 1981.
Audi, Robert, and Nicholas Wolterstorff. *Religion in the Public Square: The Place of Religious Convictions in Political Debate*. Lanham, MD: Rowman & Littlefield, 1997.

Bibliography

Augustine of Hippo. *The City of God*. Vol. 2 of *St. Augustine: The Writings against the Manicheans and against the Donatists*, edited by Philip Schaff, translated by Marcus Dods. Buffalo, NY: Christian Literature Company, 1887.

———. *On the Morals of the Catholic Church*. Vol. 4 of *St. Augustine: The Writings against the Manicheans and against the Donatists*, edited by Philip Schaff, translated by Richard Stothert. Buffalo, NY: Christian Literature Company, 1887.

———. *Political Writings*. Edited by Ernest L. Fortin and Douglas Kries, translated by Michael W. Tkacz and Douglas Kries. Indianapolis: Hackett, 1994.

Backus, Isaac. *An Appeal to the Public for Religious Liberty, Against the Oppressions of the Present Day*. Farmington Hills, MI: Gale Ecco Print Editions, 2018.

———. *A History of New England: With Particular Reference to the Denomination of Christians Called Baptist: Volumes I & II*. 2nd ed. Newton, MA: CrossReach, 2019.

Bailey, Tom, and Valentina Gentile. *Rawls and Religion*. New York: Columbia University Press, 2015.

Baker, C. Edwin. "Sandel on Rawls." *University of Pennsylvania Law Review* 133.4 (April 1985) 895–928.

Baker, Hunter. *The End of Secularism*. Wheaton, IL: Crossway, 2009.

———. *Political Thought: A Student's Guide*. Wheaton, IL: Crossway, 2012.

———. "The Secularist Biases of Rawls's 'Neutral' Roles." In *John Rawls and Christian Social Engagement*, edited by Anthony B. Bradley and Greg Forster, 91–104. Lanham, MD: Lexington, 2015.

Bantas, Hercules. *Understanding John Rawls: Justice as Fairness*. Pittsburgh, PA: Reluctant Geek, 2010.

Baptist Faith and Message 2000. "Article I: The Scriptures." https://bfm.sbc.net/bfm2000/#i.

Baranowski, Shelley. "The Primacy of Theology: Karl Barth and Socialism." *Studies in Religion/Sciences Religieuses* 10.4 (Dec 1981) 451–61.

Barbour, John D. "Review of Foundations of Religious Tolerance." *The Journal of Religion* 65.4 (Oct 1985) 570–71.

Barefoot, John Chadwick. "John Rawls' A Theory of Justice and Christian Ethics." MA thesis, Southeastern Baptist Theological Seminary, 2009.

Barth, Karl. *Community, State, and Church: Three Essays*. 1st ed. New York: Doubleday, 1960.

———. *Ethics*. Edited by Dietrich Braun, translated by Geoffrey W. Bromiley. New York: Seabury, 1981.

Bauer, Walter. *A Greek-English Lexicon of the New Testament and Other Early Christian Literature*. 3rd ed. Edited by Frederick William Danker. Chicago, IL: University of Chicago Press, 2000.

Baxter, Michael. "Murray's Mistake: The Political Divisions a Theologian Failed to Foresee." *American Magazine*, March 12, 2014. https://www.americamagazine.org/issue/murrays-mistake.

Beach, Waldo, and H. Richard Niebuhr. *Christian Ethics; Sources of the Living Tradition*. New York: The Ronald Press, 1955.

Beale, G. K. *The Book of Revelation: A Commentary on the Greek Text*. Grand Rapids: Eerdmans, 1999.

Beitzel, Barry J. "Conscience." In *Baker Encyclopedia of the Bible*, edited by Walter A. Elwell, 510. Grand Rapids: Baker, 1988.

Bibliography

Bentham, Jeremy. "Anarchical Fallacies." In *Nonsense upon Stilts: Bentham, Burke, and Marx on the Rights of Man*, edited by John Waldon, 29–46. London: Methuen and Coy Limited, 1987.

———. *Rights, Representation, and Reform: Nonsense upon Stilts and Other Writings on the French Revolution*. New York: Oxford University Press, 2002.

Bercuson, Jeffrey. *John Rawls and the History of Political Thought: The Rousseauvian and Hegelian Heritage of Justice as Fairness*. 1st ed. New York: Routledge, 2014.

Berg, Thomas C. "John Courtney Murray and Reinhold Niebuhr: Natural Law and Christian Realism." *Journal of Catholic Social Thought* 4.1 (Sept 2007) 1–21.

Berger, Peter L. *The Sacred Canopy: Elements of a Sociological Theory of Religion*. New York: Anchor, 1990.

Bevans, Stephen B. *Models of Contextual Theology*. Faith and Cultures Series. Maryknoll, NY: Orbis Books, 1992.

Boaz, David. *Libertarianism: A Primer*. New York: Free Press, 1998.

Bradley, Anthony B., and Greg Forster. *John Rawls and Christian Social Engagement: Justice as Unfairness*. Lanham, MD: Lexington, 2015.

Bratman, Michael E. "Two Problems about Human Agency." *Proceedings of the Aristotelian Society* 101 (2001) 309–26.

Brennan, William J. "Ethics as Theology: Self, World, and Time an Induction." *Trinity Journal* 21.1 (Fall 2015) 319–21.

Bresler, Kimberly A. "How the Idea of Religious Toleration Came to the West." *Theology Today* 61.3 (Oct 2004) 416–20.

Brink, David Owen. *Mill's Progressive Principles*. Oxford: Oxford University Press, 2013.

Brunner, Emil, and Karl Barth. *Natural Theology: Comprising "Nature and Grace" by Emil Brunner and the Reply "No!" by Karl Barth*. London: The Centenary Press, 1946.

Budziszewski, J. *Evangelicals in the Public Square: Four Formative Voices on Political Thought and Action*. Grand Rapids: Baker Academic, 2006.

———. *The Line Through the Heart*. Wilmington, DE: ISI Books, 2009.

———. *Written on the Heart: The Case for Natural Law*. Downers Grove: IVP Academic, 1997.

Burge, Ryan P. *The Nones: Where They Came From, Who They Are, and Where They Are Going*. Minneapolis: Fortress, 2021.

Burns, Timothy. "John Courtney Murray, Religious Liberty, and Modernity: Part I: Inalienable Natural Rights." *Logos* 17.2 (2014) 13–38.

Bykvist, Krister. *Utilitarianism: A Guide for the Perplexed*. London: Continuum, 2010.

Cadeddu, Francesca. "A Call to Action: John Courtney Murray, S.J., and the Renewal of American Democracy." *Catholic Historical Review* 101.3 (Summer 2015) 530–53.

Calvin, John. *Commentary on a Harmony of the Evangelists Matthew, Mark, and Luke*. Translated by William Pringle. Bellingham, WA: Lexham, 2010.

———. *Institutes of the Christian Religion*. Translated by Henry Beveridge. Peabody, MA: Hendrick, 1816.

———. *Institutes of the Christian Religion 1536 Edition*. Edited by Ford Lewis Battles. Grand Rapids: Eerdmans, 1995.

Carlon, Keith. "R. M. Hare and Moral Theology." *Louvain Studies* 8.1 (Summer 1980) 30–46.

Carlson, Carl Emanuel. "Need for Study of the Biblical Basis of Religious Liberty." *The Journal of Religious Thought* 16.2 (Fall 1959) 137–44.

Carson, D. A. *Christ and Culture Revisited*. Grand Rapids: Eerdmans, 2008.

Bibliography

———. *The Intolerance of Tolerance*. Grand Rapids: Eerdmans, 2012.

Carter, Stephen L. *God's Name in Vain: The Wrongs and Rights of Religion in Politics*. New York: Basic Books, 2000.

Carver, Terrell. *The Cambridge Companion to Marx*. New York: Cambridge University Press, 1991.

Cavanaugh, William T. "From One City to Two: Christian Reimagining of Political Space." *Political Theology* 7.3 (July 2006) 299–321.

———. *Migrations of the Holy: God, State, and the Political Meaning of the Church*. Grand Rapids: Eerdmans, 2011.

Cohen-Almagor, Raphael. *Speech, Media and Ethics: The Limits of Free Expression: Critical Studies on Freedom of Expression, Freedom of the Press and the Public's Right to Know*. New York: Palgrave Macmillan, 2001.

Cole, Graham. "Theological Utilitarianism and the Eclipse of the Theistic Sanction." *Tyndale Bulletin* 42.2 (Nov 1991) 226–44.

Coleman, John Aloysius. "Deprivatizing Religion and Revitalizing Citizenship." In *Religion and Contemporary Liberalism*. Edited by Paul J. Weithman, 264–90. Notre Dame, IN: University of Notre Dame, 1997.

Collins, Gary R. *Christian Counseling: A Comprehensive Guide*. 3rd ed. Nashville: Thomas Nelson, 2007.

Colson, Charles W., and Richard John Neuhaus, eds. *Evangelicals and Catholics Together: Toward a Common Mission*. Dallas: Word, 1995.

Comstock, W. Richard. "Freedom and Reason." *Union Seminary Quarterly Review* 19.2 (Jan 1964) 178–80.

Concordia Theological Seminary. "A Whole New Can of Worms: A Statement of the Faculty of Concordia Theological Seminary on Religious Liberty." *Concordia Theological Quarterly* 76.1–2 (Jan 2012) 178–81.

Coppenger, Mark T. "A Free Church in a Free State." *The Southern Baptist Journal of Theology* 11.4 (Winter 2007) 54–69.

Corvino, John, Ryan T. Anderson, and Girgis Sherif. *Debating Religious Liberty and Discrimination*. New York: Oxford University Press, 2017.

Cowling, Maurice. *Mill and Liberalism*. 2nd ed. New York: Cambridge University Press, 1963.

Cuddihy, John Murray. *No Offense: Civil Religion and Protestant Taste*. New York: Seabury, 1978.

Curran, Charles E. *American Catholic Social Ethics: Twentieth-Century Approaches*. Notre Dame, IN: University of Notre Dame Press, 1982.

D'Abrera, Bella. "Farce from the Madding Crowd." *IPA Review* 71.4 (2019) 56–61.

Dalrymple, Timothy. "If You're Selling Scorn for Conservative Christians, the Market Is Hot." *Patheos* June 11, 2012. https://www.patheos.com/blogs/philosophicalfragments/2012/06/11/if-youre-selling-scorn-for-conservative-christians-the-market-is-hot/.

Davis, Derek H. "The Enduring Legacy of Roger Williams: Consulting America's First Separationist on Today's Pressing Church-State Controversies." *Journal of Church & State* 41.2 (Spring 1999) 201.

Davis, James Calvin. *The Moral Theology of Roger Williams*. Louisville: Westminster John Knox Press, 2013.

Davis, John Jefferson. *Evangelical Ethics: Issues Facing the Church Today*. 3rd ed. Phillipsburg, NJ: P&R, 2004.

Bibliography

Dawson, Christopher. *Religion and the Rise of Western Culture*. Gifford Lectures 1948–1949. New York: Sheed & Ward, 1950.

Day, J. P. "Mill on the Moral Right to Free Expression of Thought." *Journal of Social Philosophy* 29.3 (Spring 1998) 41–45.

———. "More about Mill on Free Expression." *Journal of Social Philosophy* 31.2 (Summer 2000) 189–94.

Del Noce, Augusto. *The Crisis of Modernity*. Montreal: McGill-Queen's University Press, 2017.

Deneen, Patrick J. *Why Liberalism Failed*. New Haven: Yale University Press, 2019.

Dombrowski, Daniel A. *Rawls and Religion: The Case for Political Liberalism*. Albany: SUNY Publishing, 2001.

Doughty, Howard A. "John Rawls and The Evolution of Liberalism." *Innovation Journal* 24.3 (Summer 2019) 1–29.

Drakeman, Donald L. *Church, State, and Original Intent*. Cambridge, UK: Cambridge University Press, 2010.

Dreher, Rod. *The Benedict Option, A Strategy for Christians in a Post-Christian Nation*. New York: Penguin Random House, 2017.

Duesing, Jason G., Thomas White, and Malcolm B. Yarnell III, eds. *First Freedom: The Beginning and End of Religious Liberty*. 2nd ed. Nashville: B&H Academic, 2016.

Duke, Barrett. "The Christian Doctrine of Religious Liberty." In *First Freedom: The Baptist Perspective on Religious Liberty*, edited by Jason G. Duesing, Thomas White, and Malcolm B. Yarnell III, 7–30. 2nd ed. Nashville: B&H Academic, 2016.

Duncan, Craig, and Tibor R. Machan. *Libertarianism: For and Against*. Lanham, MD: Rowman & Littlefield, 2005.

Dworkin, Ronald. *Religion without God*. 1st ed. Cambridge, MA: Harvard University Press, 2013.

Easton, Burton Scott. "Authority and Liberty in the New Testament." *Anglican Theological Review* 35.3 (July 1953) 166–73.

Eberle, Christopher J. *Religious Conviction in Liberal Politics*. Cambridge, UK: Cambridge University Press, 2002.

Eberstadt, Mary. *How the West Really Lost God: A New Theory of Secularization*. West Conshohocken, PA: Templeton, 2013.

———. *It's Dangerous to Believe: Religious Freedom and Its Enemies*. New York: Harper, 2016.

Edwards, Jonathan. *The End for Which God Created the World: Updated to Modern English*. Edited by Jason Dollar. CreateSpace Independent Platform, 2014.

Erickson, Millard J., and L. Arnold Hustad. *Introducing Christian Doctrine*. 3rd ed. Grand Rapids: Baker Academic, 2015.

Ernst, James Emanuel. *The Political Thought of Roger Williams*. Long Island: Kennikat, 1966.

Evans, Jeremy A., and Daniel R. Heimbach. *Taking Christian Moral Thought Seriously: The Legitimacy of Religious Beliefs in the Marketplace of Ideas*. B&H Studies in Christian Ethics. Nashville: B&H Academic, 2011.

Farrow, Douglas. *Desiring a Better Country: Forays in Political Theology*. Montreal: McGill-Queen's University Press, 2015.

Feinberg, Joel. *Offense to Others*. Vol. 2 of *The Moral Limits of the Criminal Law*. New York: Oxford University Press, 1985.

Bibliography

Ferguson, Thomas P. *Catholic and American: The Political Theology of John Courtney Murray*. Kansas City, MO: Sheed & Ward, 1993.

Finnis, John. *Moral Absolutes: Tradition, Revision, and Truth*. The Michael J. McGivney Lectures of the John Paul II Institute for Studies on Marriage and Family. Washington, DC: Catholic University of America Press, 1991.

———. *Natural Law and Natural Rights*. 2nd ed. Clarendon Law Series. Oxford: Oxford University Press, 2011.

Fleming, Theodore B. "Mill and Liberalism." *American Political Science Review* 59.2 (June 1965) 466.

Forster, Greg. *The Contested Public Square: The Crisis of Christianity and Politics*. Downers Grove: IVP Academic, 2008.

———. *John Locke's Politics of Moral Consensus*. Cambridge, UK: Cambridge University Press, 2005.

Forte, David F., Matthew Spalding, and Edwin Meese III, eds. *The Heritage Guide to the Constitution*. 2nd ed. New York: Heritage Foundation, 2014.

Foss, Jerome C. "The Hidden Influence of John Rawls on the American Mind." *First Things* 61 (2016) 1–15.

———. "John Rawls: A Theorist of Modern Liberalism." *First Principles* 12 (Aug 2014) 1–9.

Foster, Michael Beresford. *The Political Philosophies of Plato and Hegel*. West Grove, TX: Russell & Russell, 1965.

Frame, John M. *The Doctrine of the Christian Life*. Phillipsburg, NJ: P&R, 2008.

———. *The Doctrine of God*. Phillipsburg, NJ: P&R, 2002.

Franck, Matthew J. "Two Tales of Freedom: Getting the Origins of Religious Liberty Right Matters." *Touchstone* 29.4 (July 2016) 19–26.

Franke, Katherine. "Religious Freedom for Me, but Not for Thee." *The Washington Post*, September 28, 2018. https://www.washingtonpost.com/opinions/religious-freedom-for-me-but-not-for-thee/2018/09/28/297fffb4-c340-11e8-8f06-009b39c3f6dd_story.html.

French, David A. *Divided We Fall: America's Secession Threat and How to Restore Our Nation*. New York: St. Martin's, 2020.

Galston, William A. "Liberal Pluralism and Civic Goods." *Liberal Pluralism* 112.3 (Jan 2002) 124.

———. *Liberal Purposes: Goods, Virtues, and Diversity in the Liberal State*. Cambridge, UK: Cambridge University Press, 1876.

Gauss, Gerald F. "The Convergence of Rights and Utility: The Case of Rawls and Mill." *Ethics* 92.1 (Oct 1981) 57–72.

Gaustad, Edwin S. *Roger Williams: Prophet of Liberty*. New York: Oxford University Press, 2001.

George, Robert P. *Clash of Orthodoxies: Law, Religion, and Morality in Crisis*. Wilmington, DE: ISI Books, 2001.

———. *Making Men Moral: Civil Liberties and Public Morality*. Oxford: Clarendon, 1993.

———. "Religious Freedom & Why It Matters." *Touchstone* 27.3 (Spring 2014) 22–29.

George, Robert P., and Mary Ann Glendon. *Conscience and Its Enemies: Confronting the Dogmas of Liberal Secularism*. 1st ed. Wilmington, DE: Intercollegiate Studies Institute, 2016.

Gewirth, Alan. *Political Philosophy*. London: MacMillian, 1965.

Bibliography

Gill, Anthony James. *The Political Origins of Religious Liberty*. Cambridge Studies in Social Theory, Religion, and Politics. Cambridge, UK: Cambridge University Press, 2008.

Gilpin, W. Clark. "Building the 'Wall of Separation': Construction Zone for Historians." *Church History* 79.4 (Dec 2010) 871–80.

Glendon, Mary Ann. *A World Made New: Eleanor Roosevelt and the Universal Declaration of Human Rights*. New York: Random House, 2001.

Goerner, E. A. *Peter and Caesar: The Catholic Church and Political Authority*. New York: Herder and Herder, 1965.

Gonzalez, Mike. *The Plot to Change America: How Identity Politics Is Dividing the Land of the Free*. New York: Encounter Books, 2020.

Goodin, Robert E. *Political Theory and Public Policy*. Chicago: University of Chicago Press, 1982.

Goodrich, Luke. *Free to Believe: The Battle over Religious Liberty in America*. Colorado Springs: Multnomah, 2019.

Grabill, Stephen J. *Rediscovering the Natural Law in Reformed Theological Ethics*. Grand Rapids: Eerdmans, 2006.

Graham, George Adams. *Morality in American Politics*. New York: Random House, 1952.

Graham, Paul. *Rawls: A Beginner's Guide*. London: One World Publications, 2007.

Gregg, Samuel. "John Stuart Mill's Intolerant Faith and the Religion of Liberalism." *Public Discourse*, June 19, 2017. https://www.thepublicdiscourse.com/2017/06/19529/.

———. *On Ordered Liberty: A Treatise on the Free Society*. Lanham, MD: Lexington Books, 2003.

Gregory, Brad S. *The Unintended Reformation: How a Religious Revolution Secularized Society*. Cambridge, MA: Belknap Press, 2012.

Greidanus, Sidney. "Human Rights in Biblical Perspective." *Calvin Theological Journal* 19.1 (April 1984) 5–31.

Grönebaum, Melissa. *John Rawls' Theory of Justice. Justice as Fairness*. Munich: GRIN Verlag, 2014.

Grudem, Wayne A. *Politics According to the Bible: A Comprehensive Resource for Understanding Modern Political Issues in Light of Scripture*. Grand Rapids: Zondervan, 2010.

———. *Systematic Theology: An Introduction to Biblical Doctrine*. Grand Rapids: Zondervan, 1994.

Guinness, Os. *The Case for Civility: And Why Our Future Depends on It*. New York: Harper Collins, 2008.

———. *A Free People's Suicide: Sustainable Freedom and the American Future*. Downers Grove: IVP Books, 2012.

———. *The Global Public Square: Religious Freedom and the Making of a World Safe for Diversity*. Downers Grove: IVP Books, 2013.

Gunn, T. Jeremy, and John Witte. *No Establishment of Religion: America's Original Contribution to Religious Liberty*. Oxford: Oxford University Press, 2013.

Gushee, David P. *The Sacredness of Human Life: Why an Ancient Biblical Vision Is Key to the World's Future*. Grand Rapids: Eerdmans, 2013.

Guterres, António. "United Nations Strategy and Plan of Action on Hate Speech." *United Nations*, May 2019. https://www.un.org/en/genocideprevention/hate-speech-strategy.shtml.

Guzman, Ralph C., James H. Sutton, and Sylvia Leal Carvajal. *The Mexican-American People: The Nation's Second Largest Minority*. New York: Free Press, 1970.

Bibliography

Hall, Timothy L. *Separating Church and State: Roger Williams and Religious Liberty.* Champaign, IL: University of Illinois Press, 1998.

Hamburger, Philip. *Separation of Church and State.* Cambridge, MA: Harvard University Press, 2002.

Hamilton, Alexander, James Madison, John Jay, and Terence Ball. *The Federalist: With Letters of Brutus.* Cambridge Texts in the History of Political Thought. Cambridge, UK: Cambridge University Press, 2003.

Hankins, Barry. *Francis Schaeffer and the Shaping of Evangelical America.* Library of Religious Biography. Grand Rapids: Eerdmans, 2008.

Hare, R. M. *Essays on Religion and Education.* Oxford: Clarendon, 1992.

———. *Freedom and Reason.* Oxford: Oxford University Press, 1977.

———. *The Language of Morals.* Oxford: Oxford University Press, 1991.

Hauerwas, Stanley. *After Christendom?: How the Church Is to Behave If Freedom, Justice, and a Christian Nation Are Bad Ideas.* Nashville: Abingdon Press, 1991.

———. *The Peaceable Kingdom: A Primer in Christian Ethics.* Notre Dame, IN: University of Notre Dame Press, 1983.

Hauerwas, Stanley, and William H. Willimon. *Resident Aliens: Life in the Christian Colony.* Nashville: Abingdon, 2014.

Hegel, Georg Wilhelm Friedrich, and Stephen Houlgate. *Outlines of the Philosophy of Right.* Oxford World's Classics. Oxford: Oxford University Press, 2008.

Heimbach, Daniel R. "Contrasting Views of Religious Liberty: Clarifying the Relationship Between Responsible Government and the Freedom of Religion." *Journal of Law and Religion* 11.2 (1994–95) 715–31.

———. "Natural Law in the Public Square." *Liberty University Law Review* 2.3 (Spring 2008) 685–702.

———. *True Sexual Morality: Recovering Biblical Standards for a Culture in Crisis.* Wheaton, IL: Crossway, 2004.

———. "Understanding the Difference between Religious Liberty and Religious Autonomy." In *First Freedom: The Baptist Perspective on Religious Liberty*, edited by Jason G. Duesing, Thomas White, and Malcolm B. Yarnell III, 125–42. 2nd ed. Nashville: B&H Academic, 2016.

Henry, Carl F. H. *Aspects of Christian Social Ethics.* Grand Rapids: Baker Academic, 1964.

———. *The Christian Mindset in a Secular Society.* Portland: Multnomah Press, 1984.

———. *Christian Personal Ethics.* Grand Rapids: Eerdmans, 1957.

———. "Dare We Renew the Controversy? Part II: The Fundamentalist Reaction." *Christianity Today*, June 24, 1957.

———. *Evangelical Responsibility in Contemporary Theology.* Grand Rapids: Eerdmans, 1957.

———. *God, Revelation, and Authority.* 6 vols. Wheaton, IL: Crossway, 1999.

———. *Has Democracy Had Its Day?* 2nd ed. Nashville: Leland House, 2019.

———. *A Plea for Evangelical Demonstration.* Grand Rapids: Baker, 1971.

———. *Toward a Recovery of Christian Belief: The Rutherford Lectures.* Wheaton, IL: Crossway, 1990.

———. *The Uneasy Conscience of Modern Fundamentalism.* Grand Rapids: Eerdmans, 2003.

Hertzke, Allen D., and Timothy Samuel Shah, eds. *Contemporary Perspectives.* Vol. 2 of *Christianity and Freedom.* New York: Cambridge University Press, 2016.

Bibliography

Hinson, E. Glenn. *Religious Liberty: The Christian Roots of Our Fundamental Freedoms.* Louisville: Glad River Pub, 1991.

———. *Soul Liberty: The Doctrine of Religious Liberty.* Cambridge, MA: Convention, 1975.

Hobbes, Thomas, and C. B. MacPherson. *Leviathan.* 4th ed. New York: Penguin Classics, 1982.

Hoekema, Anthony A. *Created in God's Image.* Grand Rapids: Eerdmans, 1986.

Hooper, J. Leon. "John Courtney Murray, SJ (1904–67) Working with God." *Theology Today* 62.3 (2005) 342–51.

Houlgate, Laurence. *Understanding Immanuel Kant: The Smart Student's Guide to Grounding for the Metaphysics of Morals.* San Luis Obispo, CA: Houlgate Books, 2018.

———. *Understanding John Locke: The Smart Student's Guide to Locke's Second Treatise of Government.* San Luis Obispo, CA: Houlgate Books, 2018.

———. *Understanding John Stuart Mill: The Smart Student's Guide to Utilitarianism and on Liberty.* San Luis Obispo, CA: Houlgate Books, 2018.

Hubbard, Arthur John. "The Fate of Empires." *Charity Organ. Review* 34.199 (1913) 40–42.

———. *The Fate of Empires: Being an Inquiry into the Stability of Civilization.* London: Pantianos Classics, 2018.

Hughey, John David Jr. "The Theological Frame of Religious Liberty." *The Christian Century* 80.45 (Nov 1963) 1365–68.

Hunter, James Davison, and Os Guinness. *Articles of Faith, Articles of Peace: The Religious Liberty Clauses and the American Public Philosophy.* Washington, DC: Brookings Institution, 1990.

Hurst, James Willard. "Justice Oliver Wendell Holmes and Utilitarian Jurisprudence (Book Review)." *American Historical Review* 92.1 (Feb 1987) 218.

Hutchens, S. M. "Toleration & Divine Forbearance." *Touchstone: A Journal of Mere Christianity* 29.4 (Summer 2016) 33–36.

Hutson, James H., ed. *Religion and the New Republic: Faith in the Founding of America.* Lanham, MD: Rowman & Littlefield, 2000.

Insole, Christopher J. "Kant on Christianity, Religion and Politics: Three Hopes, Three Limits." *Studies in Christian Ethics* 29.1 (Feb 2016) 14–33.

International Mission Board. "Engineering: A Guide for IMB Students." https://www.imb.org/students/wp-content/uploads/sites/4/2020/10/Engineering-Roadmap.pdf.

Irenaeus of Lyons. *Irenaeus against Heresies.* Edited by Alexander Roberts, James Donaldson, and A. Cleveland Coxe. Buffalo, NY: Christian Literature Company, n.d.

Jacobson, Daniel. "Mill on Liberty, Speech, and the Free Society." *Philosophy & Public Affairs* 29.3 (Fall 2000) 276.

———. "Mill's Progressive Principles." *Ethics* 126.1 (Oct 2015) 204–10.

———. "Utilitarianism without Consequentialism: The Case of John Stuart Mill." *Philosophical Review* 117.2 (April 2008) 159–91.

Jefferson, Thomas. *Thomas Jefferson, Political Writings.* Cambridge, UK: Cambridge University Press, 1999.

Jones, David W. "Evangelical Ethics: Issues Facing the Church Today." *Faith and Mission* 22.1 (Fall 2004) 120–22.

Jones, Donald G. *Private and Public Ethics: Tensions between Conscience and Institutional Responsibility.* Lewiston, NY: E. Mellen, 1978.

Bibliography

Kant, Immanuel. *Complete Works of Immanuel Kant*. London: Minerva Classics, 2013.

———. *Critique of Practical Reason*. Translated by Werner S. Pluhar. Indianapolis: Hackett, 2002.

———. *Grounding for the Metaphysics of Morals: With On a Supposed Right to Lie Because of Philanthropic Concerns*. Translated by James W. Ellington. 3rd ed. Indianapolis: Hackett, 1993.

Kant, Immanuel, and Werner S. Pluhar. *Religion within the Bounds of Bare Reason*. Indianapolis: Hackett, 2009.

Kao, Grace. *Grounding Human Rights in a Pluralist World*. Advancing Human Rights. Washington, DC: Georgetown University Press, 2011.

Kemeny, Paul Charles, ed. *Church, State and Public Justice: Five Views*. Downers Grove: IVP Academic, 2007.

Kilner, John Frederic. *Why People Matter: A Christian Engagement with Rival Views of Human Significance*. Grand Rapids: Baker Academic, 2017.

Kim, Uichol. *Individualism and Collectivism: A Psychological, Cultural and Ecological Analysis*. NIAS Reports. Copenhagen: NIAS, 1995.

Kirsch, Thomas G., and Bertram Turner. *Permutations of Order: Religion and Law as Contested Sovereignties*. Law, Justice, and Power. Farnham, UK: Routledge, 2009.

Kreeft, Peter. *A Shorter Summa: The Most Essential Philosophical Passages of St. Thomas Aquinas' Summa Theologica*. San Francisco, CA: Ignatius, 1993.

Ladd, George Eldon. *The Gospel of the Kingdom: Scriptural Studies in the Kingdom of God*. Grand Rapids: Eerdmans, 1959.

Land, Richard. "Free Exercise Issues in Supreme Court Decisions During the 1990s." *Southwestern Journal of Theology* 41.3 (Summer 1999) 92–106.

———. "Personal Prejudice and the Workplace." *Campaigns & Elections (1996)* 28.1 (Jan 2007) 70.

Larsen, Timothy. *John Stuart Mill: A Secular Life*. Spiritual Lives. Oxford: Oxford University, 2018.

Leeman, Jonathan. *How the Nations Rage: Rethinking Faith and Politics in a Divided Age*. Nashville: Thomas Nelson, 2018.

———. *Political Church: The Local Assembly as Embassy of Christ's Rule*. Downers Grove: IVP Academic, 2016.

Leithart, Peter J. *Defending Constantine: The Twilight of an Empire and the Dawn of Christendom*. Downers Grove: IVP Academic, 2010.

Leland, John. *The Writings of the Late Elder John Leland: Including Some Events in His Life*. Edited by L. F. Greene. Indianapolis: Scholar's Choice, 2015.

Lenin, Vladimir. *Collected Works of Vladimir Lenin*. Vol. 3. Translated by Julius Katzer. Moscow: Progress, 1966.

Lennox, Stephen J. *Proverbs: A Bible Commentary in the Wesleyan Tradition*. Indianapolis: Wesleyan University Press, 1998.

Lewis, Thomas A. *Religion, Modernity, and Politics in Hegel*. Oxford: Oxford University Press, 2011.

Liederbach, Mark. "The Religious and Moral Conscience: An Ethical Analysis of Bernard Häring and Helmut Thielicke." PhD diss., University of Virginia, 2000.

Ligonier Ministries. "The State of Theology." https://thestateoftheology.com/.

Locke, John, and Henry Morley. *Two Treatises of Government and A Letter Concerning Toleration*. Overland Park, KS: Digireads.com, 2015.

Bibliography

Loconte, Joe. "Faith and the Founding: The Influence of Religion on the Politics of James Madison." *Journal of Church and State* 45.4 (Fall 2003) 699–715.

———. *God, Locke, and Liberty: The Struggle for Religious Freedom in the West*. Lanham, MD: Lexington Books, 2014.

Long, Carolyn Nestor. *Religious Freedom and Indian Rights: The Case of Oregon v. Smith / Carolyn N. Long*. Landmark Law Cases & American Society. Kansas City, MO: University of Kansas Press, 2000.

Love, Thomas T. *John Courtney Murray: Contemporary Church-State Theory*. Garden City, NY: Doubleday, 1965.

Lovett, Frank. *Rawls' A Theory of Justice*. New York: Continuum International Group, 2011.

Lovin, Robin W. *Christian Faith and Public Choices: The Social Ethics of Barth, Brunner, and Bonhoeffer*. Minneapolis: Fortress, 1984.

Luther, Martin. *Luther's Works*. 55 vols. Edited by Jaroslav Jan Pelikan, Hilton C. Oswald, and Helmut T. Lehmann. Philadelphia: Fortress, 1999.

Luther, Martin, and John Calvin. *Luther and Calvin on Secular Authority*. Edited by Harro Höpfl. Cambridge Texts on the History of Political Thought. Cambridge, UK: Cambridge University Press, 1991.

Machan, Tibor R. *The Libertarian Alternative: Essays in Social and Political Philosophy*. Chicago: Nelson-Hall, 1974.

MacIntyre, Alasdair C. *After Virtue: A Study in Moral Theory*. Notre Dame, IN: University of Notre Dame Press, 1980.

———. *Marxism and Christianity*. New York: Schocken Books, 1968.

———. *Whose Justice? Which Rationality?* Notre Dame, IN: University of Notre Dame Press, 1988.

Maclure, Jocelyn, and Charles Taylor. *Secularism and Freedom of Conscience*. Translated by Jane Marie Todd. Cambridge, MA: Harvard University Press, 2011.

Madison, James. *Memorial and Remonstrance against Religious Assessments*. Early American Imprints, 2nd series, no. 48557. Boston: Lincoln & Edmands, 1819.

Markus, Robert A. *Christianity and the Secular*. Blessed Pope John XXIII Lecture Series in Theology and Culture. Notre Dame, IN: University of Notre Dame, 2006.

Marsden, George M. *Understanding Fundamentalism and Evangelicalism*. Grand Rapids: Eerdmans, 1990.

Marshall, John. *John Locke: Resistance, Religion, and Responsibility*. Cambridge, UK: Cambridge University Press, 1994.

Mathewes-Green, Frederica. "Loving the Storm-Drenched." *Christianity Today* 50.3 (March 2006) 36.

McCracken, Victor. "In Defense of Restraint: Democratic Respect, Public Justification, and Religious Conviction in Liberal Politics." *Journal of the Society of Christian Ethics* 32.1 (Spring–Summer 2012) 133–49.

Mill, John Stuart. *The Complete Works of John Stuart Mill*. Edited by W. L. Courtney. Middletown, DE: Dorrance Publishing Co., 1901.

———. *John Stuart Mill Autobiography*. London: Penguin Classics, 1989.

———. *Newspaper Writings*. Vol. XXII. Toronto: University of Toronto Press, 1986.

———. *On Liberty, Considerations on Representative Government*. Edited by R. B. McCallum. Oxford: Oxford University Press, 1946.

———. *On Liberty, Utilitarianism and Other Essays*. Edited by Mark Philp and Frederick Rosen. 2nd ed. Oxford: Oxford University Press, 2015.

Bibliography

Miller, Dale E. *J. S. Mill: Moral, Social and Political Thought*. Classic Thinkers. New York: Polity Press, 2010.

Ministerial to Advance Religious Freedom. "Statement on the Use of Technology and Religious Freedom." *US State Department*. July 18, 2019. https://www.state.gov/statement-on-the-use-of-technology-and-religious-freedom/.

Moltmann, Jürgen. *On Human Dignity: Political Theology and Ethics*. Philadelphia: Fortress, 1984.

Moore, Russell. *The Kingdom of Christ: The New Evangelical Perspective*. Wheaton, IL: Crossway, 2004.

———. *Onward: Engaging the Culture without Losing the Gospel*. Nashville: B&H, 2015.

Moore, Russell, and Andrew T. Walker. *The Gospel and Religious Liberty*. The Gospel for Life. Nashville: B&H, 2016.

Morsink, Johannes. *The Universal Declaration of Human Rights and the Challenge of Religion*. Columbia, MO: University of Missouri, 2017.

Moser, Mary Theresa. "Revising the Constitution? The Problem of Religious Freedom." *Journal of Religious Ethics* 16.2 (Fall 1988) 325.

Murray, Douglas. *The Madness of Crowds: Gender, Race and Identity*. London: Bloomsbury Continuum, 2019.

Murray, John Courtney. *Bridging the Sacred and the Secular: Selected Writings of John Courtney Murray*. Moral Traditions & Moral Arguments. Washington, DC: Georgetown University Press, 1994.

———. "Contemporary Orientations of Catholic Thought on Church and State in the Light of History." *Theological Studies* 10.2 (Nov 1949) 15–55.

———. *The Problem of Religious Freedom*. Westminster, MD: Newman, 1965.

———. "The Vatican Declaration on Religious Freedom." In *The University in the American Experience*. Edited by Leo McLaughlin, John Courtney Murray, and Pedro Arrupe, 3–16. New York: Fordham University Press, 1966.

———. *We Hold These Truths: Catholic Reflections on the American Proposition*. Lanham, MD: Rowman & Littlefield, 1960.

Murray, John Courtney, and J. Leon Hooper. *Religious Liberty: Catholic Struggles with Pluralism*. 1st ed. Library of Theological Ethics. Louisville: Westminster John Knox, 1993.

Murray, John Courtney, and D. Thomas Hughson. *Matthias Scheeben on Faith: The Doctoral Dissertation of John Courtney Murray*. Toronto Studies in Theology 29. Lewiston, NY: E. Mellen, 1987.

Naselli, David, and J. D. Crowley. *Conscience: What Is It, How to Train It, and Loving Those Who Differ*. Wheaton, IL: Crossway, 2016.

Neuhaus, Richard John. *The Naked Public Square: Religion and Democracy in America*. 2nd ed. Grand Rapids: Eerdmans, 1988.

Newman, Jay. *Foundations of Religious Tolerance*. Toronto: University of Toronto Press, 2019.

Niebuhr, Reinhold. *Christian Realism and Political Problems*. New York: Scribner, 1953.

———. *Christianity and Power Politics*. New York: Scribner, 1946.

———. *Does Civilization Need Religion?: A Study in the Social Resources and Limitations of Religion in Modern Life*. New York: Macmillan, 1927.

———. *Faith and Politics: A Commentary on Religious, Social, and Political Thought in a Technological Age*. New York: G. Braziller, 1968.

Bibliography

———. *Moral Man and Immoral Society: A Study in Ethics and Politics*. The Scribner Library 28. New York: Scribner, 1953.

———. *The Nature and Destiny of Man: A Christian Interpretation*. Gifford Lectures. New York: Scribner, 1941.

Nock, Albert Jay. *On Doing the Right Thing*. Auburn, AL: Ludwig von Mises Institute, 2011.

Noll, Mark A., David W. Bebbington, and George M. Marsden. *Evangelicals: Who They Have Been, Are Now, and Could Be*. Grand Rapids: Eerdmans, 2019.

Norman, Stan. *The Mission of Today's Church: Baptist Leaders Look at Modern Faith Issues*. Nashville: Broadman & Holman, 2007.

Nozick, Robert. *Anarchy, State, and Utopia*. New York: Basic Books, 2013.

Nussbaum, Martha Craven. *Liberty of Conscience: In Defense of America's Tradition of Religious Equality*. New York: Basic Books, 2008.

O'Donovan, Oliver. *Common Objects of Love: Moral Reflection and the Shaping of Community*. The 2001 Stob Lectures. Grand Rapids: Eerdmans, 2001.

———. *The Desire of the Nations: Rediscovering the Roots of Political Theology*. Cambridge, UK: Cambridge University Press, 1996.

———. *Entering into Rest*. Vol. 3 of *Ethics as Theology*. Grand Rapids: Eerdmans, 2017.

———. *Finding and Seeking*. Vol. 2 of *Ethics as Theology*. Grand Rapids: Eerdmans, 2014.

———. *Resurrection and Moral Order: An Outline for Evangelical Ethics*. Downers Grove: InterVarsity, 1986.

———. *Self, World, and Time*. Vol. 1 of *Ethics as Theology*. Grand Rapids: Eerdmans, 2013.

———. *The Ways of Judgment*. Grand Rapids: Eerdmans, 2005.

O'Donovan, Oliver, and Joan Lockwood O'Donovan. *From Irenaeus to Grotius: A Sourcebook in Christian Political Thought, 100–1625*. Grand Rapids: Eerdmans, 1999.

Outka, Gene H, and John P. Reeder, eds. *Religion and Morality: A Collection of Essays*. Garden City, NY: Doubleday, 1973.

Owens, Waylan. "The Divided States of America?: What Liberals and Conservatives Are Missing in the God-and-Country Shouting Match." *Southwestern Journal of Theology* 52.2 (Spring 2010) 269–71.

Packer, J. I. *Concise Theology: A Guide to Historic Christian Beliefs*. Wheaton, IL: Tyndale House, 1993.

Palmer, Tom G. *Learning about Liberty, The Cato University Study Guide*. Washington, DC: Cato Institute, 1997.

Pangle, Thomas L. *The Spirit of Modern Republicanism: The Moral Vision of the American Founders and the Philosophy of Locke*. Chicago: University of Chicago Press, 1988.

Parks, Matthew. "Can Human Beings Have Intrinsic Dignity or Equality without God?" In *John Rawls and Christian Social Engagement*, edited by Anthony B. Bradley and Greg Forster, 75–90. Lanham, MD: Lexington, 2015.

Patrick, Tom. *An Analysis of John Stuart Mill's Utilitarianism*. 1st ed. London: Macat Library, 2017.

Pelotte, Donald E. *John Courtney Murray: Theologian in Conflict*. New York: Paulist, 1976.

Perry, Michael J. *Love and Power: The Role of Religion and Morality in American Politics*. Oxford: Oxford University Press, 1991.

Pierce, Claude Anthony. *Conscience in the New Testament: A Study of Syneidesis in the New Testament*. London: SCM, 1955.

Bibliography

Piper, John, and Jonathan Edwards. *God's Passion for His Glory: Living the Vision of Jonathan Edwards*. Wheaton, IL: Crossway, 2006.

Plessis, Georgia. "The Legitimacy of Using the Harm Principle in Cases of Religious Freedom within Education." *Human Rights Review* 17.3 (Sept 2016) 349–70.

Pogge, Thomas. *John Rawls, His Life and Theory of Justice*. New York: Oxford University Press, 2007.

Pohl, Lucas. "Hegel and the Shadow of Materialist Geographies." *ACME: An International E-Journal for Critical Geographies* 18.2 (April 2019) 285.

Pohlman, H. L. *Justice Oliver Wendell Holmes and Utilitarian Jurisprudence*. Boston: Harvard University Press, 2013.

Porter, Jean. *Natural and Divine Law: Reclaiming the Tradition for Christian Ethics*. Grand Rapids: Eerdmans, 1999.

Powell, Jim. "John Locke: Natural Rights to Life, Liberty, and Property." *Cato Institute*, August 1, 1996. https://www.libertarianism.org/publications/essays/john-locke-natural-rights-life-liberty-property.

Rae, Scott. *Doing the Right Thing: Making Moral Choices in a World Full of Options*. Grand Rapids: Zondervan, 2013.

Ratzinger, Cardinal Joseph. *Western Culture Today and Tomorrow: Addressing the Fundamental Issues*. San Francisco: Ignatius, 2019.

Rawls, John. *John Rawls, A Brief Inquiry into the Meaning of Sin and Faith*. Edited by Thomas Nagel. Cambridge, MA: Harvard University Press, 2009.

———. *Justice as Fairness: A Restatement*. Cambridge, MA: Harvard University Press, 2001.

———. *The Law of Peoples: With "The Idea of Public Reason Revisited."* Cambridge, MA: Harvard University Press, 2001.

———. *Lectures on the History of Moral Philosophy*. Edited by Barbara Herman. Cambridge, MA: Harvard University Press, 2000.

———. *Political Liberalism*. Columbia Classics in Philosophy. New York: Columbia University Press, 2005.

———. *A Theory of Justice*. Cambridge, MA: Harvard University Press, 1971.

———. *A Theory of Justice*. Rev. ed. Cambridge, MA: The Belknap Press, 1999.

Rawls, John, and Thomas Nagel. *A Brief Inquiry into the Meaning of Sin and Faith*. Cambridge, MA: Harvard University Press, 2009.

Redding, Paul, and Paolo Diego Bubbio. *Religion After Kant: God and Culture in the Idealist Era*. Tyne, UK: Cambridge Scholars Publishing, 2012.

Regan, Richard J. *American Pluralism and the Catholic Conscience*. New York: Macmillan, 1963.

———. *The Moral Dimensions of Politics*. New York: Oxford University Press, 1986.

Rouner, Leroy S., ed. *Civil Religion and Political Theology*. Notre Dame, IN: University of Notre Dame Press, 1986.

Saeed, Abdullah. "Development of Religious Freedom in Islamic Thought." In *Islam and Religious Freedom: A Sourcebook of Scriptural, Theological and Legal Texts*, edited by Matthew Anderson and Karen Taliaferro, 5–6. Washington, DC: Georgetown University Press.

Sandel, Michael J. *Liberalism and the Limits of Justice*. 2nd ed. Cambridge, UK: Cambridge University Press, 1998.

Sayers, Dorothy L. *The Mind of a Maker*. London: Mowbray, 1994.

Schaeffer, Francis A. *Back to Freedom and Dignity*. Downers Grove: InterVarsity, 1972.

Bibliography

———. *A Christian Manifesto*. Wheaton, IL: Crossway, 1981.

———. *How Should We Then Live?: The Rise and Decline of Western Thought and Culture*. Old Tappan, NJ: F. H. Revell Co., 1976.

Schaeffer, Francis A., Lane T. Dennis, and J. I. Packer. *The Francis A. Schaeffer Trilogy: Three Essential Books in One Volume*. 1st ed. Wheaton, IL: Crossway, 1990.

Schreiner, Thomas R. *Romans*. Baker Exegetical Commentary on the New Testament. Grand Rapids: Baker, 1998.

Scribner, Todd. *A Partisan Church*. Washington, DC: Catholic University of America Press, 2015.

Seltser, Barry Jay. *The Principles and Practice of Political Compromise: A Case Study of the United States Senate*. Studies in American Religion 12. Lewiston, NY: E. Mellen, 1984.

Shah, Timothy Samuel, ed. *Historical Perspectives*. Vol. 1 of *Christianity and Freedom*. New York: Cambridge University Press, 2016.

Shaw, Timothy, Matthew J. Franck, and Thomas F. Farr. *Religious Freedom: Why Now? Defending and Embattled Human Right*. Princeton, NJ: The Witherspoon Institute, 2012.

Shepherd, Frederick M. *Christianity and Human Rights: Christians and the Struggle for Global Justice*. Lanham, MD: Lexington, 2009.

Shriver, Donald W. *An Ethic for Enemies: Forgiveness in Politics*. New York: Oxford University Press, 1998.

Sidgwick, Henry, and Marcus G. Singer. *Essays on Ethics and Method*. British Moral Philosophers. Oxford: Clarendon, 2000.

Simpson, Robert Mark. *Harm and Responsibility in Hate Speech: The Legal Restriction of Hate Speech*. Oxford: Oxford University Press, 2013.

Singer, Peter. *Animal Liberation*. 2nd ed. New York: New York Review of Books, 1990.

———. "The Use and Abuse of Religious Freedom." *Ethical Perspectives: Journal of the European Ethics Network* 20.1 (Mar 2013) 187–89.

Skillen, James W. *The Good of Politics: A Biblical, Historical, and Contemporary Introduction*. Grand Rapids: Baker Academic, 2014.

———. *The Scattered Voice: Christians at Odds in the Public Square*. 1st ed. Edmonton: Canadian Institute for Law, Theology & Public Policy, Inc., 1996.

Smith, Christian. *Atheist Overreach: What Atheism Can't Deliver*. New York: Oxford University Press, 2019.

Smith, Gary Scott, ed. *God and Politics: Four Views on the Reformation of Civil Government: Theonomy, Principled Pluralism, Christian America, National Confessionalism*. Phillipsburg, NJ: P&R, 1989.

Smith, James K. A. *Holdings: Awaiting the King*. Grand Rapids: Baker Academic, 2017.

Smith, Steven D. *The Rise and Decline of American Religious Freedom*. Cambridge, MA: Harvard University Press, 2014.

Strange, Sammie Pedlow. "Baptists and Religious Liberty: 1700–1900." PhD diss., The Southern Baptist Theological Seminary, 2006.

Strauss, Leo, and Joseph Cropsey, eds. *History of Political Philosophy*. 3rd ed. Chicago: University of Chicago Press, 1987.

Sullivan, Andrew. *The Conservative Soul: How We Lost It, How to Get It Back*. New York: HarperCollins, 2006.

Taylor, Bernard A., John A. L. Lee, Peter R. Burton, and Richard E. Whitaker, eds. *Biblical Greek Language and Lexicography: Essays in Honor of Frederick W. Danker*. Grand Rapids: Eerdmans, 2004.

Bibliography

Taylor, Charles. *A Secular Age*. Cambridge, MA: Harvard University Press, 2007.

Tertullian. *The Apology, in Latin Christianity: Its Founder, Tertullian*. Vol. 3. Edited by Alexander Roberts, Roberts Donaldson, and A. Cleveland Coxe, translated by S. Thelwall. Buffalo, NY: Christian Literature Company, 1885.

Tetlow, Joanne. "J. S. Mill's Religion of Humanity: Skepticism of Religion, Skepticism of Humanity, Skepticism of Liberty." *Conference Papers—New England Political Science Association* (2007) 1.

Thielicke, Helmut. *Theological Ethics*. Vol. 2. Translated by William Henry Lazareth. Philadelphia: Fortress, 1969.

Thompson, Kenneth W. *Ethics, Functionalism, and Power in International Politics: The Crisis in Values*. Baton Rouge: Louisiana State University, 1979.

Thornbury, Gregory Alan. *Recovering Classic Evangelicalism: Applying the Wisdom and Vision of Carl F. H. Henry*. Wheaton, IL: Crossway, 2013.

US State Department Office of International Religious Freedom. "2019 Report on International Religious Freedom." June 10, 2020. http://www.state.gov/reports/2019 report-on-international-religious-freedom.

Van Til, Cornelius. *Christian Theistic Ethics*. Kingsburg, CA: Dulk Christian Foundation, 1974.

———. *The Moral Disciple: An Introduction to Christian Ethics*. Grand Rapids: Eerdmans, 2012.

Van Wyk, J. H. "John Calvin on the Kingdom of God and Eschatology." *In die Skriflig* 35.2 (2001) 191–205.

VanDrunen, David. *A Biblical Case for Natural Law*. Grand Rapids: Acton Institute, 2012.

———. *Divine Covenants and Moral Order: A Biblical Theology of Natural Law*. Grand Rapids: Eerdmans, 2014.

Veith, Gene Edward Jr. *Post-Christian: A Guide to Contemporary Thought and Culture*. Wheaton, IL: Crossway, 2020.

Walker, Andrew Thomas. "Religious Liberty in Contemporary Evangelical Social Ethics: An Assessment and Framework for Socio-Political Challenges." PhD diss., The Southern Baptist Theological Seminary, 2018.

Walker, Andrew T., and Robert George. *Liberty for All: Defending Everyone's Religious Freedom in a Pluralistic Age*. Grand Rapids: Brazos, 2021.

Walton, John H. *The Lost World of Genesis One: Ancient Cosmology and the Origins Debate*. Downers Grove: IVP Academic, 2009.

Whitehead, Andrew L., and Samuel L. Perry. *Taking America Back for God: Christian Nationalism in the United States*. New York: Oxford University Press, 2020.

Wilken, Robert Louis. *The Christian Roots of Religious Freedom*. Milwaukee: Marquette University Press, 2014.

———. *Liberty in the Things of God: The Christian Origins of Religious Freedom*. New Haven, CT: Yale University Press, 2019.

Williams, Roger. *On Religious Liberty: Selections from the Works of Roger Williams*. Edited by James Calvin Davis. Cambridge, MA: Belknap, 2008.

Williams, Roger, and Perry Miller. *The Complete Writings of Roger Williams*. New York: Russell & Russell, 1963.

Witte, John. "Moderate Religious Liberty in the Theology of John Calvin." *Calvin Theological Journal* 31.2 (Nov 1996) 359–403.

Witte, John, and Frank S. Alexander, eds. *Christianity and Human Rights: An Introduction*. Cambridge, MA: Cambridge University Press, 2010.

Bibliography

Witte, John, and Joel A Nichols. *Religion and the American Constitutional Experiment*. New York: Oxford University Press, 2016.

Wogaman, J. Philip. *Protestant Faith and Religious Liberty*. Nashville: Abingdon, 1967.

Wolfe, Christopher, ed. *The Naked Public Square Reconsidered: Religion and Politics in the Twenty-First Century*. Wilmington, DE: ISI Books, 2009.

———. *Natural Law Liberalism*. London: Cambridge University Press, 2006.

Wolterstorff, Nicholas. *Art in Action: Toward a Christian Aesthetic*. Grand Rapids: Eerdmans, 1979.

———. "A Christian Case for Religious Freedom." In *Religious Freedom: Why Now? Defending an Embattled Human Right*, edited by The Witherspoon Institute Task Force on International Religious Freedom, 39–40. Princeton, NJ: The Witherspoon Institute, 2012.

———. *John Locke and the Ethics of Belief*. Cambridge Studies in Religion and Critical Thought. New York: Cambridge University Press, 1996.

———. *Justice in Love*. Emory University Studies in Law and Religion. Grand Rapids: Eerdmans, 2011.

———. *Justice: Rights and Wrongs*. Princeton, NJ: Princeton University Press, 2008.

———. *Reason within the Bounds of Religion*. Grand Rapids: Eerdmans, 1976.

———. *Understanding Liberal Democracy: Essays in Political Philosophy*. New York: Oxford University Press, 2012.

Wood, James E. "Theological and Historical Foundations of Religious Liberty." *Journal of Church State* 15.2 (1973) 241–58.

Zachman, Randall C. *The Assurance of Faith: Conscience in the Theology of Martin Luther and John Calvin*. Minneapolis: Fortress, 1993.

Zagorin, Perez. *How the Idea of Religious Toleration Came to the West*. Princeton, NJ: Princeton University Press, 2003.

Zappen, James P. "The Logic and Rhetoric of John Stuart Mill." *Philosophy & Rhetoric* 26.3 (Spring 1993) 191–200.

Zuckert, Catherine H. *Political Philosophy in the Twentieth Century: Authors and Arguments*. New York: Cambridge University Press, 2011.

Subject Index

a priori knowledge, 25–27
abortion, 75, 151
absolute certainty, 34
absolute moral values, 10, 11, 12, 124
absolute objective truth, 103
absolute submission, vs. compliance, 51
absolutism, 50
abstract choices, 70
accountability, 68
Affordable Care Act (Obamacare), 56
agency, 153. *see also* human agency
Agrippa, 76
Ahdar, Rex, 127, 129, 136–37
    Religious Freedom in the Liberal State, 122
alternative lifestyles, 31
Amazon, 155
American Catholics, 94
American Christians, 156
American Civil Liberties Union, 4
American consensus, 92
American constitutionalism, 99
American culture, 149
American proposition, 97
American Protestants, Murray and, 85
American religious pluralism, 103
American social order, 84
An Appeal to the Public for Religious Liberty (Backus), 5

Anastasius, 89
Apostolic Delegation, 87
apostolic succession, 117
Aquinas, Thomas, 34, 85
Arab Awakening, 155
Arbo, Matthew, 70, 78
argument, 91
Aristotelian philosophy, 98
Aristotelian-Thomistic philosophy, 89
Aristotle, 78, 89, 96
    philosophy of citizen, 89
    political philosophy, and Murray's social ethic, 90
atheism, 53, 89
    beliefs, 83
    Mill and, 53
    Rawls' rejection of, 64n50
Augustine, 4, 40–41, 78, 89, 158
authority, 8
    in autonomous individual, 7
    and communication, 36
    Mill and, 41
    problem of, 35–41
    of Scripture, rejection, 12
    spheres of, 135–37
    of state, 137
    submission to, 50
autonomous choice, 79

Subject Index

autonomous reason, 12, 13, 84, 88, 102
    as principle for morality, 152
    religion based on, 87
autonomy, 38, 97

Backus, Isaac, 118–19, 128
    An Appeal to the Public for Religious Liberty, 5
Bahnsen, Greg, 155
Baker, Hunter, 75
baptism, 138
Baptist Faith and Message 2000, 14
Baptists, eighteenth-century, 118–19
Barth, Carl F.H., 120
basic liberties, 62
basic principles, 62
Baxter, Michael, 94
Beach, Waldo, *Christian Ethics*, 131
Beale, G.K., 140
belief, 111
    crimes of, 137
    Dworkin on, 3
The Benedict Option: A Strategy for Christians in a Post-Christian Nation (Dreher), 18
Bentham, Jeremy, 17, 25
    fear of revolution, 20–21
    principle of utility, 23–24
bias, 52
Bible, 14, 64, 153–54
    authoritativeness of, 109
    conscience in, 13, 100, 101
    liberal Protestantism and, 12
    religious liberty and, 5, 20–21, 111
    as revelation from God, 10, 108, 109
    on submission to God, 51
biblical ethics, 14
biblical justice, 78–79
biblical theology, Mill's rejection of, 26
bigotry, 148
blessings, 113
The Bloody Tenet of Persecution for Cause of Conscience (Williams), 53–54, 117
Boaz, David, 31
boundaries
    human discernment of, 133
    in ordered world, 137
    protecting, 135
Bratman, Michael E., 67–68
Brink, David Owen, 31, 32–33, 38, 46
Burge, Ryan P., *The Nones: Where They Came From, Who They Are, and Where They Are Going*, 147

Cadeddu, Francesca, 84
Calvin, John, 71, 109, 114–16
    The Institutes of Christian Religion, 114
Carson, Don, 135, 137
categorical imperative, 25, 62
Catholic University, 87
Catholicism, 83, 94, 103. *see also* Roman Catholic Church
charity, Christian's duty and, 139
Charles of Guise, 83
choice, 70, 127
Christenings Make Not Christians (Williams), 53–54
Christian command, to obey authority, 50
Christian doctrine, 58
Christian ethics, 50
    vs. evangelical ethics, 13–14
Christian Ethics (Beach), 131
Christian Ethics (Niebuhr), 131
Christian evangelism
    challenges for, 148
    goal of, 138
Christian faith, 79
Christian mind, 52
Christian minorities, 155
Christian morality, 150, 151
    and divine relationship, 116
Christian nationalism, 156
Christian theology
    on freedom, 10
    on source of happiness, 28
Christian values, 50, 150
    vs. worldly, 117
Christianity, 50, 51, 52, 64
    ethical separation of, 111–12
    intolerance toward, 29
    Mill and, 23
    as part of social order, 137
    Rawls' renunciation of, 63
    and religious liberty, ix

Subject Index

church, 50
    Christ's rule of, 141
    dichotomy between world and, 117
    exclusive prejudice, 50
    mission of, 18
Church Missionary Society, 108
church-state relationships, 87, 93, 115
civil coercion, Puritan theology and, 117
civil duty, 129
civil law, x
civil order, 136
civil religion, 32
civil society, 83, 89, 147
civil war, threat of, 156
Civil War (U.S. 1860s), impact on Rawls, 57
civilization, permanence of, 157
classical liberalism, 2, 13, 16
    and freedom, 16
Clinton, Bill, 56
closed groups, 63
coerced doctrine, 54
coerced opinions, 53
coercion, 9
coexistence, 144
cognition, 69
    and Holy Spirit, 71
Cohen-Almagor, Raphael, 46
collaboration, 61
collective passions, rights as invention, 26
collective will, 125
collectivism
    principles of, 33
    for religious freedom, 153
collectivist, 29
Collins, Gary, 144
common beliefs, 70
common good, 75, 85, 92
community consensus, 8
compliance, vs. absolute submission, 51
comprehensive doctrine, 72, 73, 75
    and society, 74
Comte, Auguste, 32
concentration camps, 58
conscience, 34, 41, 54, 68, 99–100, 107, 116
    Calvin's belief in liberty of, 115
    creation of, 35
    and epistemology, 102–4
    evangelical theory of, 126, 128
    as guiding agent, 101
    Holy Spirit and, 127
    Murray's concept of, 101
    principle of unrestricted, 138
    religious, 127
    in religious liberty frameworks, 122
    respect, 2
    Roman Catholic concept of, 125, 126
    secular, 123, 124–25
    as social function, 100
conscienta ex lex, 99
conscientia ex lex (law is by conscience), 86
conscientious citizens, 113
consensus, 74–77, 90–92, 153
    for common good, 100
    Murray's optimism for, 105
    in Roman Catholic Church, 94
consequences, 67–68
    and moral quality of an act, 38
Conservative Soul (Sullivan), 104
constitutionalism, 85
consummation, 142–44
contractarianism, 61
    ethics, 63
controversy, 53
conviction, diminishing power of, 79
cooperation, 61
corrupted nature, 78
corruption, prophetic warning against, 118
cosmology, 16
    evangelical, 107, 111, 121
    evangelical, superiority of, 132–39
    utilitarian, 132
Council of Trent, 53
courage, 24
Cowling, Maurice, 29, 31–32, 38
creation, 40, 49, 118
    doctrine of, 123
    evangelical doctrine of, 133
    good of, 77
creation narrative, 26
crimes against society, 137

Subject Index

"A Crisis in the History of Trent" (Murray), 83
Crowley, J.D., 100
cultural closed groups, 63
cultural conservatism, and evangelical theology, 150
culture warring, 151
Curran, Charles E., 94, 98, 102–3

Davidic rule, 142
Davis, James Calvin, 116
Day, J.P., 39
Declaration for Human Rights, 104
Declaration of Independence, Murray on, 85
Declaration on Religious Freedom, 81–82
deism, 64n50
Del Noce, Augusto, 10–11, 17
deliberation, 67, 68, 69, 91
democracy, 31, 135
    liberal, 124
    pragmatism and, 134–35
    religious freedom as necessary for, 146
democratic societies, 91
democratic tyranny, 23
Deneen, Patrick, 10, 17
    Why Liberalism Failed, 13
deontology, 60, 63, 73
depression, 24–25
desire, 68
despotism, 31
dictatorships, 13
Dignitatis Humanae, 93
dignity, 97, 100, 118, 124, 126
    evangelical doctrine of, 127
disadvantaged citizens, 72
disinformation, 154
distribution of goods, 60
diversity in America, 58
divine authority, Mill's rejection of, 36
divine command theory, 128
    Rawls' rejection of, 59–60
divine judgment, evangelical belief in, 143
divine justice, 144
divine omniscience, and utilitarian ethics, 27
divine providence, 58
divine retribution, 143, 144
divine revelation, 5, 18, 20, 21–22, 42, 54, 64, 65, 88, 94, 96, 99, 110, 153
    Mill's denial of, 28, 33, 52
    rejection of, 34–35, 40, 44
divine rewards, 144
divine transcendence, 95–96, 107, 122
    and absolute morals, 124
divine will, 58
doctrine, 53
doctrine of separation, 2
dogma, 53
dominance, 49
domination, 69
Dreher, Rod, *The Benedict Option: A Strategy for Christians in a Post-Christian Nation*, 18
dual authority principle, 136–37
Duke, Barrett, 5, 139
duty, 96
Dworkin, Ronald, 3, 4

E Pluribus Unum, 103
early Christians, 113
economic inequalities, 62
ecumenical cooperation, 83
egalitarian equality, 47
egalitarianism, 22
ego, underestimating power of, 102
egoism, 32, 63, 64
    utilitarianism and, 29
emotional harm, 46
emotions, 24
    morality and, 24
empathy, 65, 80
empires, 156
empires, fall of, 156
empiricism, 12
    utilitarian cosmology and, 132
"emptythepews.com," 148
Enlightenment philosophy, 10, 145
Enlightenment rationalism, 2
Enlightenment thought, 11
epistemic reason, 47
epistemological knowledge, 34, 43
epistemological unity, Murray and, 103

Subject Index

equal treatment, 78
equality, 2, 124
equilibrium, crisis of, 10
equity, 2, 135
Erickson, Millard, 129
eschatology, 121
    evangelical, 111, 139–44
    Protestant, 141
    visions, 142
    Williams and, 117
ethical reasoning, time and, 67
ethical separation of Christianity, 111
ethics, 15
    evangelical framework of, 26
    Mill's theory, 38
eudaimonia (happiness), 90
European constitutionalism, 86
European democracies, 155
European religious wars, 82
euthanasia, 75
evangelical, classic meaning, 107
evangelical anthropology, 40, 41, 111, 121, 132, 154
    vs. secular anthropology, 145
    superiority of, 122–32
evangelical balance, 48–49
evangelical belief, 14
evangelical conscience, 123
evangelical cosmology, 107, 111, 121
    superiority of, 132–39
evangelical disengagement, 18
evangelical epistemology, 154
evangelical eschatology, 111, 139–44
evangelical ethics, 26, 36, 44, 69, 109, 143
    vs. Christian ethics, 13–14
evangelical foundationalism, 54
evangelical freedom, 131
evangelical paradigm for religious liberty, 15, 106–45, 154
    extension to all, 134
    historical definition, 145
    historical framework, 111–21
    structure, 110–11
    superiority of, 6, 107
    time in, 139
    vision, 13

evangelical religious freedom, 138
    as act of love, 139
    and ordered boundaries, 135
evangelical self, and freedom, 128–31
evangelical social ethics, 150
evangelical social policy, 143
evangelical teleology, 140
evangelical theology, 149, 150
    missiological vision, 121
    and truth, 49
    in twentieth century, 120–21
evangelical withdrawal
    from public engagement, 154
    risks from, 149
evangelicalism, 47–48, 76
    Christian nationalism and, 150
    defining, 108
    precursors, ix
    strengths and weaknesses of, 14
evil, 64, 143
evolution, 124
evolutionary cycle, 122
exclusive truth, 49
excommunication, 114

fair distribution, 61
fairness, 68–70, 73, 74, 78
    through justice, 56–80
    modern notions of, 78
faith, 76, 116, 139
    appearance of, 54
    coercion and, 114
    in Jesus Christ, 137
the fall, 26, 146
fallibility, 35
family, and instilled values, 135
Feinberg, Joel, 45–46
Ferguson, Thomas P., 90, 103
finitude, humanity's realization of, 134
First Amendment, 91
    and Roman Catholics, 85
forced prayer, 54
Foss, Jerome, 70
Founding Fathers, 86
Frame, John, 36
free choice, 37, 40, 50–51, 122, 123, 124
    identity and, 70

Subject Index

free expression, 39, 41
  absolute right to, 44
  and human complexity, 42
Free to Believe (Goodrich), 6
free voice, 70
free will, 16, 52
  and Kant, 21
freedom, 92
  apart from Christ, 130
  from arbitrary arrest and seizure, 62
  of conscience, 62. *see also* conscience
  of conscience, Calvin's belief in, 115
  evangelical concept of, 129, 130, 131
  and evangelical self, 128–31
  and liberal social ethics, 10
  liberalism's redefinition of, 11
  love of, 158
  of thought, 33
freedom of assembly, 62
freedom of person, 62
freedom of speech, 40, 48, 62
  exclusions from protections of, 46
  suppression of, 39
freedom of thought, 62
French, David, 7
French Revolution, 30
future happiness, 27
future reward, evangelical promise of, 144

gay rights, 147
Gelasius I (pope), 85, 89
general happiness, 30
  of the majority, 42
general revelation, 14, 133
George, Robert, 29, 72, 75
Gewirth, Alan, 27–28
globalization, 148
God, 28, 40–41, 69, 100. *see also* divine . . .
  accountability to, 101
  authoritative structure of, 78
  duty to, 131
  enlightenment thought on, 11
  governance of creation, 88
  and human will, 16
  love of, 131
  mission of, 121
  ordered liberty and, 8
  relationship with, 28
  revelation of, 133
  self-revelation, 14
  service to, 131
  as source of U.S. Constitution, 86
  sovereignty of, 85, 86, 120
  submission to, 51
  voice of, 99
  will of, 58, 127
  will of, Rawls on, 64n50
  word of, 41
  wrath of, 113
God's image, 71
God's Spirit, 41
God's word, 107
Goerner, E.A., *Peter and Caesar*, 98
good, 70, 77, 78, 143
  competing visions of, 60
  definition of, 65, 72
  perspective on, 66
  vs. right, 71–74, 77–78
  right to choose, 72
  shared vision of, 96
goodness, measure determining value, 12
Goodrich, Luke, 147
  Free to Believe, 6
goods, fair distribution, 60
governance, 9
government
  consensus and, 92
  purpose of, 64
  and restraint of sin, 119
government structures, within evangelicalism, 147
grace, 99
Graham, Paul, 73–74
Great Commandment, 130, 131
Great Commission, 138
Great Depression, 84
Greek philosophy, 24
  on freedom, 10
Gregg, Samuel, 29, 36
Groundwork of the Metaphysics of Morals (Kant), 57
Grudem, Wayne, 125
guilt, 68, 101

Subject Index

Guinness, Os, 5, 76, 148
Guterres, António, 148

happiness, 69, 90, 140, 145
    general vs. individual, 30–31
    as highest good, 153
    Mill and, 25, 28–29
    of society, 26, 39
    utilitarianism and, 59
harm, 44, 48
harm principle, 45–48, 153
hate speech, 154
    global strategy to end, 148
hate speech laws, 47
Hauerwas, Stanley, 14n67
hedonism, 32
Hegelian principles, 98
Heimbach, Daniel, 5, 7, 88, 104, 143
Henry, Carl F.H., 4, 5, 12, 14, 18, 109, 123, 124, 126–27, 134, 149
heretical beliefs, 83
Hiroshima, 58
historicism, Murray's dependence on, 98
Hoekema, Anthony, 24, 50–51, 77
Holmes, Oliver Wendell, 39
Holy Office in Rome, 87
Holy Spirit, 41, 127, 130
    and cognition, 71
homosexual marriage, 73
homosexuality, 75
Hooper, Leon, 84, 87
hope, 144
hopelessness, 144
hostile society, 113
Houlgate, Laurence, 45
Hubbard, Arthur John, 156
Hueber, Harry, 14n67
Hughes, Emmet John, 84
human advancement, 123
human agency, 56, 67, 80, 109, 118
    biblical view of, 71
    factors, 70
    and salvation, 114–15
    theory, 69–70
human associations, 90
human consciousness, 49
human consensus, 93

human dignity, 49
    Murray on, 97
human flourishing, 90, 146
human identity, 70
human knowledge, development phases, 32
human mind, fallibility of, 34
human nature, 105
human progress, freedom of thought and, 23
human reason, 28, 34, 41, 66
    as foundation of liberty, 33
    limitations of, 34
    metaphysics, 23
    religion of, 32
human reflection, 48
human rights, 41, 120, 124
human will, 111
humanity, 41
    freedom of choice, 5
    perfectibility of, 96
    reason for creation, 69
    role as image-bearer, 147
Humean philosophy, 23

idealists, xi
ideas, clash of, 43
identity politics, 71
identity-based social hierarchies, 46–47
image of God, 15
    Calvin on, 114
imago Dei, 124, 125, 126, 128, 154
    evangelical doctrine of, 127
immoral, 70
inaugurated kingdom theology, 142
incarnation, 118
    classic liberalism and, 17
incarnation theology of Williams, 116
inculated submission, 51
independence, 28
individual, and society, 95
individual accountability before God, 100
individual autonomy, 28
    and communal authority, 7
individual choice, religious liberty and, 80
individual happiness, 30
individual liberty, 39, 44, 45

individual rights, Mill on, 22–23
individualism, 86, 87, 153
   principles of, 33
   and statism, 13
Industrial Revolution, 32
injustice, 57, 125, 143
inseparability concept, 40
The Institutes of Christian Religion
   (Calvin), 114
institutions, 146
instrumental reason, 35
intellectual minority, 38
intellectual reason, 40
interdenominational movement,
   evangelicalism as, 108
interfaith cooperation, 120
interfaith services, 150
interference harm, 45–46
International Mission Board, 18
intolerance, 148
intuitionism
   and justice standard, 59
   Rawls' rejection of, 59
Islam, 150
   religious freedom and, 155
Islamic "fundamentalists," 150
Islamic jurisprudence, 155
Israel
   God's covenant with, 116
   political entity, 117

Jackson, Robert H, 1
Jacobinism, 85, 93
Jacobson, Daniel, 31
James, 28
January 6, 2021 U.S. Capitol attack, 156
Jesus, historic, 18
Jesus Christ, 14, 49, 52, 129
   all authority to, 137
   as arbiter of good and evil, 140
   command to make disciples, 138
   ethics of, 50
   faith in, 137
   incarnation, 116–17
   inner call of, 116
   as judge, 140
   law of love, 69
   millennial reign of, 117
   submission to, 107
John (apostle), 121
John of Paris, 85
joy, 28
Judaism, 103
Judeo-Christian framework, 103
judgment, 140, 142
   evangelical vision of, 144
   final, 121
   moral, 126
   Tertullian's beliefs on, 114
just principles, Rawls on, 62
just society, 83
justice, 58, 59, 61–62, 74–75, 77, 78, 106,
   149, 153. *see also* fairness
   biblical, 78–79
   divine, 144
   as fairness, 56–80. *see also* fairness
   pleasure and, 65
   Rawls' theory of, 58–59
   and secular social ethics, 143
   structure for adjudicating, 136
   traditional ideas of, 78
   utilitarian, 132

Kant, Immanuel, 25, 57, 62
   flaws in social contract theory, 60
   Mill on philosophy, 26
   Mill's rejection of ethics, 27
   on religious liberty, 21
Kantzer, Kenneth, 6
Kennedy, John F., 87–88
Kilner, John, 42
kindred relationships, 105
kingdom of God, 15, 121
   time and, 116
kingdom theology of Calvin, 115
kinship relationships, 91

Ladd, George, 141
law, formation of, 72
League of Women Voters, 57
Leeman, Jonathan, 136, 141, 143, 151
Leigh, Ian, 127, 136–37
   Religious Freedom in the Liberal State,
   122

Subject Index

Leland, John, 118
Lenin, Vladimir, 12
Leo XIII (pope), 82–83, 85, 87, 99
liberal democracies, 47, 124, 147
liberal philosophies, and autonomous freedom, 128
liberal political philosophers, 2
liberal social ethics, 10
liberalism, support of religious liberty, 20
libertarians, 22, 29, 31, 33, 44
libertine freedom, 11–12
libertinism, 157
liberty, 10, 33, 38, 43, 45, 49. *see also* freedom
    argument for, 37
    origins of, 28
Liederbach, Mark, 102
Liognier Ministries, 150
Locke, John, 25, 86
    flaws in social contract theory, 60
    influence of, 20
    Mill's rejection of ethics, 27
locus in society, vs. God, 8
logic, inconsistencies in Mill's, 39
loneliness, 24
love
    Christ's law of, 69
    for neighbor, 131, 138
love of God, 131
Lovett, Frank, 68, 74
Luther, Martin, 9, 51, 77, 125–26
    two kingdom's theology, 141
Lutherans, 102
Lyons, David, 56

Maclure, Jocelyn, 147
majority, 42
    ideology of, 42
    tyranny of, 37
majority opinion, vs. public consensus, 91
majority rule, and minority oppression, 23
Marsden, George, 108
martyrdom, 51
Marxism, 17, 63
Maryland, 57

material inequalities, 62
material liberties, 143
material world, 143
materialistic freedom, 28
media, misunderstanding of evangelicalism, 108
mental cultivation, 38
mental energy, 40
Messiah, 140
metaphysical realities, Rawls and, 106
metaphysical unity, 103
metaphysical world, 76
metaphysics, 23n21, 28, 32, 34
    Mill's rejection of, 26, 40, 52
Middle East, 155
middle ground, fallacy of, 52
Mill, James, 23–24
Mill, John Stuart, 4, 7, 17, 57, 152
    autobiography, 32
    biography of, 22–25
    on conscience, 122
    doctrine, 37
    education of, 23–24
    ethics, 106
    framework for religious freedom, 153
    harm principle, 45–48
    influence of philosophy, 29
    On Liberty, 30–33
    on modern religious liberty, 20–55
    on moral vision, 124
    philosophical inconsistencies, 29
    on rights of conscience, 125
    on rights of individuals, 22–23
    on truth, 134
    Utilitarianism, 33
    utilitarianism of, 21–22, 106
minor offenses, 46
minority, 23
minority groups, 42, 49
    beliefs, 7
    opinions, 42, 44
mission, world and, 137–39
mission of God, 15, 121
missions, 109
modern liberalism, 10
modern religious liberty, 56–105
modern social ethics, 45

Subject Index

modernism, danger of, 82
Molher, Albert, 5
Moore, Russell, 141, 149
moral, 70
moral actions, 24, 68, 126
moral agents, 52, 65, 67, 111
moral authority, 36
   and class, 37
moral decision-making, 126
moral framework, 77
moral judgment, 126
moral law, 100
Moral Man and Immoral Society
   (Niebuhr), 95
moral norms of America, 149
moral pattern, through life of Christ, 116
moral philosophy
   of Mill, 25
   Rawls' degree in, 58
   in twentieth century, 59
moral pluralism, increasing, 147
moral progress, 50
moral realism, 132
moral reality, 43
moral reasoning, 34–35, 67
   emotions and, 24
moral reform, 127
moral relativism, 127
moral rights, Mill on, 44
moral theology, Roman Catholic, 125
moral truth, 49
   Evangelical ethics and, 109
moral values, universal absolute, 122
morality, x, 12, 42, 49, 70
   framework to judge, 26
motivation, 68
Murray, Douglas, *The Madness of Crowds*, 93
Murray, John Courtney, x, 5, 7, 81–105, 145, 152, 153
   biography of, 82–84
   and conscience, 102–4
   early work of, 83
   and the individual vs. society, 95
   justification to non-catholics, 87–88
   natural law philosophy and, 88–92, 106–7
   and perfectionism, 95–96
   principle of consensus, 90–92
   The Problem of Religious Freedom, 98
   purpose of, 85
   and social vision, 95–96
   Theological Studies, 87
   "The Vatican Delcaration on Religious Freedom," 98
   We Hold These Truths, 99
   weakness in relationship to self, 99
   weakness in relationship to time, 96–97
mutual benefit of society members, 61

Nagel, Thomas, 56
National Humanities Medal, 56
Native Americans, 54
natural law, 5, 8–9, 72, 75, 86, 92
   conscience and, 99–102
   Mill's denial of, 52
   Murray on, 99–102
   principles, 97, 98
   rejection of, 54
natural law ethics, 109
natural law philosophy, 7, 81–105
   vs. natural law theology, 88–89
   religious freedom and, 87
   Thielicke on, 103–4
natural law theology, 17, 91
   Murray on, 106–7
   vs. natural law philosophy, 88–89
natural law theory, 64
natural process, 133
natural rights, 60, 86–87
natural rights philosophy, 17, 20
natural rights theory, 25, 30
naturalism, 12
   secular theories and, 122
naturalistic fallacy, 36
naturalistic teleology, 60, 63, 73
nature, 49
Nazi Germany, 102
Nazism, 36, 63
negative consensus, 93
neutrality, 74
New Deal, 84
Newman, Jay, 41

Subject Index

Niebuhr, H. Richard, *Christian Ethics*, 131
Niebuhr, Reinhold, 102, 134
  Moral Man and Immoral Society, 95
Nietzsche, Friedrich, 96
Noachian covenant, 136
Noll, Mark, 107
nominalism, 87
non-believers, 6
The Nones: Where They Came From, Who They Are, and Where They Are Going (Burge), 147
nonvoluntarist theism, 64n50
North Africa, 155
Nussbaum, Martha, 4, 56

Obamacare, 56
obedience, 113, 115–16
  to Christ, 144
  to God, 121
Obergefell v. Hodges (2015), 11
objectivity, 76
obligation not to harm, 45
O'Donovan, Oliver, 15–16, 18, 21, 24, 36, 49, 67, 77, 126, 129–30, 132, 141, 152
  Resurrection and the Moral Order, 16–17
Old Testament, 78
Old Testament covenant, 116
omniscient being, Mill and, 34
On Liberty (Mill), 22, 30–33, 152
opinions, 39, 48, 53
oppression, 47
  of minorities, 51–52
ordered authority, 8
original position theory, 61–63
orthodox Christianity, Rawls abandonment of, 58
outlaw conscience, 99
overlapping consensus, 80

pagan world, sex in, 143
pagans, 151
pain, 45
Papists, 52
parochialism, 84
partial truth, 110, 149

partiality, 49
partisanship, 49
passivity, 155
past experience, 67
paternalism, 8, 54
  of Mill, 42
paternalistic structure, 37
patience, 144
Patient Protection, 56
Paul, 34, 48, 51, 76, 78, 101, 125, 130, 133, 144, 151
Pelotte, Donald, 84, 87–88
perceived goods, 66
perfectionism, xi, 95–96
  of Mill's assumptions, 35
  utilitarianism and, 59
Perry, Samuel L., 148, 150
personal freedom, 33
personal happiness, social concern and, 31
personal opinions, 43
personal restraint, 10
Peter (apostle), 51, 121
Peter and Caesar (Goemer), 98
Pew Research, 147
philosophy, 57, 82, 87
  mixing Scripture with, 14
  without divine revelation, 21–22
physical harm, 46
Pierce, Claude Anthony, 101
Piper, John, 28
Pius IX (pope), 82–83, 85
Planned Parenthood v. Casey (1992), 151
Plato, 78
pleasure, 28, 37, 38, 45
Plessis, Georgia, 46
pluralism, 146
pluralistic society, 80
  diverse religious convictions, 103
  ordering right over good, 74
  toleration and, 42
plurality, 38
Pogge, Thomas, 58, 59, 64
polarization, 154
political animals, 90
political community, 91
political concepts, 74
political engagement of church, 148

Subject Index

political government, vs. spiritual government, 115
Political Liberalism (Rawls), 74, 79
political liberty, 62
political philosophy, 63–64, 110
political relationships, 142
political secularity, 3, 4
political structures, 73
politics, 9
polytheism, 150
post-Christian America, 149
post-modern era, 10n49
Powell, Jim, 20
power, 49, 69
    balance between civil and church authorities, 136
    of society over individual, 30
pragmatism, 134
prejudice, 49, 51–52
    of opinion, 50
presidential election of 2016, 108
priest and king, duality between, 89
primary good, 65
    Rawls' definition of, 62
    self-worth as, 72
Princeton University, 57
principatus sine modo sine lege (without the government no law), 86
principle for reducing harm, 45
principle of utility, 23–24
principled pluralism, 146
principles, 72
privatized religion, 8, 79–80
The Problem of Religious Freedom (Murray), 98
procedural justice, 153
progress, controversy and, 53
progressivism, 22, 44
proof, Mill's definition of, 27
proselytizing, 47–48, 139
Protestant eschatology, 141
Protestant social ethics, 11–12
Protestantism, 9, 52, 54, 83, 89, 103
    classic vs. liberal, 12
    religious freedom and, 87
psychological harm, 46, 47, 48
public acts, 3

public consensus, vs. majority opinion, 91
public engagement, 66
public morality, 149
public principles, 77
public spaces, 8
Puritan theology, 117

Qohelet, 24–25, 67
Qur'an, 155

racism, 47
radical individualism, 22
rational, vs. reasonable, 66
rational agents, 62
rational system, 118–19
rationalism, 87
rationalist philosophy, 23
rationality, 65–66
Ratzinger, Joseph, 9–10, 11–12
Rawls, Anna, 57
Rawls, Bobby, 57
Rawls, John, 4–6, 7, 8, 56–80, 96, 152
    agency and time problem, 67–69
    biography of, 57–64
    on conscience, 122
    ethics, 72
    human agency, 64–71
    on humans as truth-seekers, 135
    and metaphysical realities, 106
    model for religious freedom, 153
    on moral vision, 124
    overlapping consensus, 74–77
    Political Liberalism, 74
    principles, 56, 69
    purpose of work, 58–61
    on rights of conscience, 125
    A Theory of Justice (*TJ*), 59, 60, 63, 69, 79, 96
    views and, 57
    volition and cognition problem, 69–71
Rawls, Tommy, 57
Rawls, William, 57
realism, moral, 132
realistic utopia, 59
reason, 10, 21, 33, 39, 65, 69, 99
    Mill and, 38
    vs. reasonability, 74

Subject Index

reasonability, 66
reasonable, vs. rational, 66
reasoning, bias in, 52
reciprocity, 75
reconstructionism, 155
redeemability, 64
reflection, 67, 68
Reformation doctrine, 108
reformers, and Catholic Church, 83
regeneration, 127
relativism, 11
religion, x
   in America, 103
   and cohesive society, 157
   privatized, 79–80
religious beliefs
   privatization of, 56
   and public policy, 73
religious conscience, 127
religious doctrine, 72
religious duty, 128
religious expression, 43, 49
   vs. religious tolerance, 41–43
religious freedom, 53, 64–65, 71, 79
   in America, 92
   Catholic Church opposition to, 84
   Catholic thought, 83
   as essential good, 146
   limitation on, 76
   Murray's analysis of, 99
   Murray's theory of, 95–96
   overlapping consensus and, 75
   Rawlsian argument for, 66
   Rawls' framework for, 80
   source of argument for, 111–14
   threat to, 148
   tradition opposed to, 83
Religious Freedom in the Liberal State (Leigh), 122
religious institutions, and instilled values, 135
religious liberty, 65, 81, 88. *see also* evangelical paradigm for religious liberty
   consequence of time, 98
   current views, ix
   defined, 1–2

ethical assumptions of, 2
ethical foundation, 109
ethics, xi
evangelical framework for, 152
evangelical vision of, ix–x
free speech and, 47
for individuals, 117
Mill on, 22
Mill's premise one on reason, 33–43
Mill's premise two on truth, 43–49
Mill's premise three on prejudice, 49–52
Mill's premise four on coerced opinions, 53–54
Murray's work on, 105
need for evangelical framework, 6
as ordained by God, 133
positive and negative, xi
preserving, xi
problem, 4–6
right to, 72
social consensus, 95
as temporary condition, 144
theological foundations, 120
religious minorities, 155
religious people, rights of, 80
religious persecution, 51
religious pluralism, 137, 150
   intolerance toward, 82
religious practice restrictions, 8
religious prejudice, Mill on, 51–52
religious principles, 63
religious society, 89
religious toleration, 4, 7, 54, 82–83
   vs. religious expression, 41–43
repentance, 48, 113
respect, 72
responsibility, 70
Resurrection and the Moral Order (O'Donovan), 26
resurrection of Christ, 16–17, 130
revelation, 11
   of God, 133. *see also* divine revelation
revolution, fear of, 20
reward, evangelical promise of future, 144
right to hold private property, 62
right vs. good, 56, 71–74

Subject Index

rights
  of black Americans, 57
  of minorities, 148
Roman Catholic Church, 52, 54, 63, 83
  and Americanism, 85
  civil engagement, 84
  consensus in, 94
  doctrine, 81, 87
  history, 93
  history opposing religious freedom, 96–97
  hostility toward, 84
  moral theology, 125
  natural law, 8, 54, 107, 132, 140, 152–53
  opposition to religious freedom, 81–82
  overlapping consensus bias against natural law, 75
  political philosophers, 75
  precedent for theory, 89–90
  social ethics, 5, 145, 152
  social ethics, Murray and, 84
Roman Gregorian University, 82
romanticism, 25
Rome, 82
Rousseau, Jean-Jacques, 60
Rutherford House lectures, 109

sacred beliefs, vs. secular crimes, 136
sacred society, 98
Saeed, Abdullah, 155
salvation, 108, 133
same-sex marriage, 11, 56
sanctification, 111
Sandel, Michael, 69, 73, 79
Santeria, 52
Sayers, Dorothy, 41
scale to judge pleasure, 25
Schaeffer, Francis, 48, 122–23, 124, 128–29, 150
Schenck v. The United States (1919), 39
scriptural revelation, 109
Scripture. *see* Bible
secular anthropology, vs. evangelical, 145
secular beliefs, 50
secular conscience, 123
secular crimes, vs sacred beliefs, 136

secular ethics, 12, 109
  problems in, 152
secular liberalism, 13
secular monism, 99
secular philosophy, 7, 18, 28, 35, 122
secular social ethics, 145
  and justice, 143
secular state, 74
secularism, 3–4, 93, 103, 149
  Mill and, 26
  post-war rise in, 84
  and religious liberty, 29
secularists, ix–x
self, 15–16, 70
  Calvin on, 115
  weakness in relationship to, 99
self-authentication, 65, 80, 129, 131
self-evaluation for evangelicals, 149
self-governance, 10
self-interest, conscience and, 102
selfishness, 63
self-knowledge, 71
self-perception, 42
self-refutation, fallacy of, 34
self-restraint, 124
self-worth, 72
separation of church and state, ix–x, 2, 152
September 11, 2001 terror attacks, 149
sexual freedom, 143
sexual revolution, 11
Sidgwick, Henry, 30, 57
Simpson, Robert Mark, 46
sin, 70, 93, 106, 113, 126, 146
  effect on human relationships, 102
  evangelical doctrine of, 127
  Murray's failure to recognize realty of, 94
  Rawls concept of, 64
  Rawls' definition of, 63
  and religious persecution, 51
  social order and, 119
  state's role to restrain, 78
  Williams on, 128
Singer, Peter, 124
skepticism, 37–38, 39, 40
Skillen, James, 155
slavery, 57, 130
  abolition of, 125

Subject Index

Smith, Alfred, 88
Smith, Christian, 12
Smith, Gary, 147
social animals, 100
social bonds, 70
social cohesion, 61, 70, 79
social consciousness, 98
social consensus, 104
social contract, 60
    Rawls' argument for balance, 61
social cooperation, 62, 75, 92
social ecology, 119
social engagement, 142
social ethics, 21, 57, 60, 64, 66, 151
    ability to discern, 88
    Rawls' framework for, 56, 63–64
social function, 100
social goods, 33
    religious freedom as, 65
    unfair distribution of, 59
Social Gospel Movement, 104
social hierarchies, identity-based, 46–47
social impulse, 102
social inequalities, 62, 64
social interests
    harm principle and, 45
    of the people, 31
social life, 91, 97, 100
social media, 155
social norms, 125
social order, 30, 39, 136
    Christians as part, 137
    sin and, 119
social principle, 97
social progress, 33, 38
    restriction of, 50
social realm, 100
social secularity, 3
social splintering, 70
social structures, 61, 72
    Calvin's theory of, 115
social tension, 72
social utility, 41
social vision, 95–96
societal action, 45
society, 119, 149
    Christians in, 113
    common good, 2
    crimes against, 137
    individual and, 95
    perfectibility of, 31
    protection of, 37
    as system of cooperation, 61
Sola Scriptura, 12
Solomon, 27, 36
soul, 114
sovereignty, 147
speech. *see also* freedom of speech
    limits of, 39
    and physical acts, 40
Speech, Media, and Ethics: The Limits of Free Expression (Cohen-Almagor), 46
spiritual beliefs, 100
spiritual citizens, Christians as, 89
spiritual crimes, 137
spiritual government, vs political, 115
spiritual liberties, 143
spiritually transformed life, 109
Stace, Walter T., 57
state, 98
    neutrality toward religion, 2
    role of, 78
state authority, 137
state control, requirements, 13
state of nature, 60
The State of Theology 2020, 150–51
statism, and individualism, 13
Stettin Wittenberg, Luther's letter to, 51
Stott, John, 108
structural pluralism, 147
submission, 50
    to authority, 50
suffering, 28
Sullivan, Andrew, *Conservative Soul*, 104
superiority, 157
supernatural authority, 104
supernatural theism, 4
supernatural world, 152
suppression
    of atheistic beliefs, 83
    of heretical beliefs, 83
    of speech, 39
Supreme Court, 73
    ruling on same-sex marriage, 56
Suum cuique, 5

Subject Index

"swine" ethic, 29
synchronization, 52
syncretism, 50

Taylor, Charles, 147
technology, and religious freedom, 154
teleologic moral philosophy, Rawls' rejection of, 59
teleological philosophy, 96
temperance, 24
terrorism, 150
Tertullian, 111–14
   The Apology, 111
Testem Benvolentiae, 82
theism, 3, 24
Theological Studies (Murray), 87
theological truths, 120
theology, 21, 32, 82
theonomy, 155
theoretical reason, Mill rejection of, 23
A Theory of Justice (Rawls), 56, 59, 60, 63, 69, 79, 96
Thielicke, Helmut, 77, 103–4
thin theory of the good, 69n78
Thomas (saint), 89
Thomistic natural law, 89, 99
Thornbury, Gregory, 108, 148
thought, and speech, 40
time, 15–16, 17
   evangelical concept of, 107–10, 139, 140, 143
   and God's kingdom, 116
   God's understanding of, 119
   Williams on purpose, 118
   Williams' theology and, 117
Time magazine, 88, 93
tolerance, 7, 41
toleration, ix
totalitarian authority structures, 153
totalitarian control, alternatives, 5
traditional marriage, 73
transcendence, secular ethics and, 109
transcendent realities, 135
transcendent truth, 105
Treaty of Westphalia, 82–83
triadic structure, 52
tribalization, 70
Trinity, 40–41
true church, 117
Trump, Donald, 107–10, 148
truth, 44, 50, 52, 55, 65
   Bible as source for, 109
   church and, 83
   establishment of, 43
   evangelical paradigm of, 48–49
   humans as seekers of, 133
   opinions and, 43
   partial, 110
   pursuit of, 134
   Rawls on humans as seekers, 135
   right to pursue, 139
   treatment of, 47
tyranny, 8

United Nations, 148
United Nations Secretary-General, 148
United States, 148
   culture, 151
   political discourse, 145
U.S. Capitol Building, 156
U.S. Constitution, 86, 100
   First Amendment, 85, 91
U.S. State Department, 154
U.S. Supreme Court, 91, 103
U.S. v. Windsor (2013), 73
universal church, breakdown of, 31
universal moral boundaries, secular theories and, 128
universal truths, 109
universal values, 124
unregenerate mind, 132
utilitarian consequentialism, 27
utilitarian cosmology, 132
utilitarian ethics, 30, 44, 54, 139
   and divine omniscience, 27
   fallacies of, 28
utilitarian frameworks, 49
utilitarian justice, 132
utilitarian reason, 27–28
utilitarian social ethics, 17
utilitarian theory, 7, 60
utilitarianism, 20–55, 63, 152, 153
   and boundaries, 135
   and humans as truth seekers, 134

Subject Index

and justice standard, 59
Mill and, 25–30, 106
philosophers, 45
political philosophy, 7–8
as religion, 24
social contract theory and, 61
Utilitarianism (Mill), 33
utility, 38
utopian teleology, Rawls support for, 106
utopianism, 32, 64, 143

values
    relationships and, 124
    system of, 129
    universal, 124
    worldly vs. Christian, 117
van Wyk, J.K., 115
Vatican, 87
Vatican II, 81–82
veil of ignorance, 62, 65, 135
Veith, Gene, 149–50
Verilli, Donald, 11
virtue, 96
    cultivation of, 91
virtue ethics, Rawls' rejection of, 59–60
voluntarism, 16
voting constituency, evangelicals as, 107

Walker, Andrew, 2, 6, 15, 110, 121, 136, 137, 144, 151
war, restrictions to free speech, 39–40
Warren, Max, 108
We Hold These Truths (Murray), 88, 99
weakness, 93–96

welfare state, 2
West Virginia State Board of Education v. Barnette (1943), 1
Western political culture, 9–10
white Christian nationalism, 150
white evangelicals, 156
    and Trump, 107
white nationalism, 150
Whitehead, Andrew L., 148, 150
Why Liberalism Failed (Deneen), 13
Wilken, Robert Louis, 111
will, 69
will of God, 127
Williams, Roger, 5, 51–54, 116–18
    The Bloody Tenent of Persecution, 53–54, 117
    on sin, 128
witnessing, 76
Wogaman, J. Philip, 14n67, 138
women's rights, 125
    advocate for, 57
Wood, James E., Jr., 120–21
Woodstock College, 82, 84
world, evangelical concept of ordered, 137
World War II, 57, 84, 153
worldly values, vs. Christian, 117
worldview, 72
worship, 42–43, 80
wrath of God, 113

"x-evangelical," 148

Yoder, John Howard, 14n67

Scripture Index

OLD TESTAMENT

Genesis

1	26
1:26–28	40
1:28	71
8:22	9, 77
9	136
	136

Leviticus

19:18	158

Joshua

24:14–15	51 |// Job
12:7–25	133

Psalms

51:16–17	51

Proverbs

16:9	17
19:20	36

Ecclesiastes

3:11	67

NEW TESTAMENT

Matthew

13:24–30	143
13:30–38	5
18:18–20	137
22:36–39	131
28	136, 137
28:19	115
28:19–20	138, 139

Mark

12:13	135–36

John

1:1–3	109
5:22–23	129
6:63	114
14:15	131
15:9	113

Scripture Index

Acts

4:19	121
5:29	51, 121, 130
17:22–23	133

Romans

1:12	34
1:18	115
1:18–19	132
1:18–23	48, 75
1:18–32	14
1:19–20	100
2	125
2:14–15	100
2:15	34
2:16	100
3:25	78
7:7–8	129
9:1	127
12:19	143
13	78, 136
13:1	51
13:1–4	136

1 Corinthians

8	101
9:25	144

2 Corinthians

5:20	142

Galatians

5:1	130
5:13	131

Philippians

2:9–11	144
2:13	130

Colossians

1:15	71
1:15–20	107
1:16	136
1:28	151
2:10	141

Hebrews

1:1–2	44
11:3	49, 109

2 Peter

3:18	44

James

1:3	28
4:1	105

1 John

4:19	131

Revelation

13	78
22:13	140

www.ingramcontent.com/pod-product-compliance
Lightning Source LLC
Chambersburg PA
CBHW051737230426
43670CB00012B/2054